Susie Kelly emigrated from London to Kenya with her parents at the age of seven, and endured a convent education until she was expelled for refusing to devote her Saturday mornings to making doll's clothes, as she preferred to go horse riding. In 1973 she returned to live in England with a husband and two small children. Since then she has acquired a second and much better husband, a fine son-in-law and four gorgeous grandchildren – Catherine, Jamie, Jasmine and Leonie. Home is an ancient farmhouse, in the process of renovation, in southwest France, shared with a menagerie of goats, horses, dogs, cats, parrots and fish. Her previous memoir, *Best Foot Forward*, is also published by Bantam. You can visit the author at www.susiekelly.co.uk

Also by Susie Kelly

BEST FOOT FORWARD

TWO STEPS BACKWARD

Susie Kelly

BANTAM BOOKS

LONDON · NEW YORK · TORONTO · SYDNEY · AUCKLAND

TWO STEPS BACKWARD
A BANTAM BOOK : 0 553 81620 9

First publication in Great Britain

PRINTING HISTORY
Bantam edition published 2004

1 3 5 7 9 10 8 6 4 2

Set in 11/12¾pt Times by
Kestrel Data, Exeter, Devon.

Bantam Books are published by Transworld Publishers,
61–63 Uxbridge Road, London W5 5SA,
a division of The Random House Group Ltd,
in Australia by Random House Australia (Pty) Ltd,
20 Alfred Street, Milsons Point, Sydney, NSW 2061, Australia,
in New Zealand by Random House New Zealand Ltd,
18 Poland Road, Glenfield, Auckland 10, New Zealand
and in South Africa by Random House (Pty) Ltd,
Endulini, 5a Jubilee Road, Parktown 2193, South Africa.

Printed and bound in Great Britain by
Cox & Wyman Ltd, Reading, Berkshire.

Papers used by Transworld Publishers are natural, recyclable
products made from wood grown in sustainable forests.
The manufacturing processes conform to the environmental
regulations of the country of origin.

To my husband Terry, whose determination,
persistence and hard work has kept
the boat afloat

Acknowledgements

Dear Maggie Noach, my agent, and her right-hand woman Camilla Adeane have been a source of endless patience and encouragement, infinite wisdom, luscious meals and bowls of Friars Balsam.

Nobody could wish for kinder, more tolerant neighbours than Paulette and Clovis Meneteau, Eglantine Grimaud, Maurice Royer and Jean-Luc Garnaud. They have all, over the years, helped me in countless ways, as well as offering an intriguing glimpse into life in our hamlet during the decades before my arrival.

At Transworld, Francesca Liversidge has been enormously kind and done so much to make me feel at home there. Sadie Mayne and Nancy Webber's sympathetic and painstaking editing has brought order to the manuscript where there was none, and Michelle Bruchez's legal advice has been very valuable. Marie Gallagher is always most helpful.

Bill Hughes and Gloria Hughes, who have so good-naturedly given their approval to the inclusion of the episodes concerning them, added a memorable ingredient to living here that I fear will never be repeated.

My sincere thanks to all of them.

Prologue

Twenty hours ago we drove away, for the last time, from the cottage that once belonged to us, but which the building society has reclaimed. In the hired truck are our five dogs, two parrots and such few twigs of furniture as we still own. Latter-day Darling Buds of May. We disembarked from the ferry at Cherbourg into the rolling green orchards of Normandy, and drove past voluptuous cattle with the big fat bottoms and bosoms of saucy sea-side postcard ladies, and timbered cottages with thatched roofs topped by small narrow plateaux crowned with flowers.

The smooth grey ribbon of road has led us through rises and dips, a gentle switchback, on and on, until Normandy's lush pastures and hills gave way to the more level land of the Touraine, with its sun-sodden golden seas of wheat, where the early evening air was hot and the sun still high. The road reached seemingly into infinity; over the modest river Loir, and half an hour later, on the fringes of Tours, his regal sister, the great Loire herself.

It is late dusk as we reach the space-age landscape of Futuroscope, on the outskirts of Poitiers, in the Poitou-Charentes region. Thirty kilometres from there our new home awaits our arrival.

Because we are tired we take a wrong turning, arriving in the centre of a small town where a *gendarme* steps in front of the truck with an upraised hand. Panic floods me; what can we have done, even before reaching our destination, to attract the attention of the law? What if he searches the vehicle, asks to see paperwork for the animals? We have none. What if now, so close to our destination, the truck is searched and it all goes horribly wrong? People in England had proffered conflicting advice as to what we should do about bringing our animals into France: at one end of the scale we were told the French authorities would demand proof of ownership, vaccination certificates and pedigrees for each animal, which we must produce the moment we landed on French soil, or risk their being forbidden entry into the country; somebody else had advised that whatever we did, we mustn't start waving fistfuls of documents at the customs officers, who would much prefer that we didn't bother them, and that if we did so we'd find ourselves tangled in bureaucracy for months to come. 'Just drive quietly past. They're not interested in a few dogs.' It had sounded the simpler option so that's what we'd done. We did know that the maximum permitted number of dogs entering the country per family was four, and we had five, but one was very small and perhaps we could say he was a rare English breed of cat.

The *gendarme* simply smiles and signals we should wait: round a corner a procession appears. It looks like the entire population of the town: ancients leaning on supportive arms, infants in buggies, young, old and those in between, a dozen strutting dogs, all marching down the street behind a spirited brass band, singing merrily and waving candle-lit paper lanterns on sticks. Somebody bangs on the side of the truck, calling, 'Come on out, join us!' We only smile and shake our heads; to try to explain that we have been driving for twenty hours with five dogs, two parrots and a fitted kitchen would confirm the generally held belief that all the English are crazy. The procession passes, the *gendarme* waves us on, and ten minutes later we are rolling again, so close now, until we drive into la Petite-Eglise, the last village before our hamlet, and straight into the heart of another mass of merry-makers making an early start to France's national day.

Apart from several dozen flickering paper lanterns, the only light in the village square, which is actually an oblong, comes from the bar, with its slightly eccentric English telephone box (circa 1970) just inside the doors. Tables and chairs are set on the pavement outside the bar and the adjacent restaurant, and children skip and chase each other around the stone fountain whose jets of water leap and chuckle in the night air. Grouped around the oblong are the restaurant and bar, a bakery, a hair-dresser, a chemist and a manufacturer of the local speciality, *le farci poitevin* – a sort of stuffed cabbage. Fifty metres down the road the lovely old twelfth-century Romanesque church sits on the bend where a narrow stone bridge spans a winding stream, while a modestly imposing and rather severe seventeenth-century château gazes down on the scene from a steep bluff.

Somebody is trying to marshal the crowd around the bar into an orderly line, clapping their hands and trying to make themselves heard over the chatter and laughter and squeals and clinks of glasses and bottles. It is a quintessentially French scene and we could not have chosen a better moment to arrive if we had tried. I feel a lump in my throat, as Terry says: 'Well, welcome to France!'

Again the local citizenry beckon to us, calling out that we English should come and share their celebrations; we feel really quite awful that we can't join them, and must

11

appear unsociable when all we are is absolutely dog-tired. But we wave and yell loudly '*Vive la France!*' which is greeted with laughter and applause, and begin the four remaining kilometres to our new home.

The closer we get, the quieter we become, the less we talk. This is a high-drama event, the climax of long months of planning and preparation; a momentous day in our lives, the beginning of a new future, and a step into the unknown. Driving the last few metres up the lane into the hamlet, I'm overwhelmed with a powerful feeling of coming home to where we belong, to the place that has been waiting for us for years. At the same time I can't deny an underlying sorrow, because for the foreseeable future Terry and I will be living apart for much of the time, not knowing how often or when we'll be able to see each other. Life from now on is going to be strange, exciting and rather frightening. I know that Terry's thoughts are similar. I've said my '*au revoirs*' to our children – our son Rob and his girlfriend, and our daughter Julie, whose husband Steve is in the Royal Air Force. They both have careers and children of their own, and understand our circumstances, have been aware of our desire to move to France for a long time, and support our decision. I am sad at the thought of moving so far away from them, but look forward to them visiting us in our new home.

Terry halts the truck on the grass outside the house, switches off the engine and the lights, and for two minutes we sit in silence in the dark cab, as if savouring the moment, delaying taking that final, decisive step, before climbing down into the night. When we open the back of the vehicle, the dogs spill out in a flurry of legs and tails, and dash around ecstatically snuffling and snorting in the dark as they explore; as they take their noise further away, we can hear the crickets creaking.

From every direction come the rumbles and cracks of

exploding fireworks in nearby villages, heralding the arrival of *le quatorze juillet*, and as the rockets light the sky, the ridge of the hill that faces our house stands out on the skyline. Beneath a black velvet canopy engraved with a hundred million stars, we stand outside on the grass, warm in shorts and T-shirts, sipping champagne from star-filled wine glasses, listening to our dogs and the crickets and the fireworks.

Against the darkness of the night, the darker outlines of our farmhouse and her outbuildings stand out, along with the silhouettes of trees. Their bulk is reassuring, protective. They tell us that we are welcome here among them, and safe.

Chapter One

Where the bottom of the front door had succumbed, over the years, to damp and wear, a ragged two-inch gap allowed a radiant ribbon of moonlight to slide beneath it. From half-sleep, a persistent rattling, scuffling sound caught my attention, and in the bright glare an unwieldy black shape scrunched itself – with difficulty, but considerable determination – through the space.

Terry had heard the noise too and got up quietly to put the stag beetle outside. On the lumpy sofa bed we had set up in the living room we both lay awake, silent with our own thoughts. The beetle forced itself back in beneath the gap again.

While the wilful insect scrabbled around the ancient grimy floorboards for whatever reason it might have, I relived in my mind our first sight of the farmhouse eleven months before. It was the culmination of two exhausting and frequently demoralizing days of driving around the region with an estate agent, viewing twenty-four properties none of which was quite, or in some cases anything even remotely like, what we were looking for. As we began to run out of time, there were just two more candidates to view, and we were heading for somewhere represented most unattractively on a smudgy grey photocopied sheet, with exceedingly sparse details and a

15

photograph depicting something resembling the after-math of a nuclear strike. But from the first moment I saw those unprepossessing details, something had stirred me (possibly the ridiculously low price that we could almost, but not quite, afford). The nearer we got, the stronger was my feeling that this was the place that had our name on it. Along a narrow track leading off a minor road, across a small stone bridge spanning a seep which in times of heavy rain became a trickle, the car bumped over the uneven surface into a huddle of a dozen houses, scattering scraggy chickens, and halted beside an old stone well where the track came to an abrupt end in the very heart of the hamlet whose population, we learned, numbered a modest eleven: some retired farmers, a couple of elderly widows, two bachelors. Several of the houses were uninhabited. Our guide, Valérie, a pretty dark-haired girl with doe eyes, gestured triumphantly, like a magician producing an elephant out of a top hat, at the collection of piles of stones that represented a farmhouse and assorted outbuildings in a state of semi-collapse. *Et voilà! C'est superbe, n'est-ce pas?'*

The farmhouse, dating back to 'about the eighteenth century', said Valérie rather vaguely, was a long, rectangular building. One-third comprised the two rooms that made up the 'living' part. The main room was 20 feet by 12, with a beamed timber ceiling and two inbuilt cupboards stuffed with spiders' webs, and had originally, decades ago, acted as kitchen, dining and living room to the previous family of mother, father and five children, and the parents' bedroom too. The perimeter of the wooden floor was collapsing, and the boards were tempered by generations of food preparation and foot traffic. A livid green shiny paint was unpeeling itself in neat little curls from the walls, and a battered door led into the garden. The kitchen element had consisted of a wood-burning stove standing to the side of the fireplace, its pipe running into a hole knocked into the chimney breast; the stove had long gone, but the hole remained, rather spoiling the charm of the fireplace with its traditional stone mantelpiece. In one corner of the room was the shallow stone sink with a small oval *œil de bœuf* window over it, a characteristic feature of the area. Suspended from a lump of wood nailed to a beam, a length of flex bearing a single light bulb dangled incongruously three feet from the floor. Another door led to the adjacent room of 8 feet by 12 that had long ago served as a bedroom for the children, where the floorboards had subsided onto the dirt beneath, and mushrooms and other miscellaneous fungi were thriving on the walls. Ancient shutters clung with lost hope to the cracked windows.

Those two rooms were the full extent of the living accommodation. Above them was an empty loft space. There was no sanitation, no water supply inside the house, and the electrical installation looked as if it might have been fitted by Noah. The remaining two-thirds of the building was animal housing, and there was nothing between the compacted earth floor and the undersides of the roof tiles 20 feet above, through which in several places the sky peered in.

The children who had been born and grown up in the house were now into their sixties and their widowed mother was in a nursing home. I thought rather wistfully that if a family of seven had managed to live and grow in such a very basic environment, it was a shame that I didn't feel I was going to be able to manage without a fridge/freezer, a washing machine, hot and cold running water and a power supply that did not date back to 1934, when electricity had first arrived in the hamlet, thirty years before running water.

Facing south-east, the front of the house benefited from the sun from first light until midday, and was sheltered from the intense heat of summer afternoons. Walls 3 feet thick comprised flints and limestones piled next to and upon each other, the intervening spaces occupied by pockets of earth, desiccated animal manure and a variety of scurrying wildlife. I wondered how long it had taken to collect the hundreds of thousands of stones necessary to build these places, and how the massive beams had been hoisted into place, and what those ancient builders would think if they could see modern construction techniques that can have a house erected in just a few days.

As well as the farmhouse with its two barely habitable rooms was a collection of quaint and crumbling outbuildings. Two small stone sheds, formerly accommodation for goats or pigs; one large open-fronted barn that was home to some agricultural machinery and bales of hay; one decrepit dirt-floored building acting as a garage; one murky small hovel with a rough cobblestoned floor and caved-in ceiling, with the old wooden shelf that was used to store bread out of reach of rodents still hanging from a beam. The mellow stones and mossy pantiles of the roofs blended modestly into the landscape.

There was an acre and a half of land standing on a slight incline facing a gentle slope blazing with sunflowers, and offering a foothold to various trees. The land was roughly fenced and hedged, and maintained in an orderly state by a small family of rapacious sheep. One of the leaning fence posts supported a rakish scarecrow dressed in black trousers and shirt. The land would not look after itself. Most of it was grazing, but horses don't eat stinging nettles, and they don't eat brambles; nor would they eat the hundreds of infant sloe bushes that were creeping steadily across the field. All these, and thistles, and ragwort which is so poisonous to horses, would have to be regularly and laboriously uprooted. Small volcanoes of crumbly earth indicated the presence of moles that would have to be persuaded to move elsewhere, and I could hardly begin to imagine how many hundreds of garden pests lurked waiting to wage war.

Looking around at all this, my head and heart started an argument. Heart said it felt exactly right for us, despite the fearsome amount of work that was going to be needed to make this place habitable. Head said that this was far too big a project for paupers with no experience of building and no particular skills. While they were arguing, the pastoral scene was suddenly rent by the most horrible noise I'd ever heard.

Try, just for a moment, to imagine what a human sacrifice victim would sound like during the event: a repeated wail of pure terror and unspeakable pain, punctuated by bowel-rending shrieks. Someone, or something, was *in extremis*.

'Whatever is making that terrible noise?' I asked Valérie.

'Probably,' she shrugged in the prosaic manner of a country girl, 'they are killing the turkeys.'

My heart, which had been singing while it argued, plummeted like a lift with a broken cable. Well, that was the end of the matter. I wouldn't live anywhere, even in the kingdom of the perennial money tree and eternal youth, if hapless creatures were going to be massacred on our doorstep. I was ready to leave, but Valérie kept steering us determinedly round the property, helping herself along the way to handfuls of purple plums. 'I'm very greedy,' she laughed, rolling her eyes and reaching for another helping. She pointed out the trees: oak and linden, walnut, apples, pears, plums, greengages, and the unspoilt view, while I made a loud humming noise that I hoped would smother the tortured screams, which it didn't. We explored the hamlet, drawing steadily nearer to the barn, some fifty metres from 'our' house, from where the agonized yells were escaping. As we drew abreast, the appalling sound reached an impossible climax, a long drawn out shrieking screech. I stopped and shook my head to indicate that I'd gone as far as I was going.

Valérie laughed. 'Look!' She took me by the arm and turned me so we were facing the source of the racket. Perched majestically within a large ornate wrought-iron cage sat an apricot-white Moluccan cockatoo, his flamboyant blushing crest raised, and his clever boot-button black eyes studying our reaction to his vocal efforts. Encouraged by our attention, he swayed slowly and rhythmically from side to side like an elegant feathery pendulum, smoothly escalating the volume until it went right off the scale.

My heart shot up again and I stopped the humming noise.

We walked around the property a second time. From a small adjacent orchard the sheep glared indignantly as we stood absorbing the peace, the stillness, the herb-scented grass. Head was estimating the time and work, and particularly the money that we didn't have, that it was going to take to make this place habitable. It was not a project for the faint-hearted or financially challenged.

Heart, who was determined to win the debate, said slyly: 'It's so ridiculously cheap. We won't find anything else at this price. We may never again find anywhere that feels so absolutely right for us. We could end up regretting it for the rest of our lives if we miss this opportunity.'

'OK,' said Head, giving in just as I knew it would. 'Let's do it!'

Terry and I looked at each other; I nodded at him, and he nodded back. When we'd started out on the search for a house in France, Terry had chosen the area, based on weather, (not too far north because the weather there could be rather English, not too far south because I don't like it too hot), accessibility, and price. I had the choice of house.

Oui, we agreed with Valérie, *c'est vraiment superbe*.

We'd read a great deal about the pitfalls of buying property in France, and knew that the cardinal rule was: DO NOT IN ANY CIRCUMSTANCES, SIGN ANYTHING WITHOUT FIRST TAKING PROFESSIONAL ADVICE FROM AN ENGLISH SOLICITOR. Disastrous purchases were made in haste: a rash signature on a *compromis* – a binding agreement to purchase – and there you were landed with nothing but trouble: boundary disputes that were impossible to settle, neighbours who had the right to drive their tractors through your bathroom, houses that it was illegal to inhabit and you couldn't sell. You simply couldn't be too careful. And so, naturally, we found ourselves knocking on the door of M. Royer, a gentle, shy bachelor in his late sixties, who lived about a hundred metres away in a neat white house and was one of the children born in 'our' house. His mother, in the nursing home, had charged him with selling it. I asked him whether he was sad to be doing so, but he smiled and shook his head.

'No, not at all. It's a lot of work to maintain so many old buildings.'

'Please tell your mother,' I said, 'that we will love her house very much.'

He smiled and tilted his head in acknowledgement, and at his invitation we sat round his kitchen table, drinking vintage cider and writing, quite untruthfully, on nine successive pages of a *compromis* of which we could understand hardly a word, '*Lu et approuvé*' followed by our initials. We had just taken an irrevocable step towards buying a French farmhouse.

That was in August. Under French law, the organization known as SAFER has the pre-emptive right to purchase any agricultural property for its own use. SAFER have to be advised by letter that the property is for sale, and they have two months in which to exercise their right. I could not imagine that they would not covet our little field, and waited daily to hear that they had swiped it from under us. We sent a copy of the contract to an English solicitor to check that it contained no unwelcome surprises, which it didn't. The whole transaction went smoothly and without any hitches at all, and by early November all the necessary formalities and paperwork had been completed; in the elegant office of a charming local *notaire* we signed the *Acte de Vente* and the property actually became ours. Eight months later, we arrived with dogs, parrots and the ashes of our previous existence.

We hadn't always been impoverished. Until three years earlier we'd enjoyed a comfortable lifestyle and a plentiful income, and dreamed of owning a house in France one day. Because of a combination of factors, triggered by the recession of the early 1990s, our business failed. In a fast-moving year, we lost all our material wealth: house, savings, anything at all that had any monetary value. The furniture was sold off to buy food. Friends were aghast as the auctioneer's van drove away loaded with anything that could be converted into cash.

'Oh, my God, how awful for you,' they sympathized. As a matter of fact, my predominant thought was, 'Thank heaven I'll never again have to worry about polishing all that stuff, or scratching it.' (I'm not tremendously into housework.)

Not having money didn't make us unhappy; it was simply an inconvenience. Because we'd been unable to pay our electricity bill, the electricity company had installed a meter that we had to feed, and we were very aware of the cost of energy. We allowed ourselves one kettle of boiling water each morning for washing, and once a week put the immersion heater on for a couple of hours so we could enjoy a shower. If we kept very quiet and refused to open the door to the bailiffs who hammered upon it continually, they would eventually go away. There was no point in talking to them, anyway: there was nothing left for them to take. You can't get gold dust out of grass seeds. And we learned who our friends were – or, in several cases, weren't. People whom we'd regarded as close friends, people we'd shared holidays with, entertained and lent money to, started crossing the road when they saw us coming. Initially this was a shock, and then I started looking at it as an advantage, because if ever we won the lottery we'd know whom not to invite to the celebrations.

But other people, some of whom we knew only casually, rallied round supportively and very tactfully. We found Tupperware containers on our doorstep, with little notes saying: 'Can you possibly use this? I got carried away and made far too much, and we can't eat it all.' Anonymous food parcels appeared. Somebody arrived with sacks of coal that they said were 'surplus'. These were true friends in need.

Unless we were invited out, we usually lived off the food left on the doorstep, or packet mashed potatoes. Sometimes we added pickle, and on special days some grated cheese. This lasted for about four months, and we suffered no ill-effects. We managed to keep the dogs fed, and a very special lady called Sandra took our two ancient, retired horses under her generous wing to ensure that they too were fed and housed.

Widespread unemployment meant that we couldn't find work; we no longer came within a productive age bracket. So for a while we both did any odd jobs that came along: ironically, given my loathing for house-work, I worked as a cleaning lady, in three different establishments, for 28 hours each week. Terry did odd jobs for people. We had successfully kept the building society at bay for many months, but they were stealthily closing in and couldn't be fended off indefinitely, so we had begun to hunt for rented accommodation. There was plenty to choose from provided we didn't have any animals. No landlord was prepared to welcome five dogs and two parrots. Absolutely not. What to do? We would never separate the dogs from each other – we had a mother and three of her offspring who had been together since birth, and a small terrier; they were all now middle-aged. Nobody would take them as a job lot, except, it seemed, for some creditors who were not satisfied with their pickings from our threadbare assets. They wanted more, and we were summonsed to court to declare the resources that we had already told them many times we didn't have. Our adversary's solicitor was a pleasant and sympathetic lady who seemed rather embarrassed by her part in the proceedings. We listed our virtually non-existent belongings, and after glancing at the form she remarked that we hadn't mentioned the valuable dogs and horses that her clients had instructed her to try to sequester. The idea that anybody could regard five middle-aged dogs with ravenous appetites, or two similarly voracious horses in their mid-twenties who served no useful purpose at all, as assets, made us smile. To us they were dearly loved liabilities whose welfare was a massive drain on our tiny resources and whose existence was the cause of our difficulty in finding somewhere to live. The solicitor closed her file and secured it with an elastic band, said she doubted very much that in the circumstances her clients would pursue their interest in the animals, shook our hands and wished us the very best of luck.

Nobody would take us as tenants, and buying another house in England was out of the question. In our interesting new condition, almost penniless as we were, our thoughts returned to France, where property could still be bought for peanuts in some places. Not the modest little château that Terry would have liked, nor the perfect farmhouse with stables and ranch fencing that I'd dreamed of. It would have to be something very humble. We would work like devils at no matter what menial tasks we could find, scrimp, save and borrow if necessary, to buy somewhere as a haven for ourselves and our animals. And that's what we'd done and why we were here. It's funny how things turn out sometimes.

The moonlit strip under the door vanished in favour of brilliant early-morning sunshine, and we got up to settle our furniture into place and to explore our new home.

We walked round measuring rooms and outbuildings and planning what we would do with them; M. Royer had cleared them of any remaining bits and pieces, and had swept from the dirt floors every trace of straw, dust and cobwebs, leaving them spotlessly tidy. Several of the elderly oak doors on the outbuildings, secured with their original hand-forged iron hinges and bolts, were impossible to open, because ivy, brambles and grass had grown over and around them. Those we'd leave for another time, and we laughed at the thought of owning rooms we hadn't even seen into yet. We stroked the trunks of the trees, traced the fossils embedded in the limestones, and picked the wild mint and thyme in the field, crushing them between our fingers to savour their perfumes. We sipped wine and watched the dogs who, undecided as to which direction to investigate first, dashed hither and thither with tails wagging their delight, occasionally digging wildly at mole hills or chasing butterflies through the long grass; and we marvelled that this little kingdom really was in our keeping.

*   *   *

Three days after we'd arrived Terry climbed into the truck, smiling his enthusiastic smile, blowing a kiss and waving as he vanished into the distance, heading back to England to look for a way of making a living to support us all, as we had planned. He was cheerfully resigned to catering for himself and providing for me and the dogs. I thought how very fortunate I was to have such a generous husband. Watching him pulling away, I wondered how one person could be so eternally, unquenchably positive and optimistic after the events of the previous few years. About five foot six, with broad shoulders, blond hair and grey eyes, his strong face reflecting his very determined personality, no matter what disaster arrived on our doorstep he faced it heroically and worked at overcoming it. Defeat was not a word in his vocabulary. There was no such thing as a problem – only a situation.

Alone and lonely in the empty van, Terry would be asked very nicely by the immigration officials at Portsmouth to lift the roller door 'to make sure there were no other people in the back', when all that was in there were a few forlorn empty cardboard boxes, a reminder that he had left everything behind across the Channel.

We were both simultaneously sad and happy, each feeling as if we were abandoning the other to survive by themselves. While I'd have to cope with the unknown, Terry would be living in a small flat and fending for himself in the kitchen, which was something he knew precisely nothing about, and at the same time finding a way to keep us all by whatever means he could. How often he was able to visit would depend on what he could earn. He would have to put aside whatever he could for building materials and travel, and when he could get here for a few days he'd have to tackle the monumental task of renovating the place himself, because there would be no money to employ anyone else and there was little that I'd be able to do when it came to building. At most we anticipated seeing each other for three or four days a month. It was a brave and exciting time, because together we'd achieved what we had wanted. And it was exhilarating because we were starting a fresh chapter in our lives and the grass was definitely green in our garden.

Terry tooted a couple of times before he disappeared from sight, and I listened to the engine as the sound grew fainter and fainter, until it faded into penetrating silence. It felt like that moment when you pass your driving test, and the examiner hands you a piece of paper authorizing you to drive a motor vehicle, unaccompanied, on the public roads, and you are suddenly not at all confident that you're ready for it. I felt very alone, suddenly uncertain as to whether I was up to the job of living here by myself for much of the time and coping with whatever was sent by the fates. I didn't know how to wire a plug or change a fuse. But I was soon going to learn.

The dogs milled around, feeling my unease and pushing their snouts at me to say: 'It's OK, Mum, we're here, everything will be fine.'

Our canine matriarch was Natalia, a Hungarian Vizsla, a breed that personifies beauty, gentleness and elegance with their smooth russet coats and sincere hazel eyes. She was a faithful companion to us and a doting mother to her children. When we arrived she was already 12 years old, and although physically in remarkably good condition (she would eventually live to be 17), she was becoming a little fragile in the upper storey, and spent hours wandering round and round with a wrinkled forehead as if trying to puzzle out why she was doing so.

Hecate, her daughter, was an affectionate, strong-willed and very independent creature, who did exactly what she wanted to do, where, when and however it pleased her, and didn't let any kind of discipline influence her behaviour. Her two brothers, Wizzy and Vulcan, were the principal trouble-makers, forever escaping and vanishing for days on end. Wizzy was so handsome and noble in appearance that wherever he went people stopped to talk to him, even people who normally didn't like dogs. Vulcan, on the other hand, was slightly timid and wore a permanently perplexed and suspicious expression as if he never quite understood what was going on. In contrast with the Vizlas' russet-coated elegance, the little fellow Max, an Affenpinscher, looked like a black wig in a gale, and radiated charm and high spirits. When he had first joined the household the Vizslas had been horror-struck and for several days ignored him and rebuffed his attempts to integrate; but his cheerful persistence soon won them over, and he became their friend, their toy and at night their happily compliant pillow.

They were our reason for being here, and reminded me that they were waiting for their breakfast.

Chapter Two

One hundred metres from our house a large battered furniture removal van, bearing an English name and address, stood outside the barn where the cockatoo had screamed the previous year, but now there was no sign of life. The barn, which was separated from our house by an empty cottage, looked as if somebody had started to think about developing it and then changed their mind. There were piles of breeze-blocks and sacks of hardened cement, scaffolding poles and old tyres all over the place, and a rusty cooker peering through the undergrowth. I wandered round and narrowly failed to break my neck in a vast pit hidden in shoulder-high stinging nettles. The pit, 3 metres deep and 9 metres square, had been prepared to receive a septic tank and was thoughtfully camouflaged in the undergrowth with no indication of its presence until you were about to topple into it. This corner was the only part of the hamlet that was untidy, and I looked forward to the time when whoever owned the place would arrive and clean it up.

The first few days on my own passed in a maelstrom of washing, wiping, scraping, clearing and painting, which made no noticeable difference to the appearance of our new home and with which I was soon very bored and worn out. Apart from a couple of phone calls from Terry, when we assured each other that we were well, I hadn't seen or spoken to anybody, because our home was located in a cul-de-sac at the heart of the hamlet and not overlooked by any other property, and I'd not yet gone further afield than the cockatoo barn. On a blazing afternoon I pulled open a cardboard box of books and settled down in a deckchair in a corner of the parched earth that was the garden. Doing this, when there was such an overwhelming mound of tasks waiting to be done, made me feel very guilty, but in view of how crowded my life was to become it was just as well I did have a few moments to myself to look back on. To my right was a small building, an old goat shed, and behind that the immaculate vegetable garden of M. Meneteau, the brother-in-law of M. Royer who had sold us the house. Mme Meneteau had also been born in our living room. I don't know what it was that made me look up from my book, but when I did I saw a moving shadow at the end of the animal shed, which unmistakably belonged to a person trying to peer round it at me.

I called out 'Bonjour!' and climbed out of the deckchair and walked to the corner of the shed. He looked a little startled and puzzled as to how I had known he was there; we shook hands, and I said, in my stumbling French, how very pleased I was that we were neighbours and asked how his garden was doing, which is always an excellent way to start a conversation with a Frenchman. He shrugged and said it was OK, but very dry. We needed some rain. Did he think we'd get some soon? He shook his head. No, not until there was a wind from the west. That's where the rain came from. Today there was just a puff of breeze from the opposite direction – that's why, he explained, we could hear the church bells from a small village a few miles away to the east.

M. Meneteau was a retired farmer, a short little man whose out-thrust chest and very dark round eyes reminded me of a bird. He'd had five-way heart bypass surgery, and was meant to take life easy, but he was always on the go, working in his vegetable patch, harvesting grapes from his vineyard 2 kilometres away (from which he made 500 litres of wine a year, and their own vinegar), or weaving decorative little bowls and baskets using bramble branches, a craft his mother had taught him.

I mentioned the English furniture truck that was parked outside the nearby barn. Did he know who owned the property?

Yes, an Englishman. Called Bill, or something like that. He owned the barn and the furniture truck, and stopped off here from time to time for a few days and did some work on the property. Sometimes he came in a truck, sometimes in a car. He unloaded things, and didn't always leave in the same vehicle he arrived in. There was usually an assortment of different trucks and cars parked around the place. M. Meneteau thought he travelled between Spain and England, but their conversations were limited, as Bill didn't speak any more French than M. Meneteau spoke English.

When did he think Bill might be back?

He pulled a face and raised his shoulders half an inch. No idea. He came and went about once a month. Maybe he'd be here fairly soon.

Bill did indeed turn up a few days later, with the cockatoo. He came across and introduced himself, a pleasant and courteous man who made his living moving furniture between Spain and England, using this place as his halfway point. Contrary to my vision of a big burly man, he was slightly built and not very tall, with a good thick head of grey hair and thick-lensed glasses, and looked more like a school teacher than a removal man, apart from his boots, whose steel toecaps glistened through where the leather had worn away. He explained

31

his plans for developing his property: the barn would become three houses, two for letting and one for himself. On another plot that belonged to him in the hamlet he was planning to build several bungalows for elderly people. He would supply a community bus for them, and there were to be ponds and fountains, stained glass windows and spiral staircases. It all sounded quite charming. The important thing, he underlined, when renovating these ancient properties, was to do so sympathetically and in keeping with tradition. I nodded politely and tried to remember where I had last seen a French farmhouse with a stained glass window.

We shared a couple of glasses of wine, and I found myself agreeing to caretake Sinbad the cockatoo 'for a few days'. Bill was heading to England and somehow Sinbad was in danger of having to learn self-catering as he couldn't be taken into England, couldn't be got back to Spain, and had no-one else here to look after him. I did wonder rather vaguely at the time what would have happened if I hadn't been there. The following day the bird and its titanic cage were manoeuvred into the living room alongside our two parrots, and Bill set off northwards.

I hadn't expected, and didn't know whether I was pleased or otherwise, to find another English resident in the hamlet. My dream of being the only English person for miles around and totally immersed into French rural life was rather shattered; on the other hand it was comforting to know that there would be, from time to time, somebody with whom it would be possible to hold a conversation that both sides fully understood.

Our nearest village, Saint-Thomas-le-Petit, seemed, on the surface, more moribund than sleepy. On sunny days the elderly residents sat cross-armed and cross-ankled on benches outside their houses, watching the intermittent passing traffic with stony faces. There was a *boulangerie*, a very pretty church, the *mairie*, a café/bar and restaurant, a cemetery, and on the outskirts of the village an agricultural workshop. When I first arrived there was a sub-post office, too. It opened only in the afternoons, theoretically between 2.00 p.m. and 4.00 p.m. Theoretically, because the girl who ran it was also the waitress at the restaurant, and on busy days the post office waited while she finished waiting. Two of our neighbours, Mme Grimaud and Mme Meneteau, told me that years ago there had been six cafés, two blacksmiths, and several builders, joiners and other craftsmen trading in the village. It was hard to imagine life in the area in the days when there had been a thriving community of dozens of small busy farms, before they were taken over by co-operatives, who gouged up the hedges to make larger, more convenient fields that could be worked by huge machinery.

Fairly frequently, Saint-Thomas became vibrantly alive. Cars lined the road, and the local inhabitants and those from the surrounding hamlets stood around outside the church in their best clothes, laughing and chatting. This signified that a funeral was just about to take place. When somebody died in the commune, everybody from that commune attended the funeral – unless the deceased hadn't attended their family funerals. If people didn't come to your funerals, you didn't go to theirs.

If you didn't know better, you might have thought nothing else ever happened in Saint-Thomas-le-Petit. But there was a dedicated football team, and regular tombola or *belote* evenings (a bit like a whist drive); and the huntsmen's dinner, the fishermen's dinner, the blood donors' dinner, the football team dinner, 14 July celebrations and the re-enactment of the burning of Joan of Arc ensured that there was an active social life in the village.

Life moved at a very different tempo here from life in England. The local people went about their daily business at an unalterably leisurely pace, and must have been highly amused and puzzled by the frantic antics of English drivers hooting and swerving around the roads (rather like French drivers) in an impatient and frenzied attempt to overtake the tractors and combine harvesters wending their dignified ways. Coming so recently from the rat race, it took me quite a while to adapt to not rushing everywhere. I bought a cookery book at the supermarket, and as the cashier passed it over the barcode reader she flicked through it unhurriedly. She asked the queue, about six strong behind me, whether they thought 200 grams was too much sugar in a particular recipe. The lady behind me disagreed; the one behind her said she always used brown sugar; another woman always added a pinch of cinnamon, we learned, but somebody else shook her head disapprovingly: that was not the traditional recipe. Quite a lively discussion built up about the recipe and cooking in general, while I stood treading impatiently from one foot to the other, instead of enjoying the event like everybody else, and for absolutely no reason at all. Five more minutes there would make no difference whatsoever to the rest of my day, but old habits died hard.

Friends from England, worried about the primitive area they supposed was our new home, sent out boxes of provisions, like Red Cross parcels, which was kind of them and saved me quite a bit of money, but was completely unnecessary. The local supermarket shelves were stocked with most things essential to the English abroad – there were dozens of varieties of breakfast cereals, including cornflakes and porridge amongst the more bizarrely named Smacks, Kix and Felties. The fish counter offered kippers, sprats and smoked haddock amongst the *rascasse*, oysters, and live lobsters and crabs.

There were Indian, Mexican, Chinese and Italian ingredients and ready meals, marmalade, chocolate spread, Guinness, gin and tonic. Dishwashing liquid came in a wide variety of 'flavours' – green apple, mint, raspberry vinegar, blackcurrant and grapefruit. The supermarkets also sold garden furniture, car parts, sit-on mowers (damned awkward getting them into the trolley), assorted ammunition and, in a refrigerated unit, neat little transparent containers of gently heaving maggots, writhing worms and other squirming live bait, some with legs, some without.

The supermarkets served for more than just the weekly shop. They were places to meet friends, old and new, to catch up on gossip, and to stare at peculiar vegetables and culinary ingredients. There was always somebody happy and willing to give advice and explain how to prepare and use these mysterious products. Impromptu comedies were sometimes enacted there, too. On the day the electricity failed in the supermarket, leaving the tills out of action with a queue of shoppers at each checkout, the poor cashiers were given pencils and pieces of paper and had to work out each customer's bill with hand-held calculators. It was unbelievably time-consuming, but everyone entered merrily into the spirit of the event and waited patiently, while discussing the improbability that anybody's bill would be accurate.

No more than a week later, about a dozen of us were queuing outside the supermarket, waiting for it to open at the specified time of 2.30 p.m. But it didn't. The doors remained firmly closed. People started walking at them purposefully, pushing trolleys at them, and waving their arms at the mechanism that should have caused them to slide apart. One man tried to lever them ajar. But the doors still stayed closed. There were lights on inside, and a woman kept peering out furtively from the manager's office. The growing crowd laughed, waved and whistled, and banged playfully against the doors with their trolleys. The furtive woman vanished, and a few moments later peeped out again, and slammed the door quickly. Finally, after we had stood there for 25 minutes, she came out, shouting something over her shoulder at the office door, and looking pale, frightened and guilty. She pushed a card into a slot beside the doors which slid open sufficiently to allow her to talk through them, but not wide enough for the more determined among us to shove our trolleys through. The tills were out of order, she said, flinching as if expecting the mob to start stoning her. How long before they would be functioning again? people wanted to know. When would the store open? She couldn't give an answer.

So we all cheerfully replaced our trolleys, got in our cars, and drove to the other supermarket on the far side of town.

Around there, that qualified as quite a noteworthy event.

Erratic opening hours meant that we were always driving backwards and forwards to town. Having been used in England to shops that were open six, sometimes seven, days a week, and didn't close for lunch, learning the timetables of the local commerce required a mental effort akin to taking a degree in nuclear physics. It took several months to become used to the fact that almost nothing opened on Mondays (especially banks except for *La Poste*), apart from the supermarkets, although one of the DIY stores did open in the afternoon. The very few shops that did open on Mondays closed on Tuesdays. One supermarket closed for lunch half an hour earlier than the other, and opened fifteen minutes earlier in the afternoon. Both supermarkets stayed open all day on Saturdays, although they closed half an hour earlier than on weekdays, and one opened on Sunday mornings in July and August. The *mairie* was open one full day and two half-days per week, and the village restaurant only opened in the evenings by previous arrangement. Local bakeries had their day off on a rota system that had to be learned by heart. Relatively simple tasks could take an unreasonably long time; maybe it was just one screw that was needed to finish fitting something up, and one of us would shoot into town and arrive at the store one minute after it had closed, or on Monday morning having forgotten it didn't open until the afternoon. The supermarket that was still open probably only sold the screws in boxes of 500, so we would drive back home and wait the two and a half hours before the shop with the single screw we needed had opened again. Forty kilometres and three and a half hours just to buy one screw. It happened. And just when you were confident of knowing exactly who opened when, you could arrive to find that they were enjoying a '*fermeture exceptionelle*', or closed for stocktaking.

Although I had been an ardent Francophile since long before I knew what the word meant, for some reason that I couldn't rationalize I was uncertain about most things French before I went to live there. Chief amongst these was their vets, who would probably be hopelessly behind the times and unable to tell a dog from a cat. I'd hardly been there any time at all before our dogs gave us regular and frequent opportunities to put the local vets to the test. In England, in the days when money hadn't been a constant worry, they'd never needed veterinary attention. But now, in lamentably rapid succession, they had between them produced a torn dew-claw, a tumour, and a terrible injury caused by entanglement with a barbed-wire fence. These were dealt with so effectively and gently that any doubts I had were erased.

M. Audoux, the vet, was of medium height, with dark crew-cut hair and large, sad dark eyes. When I first met him I thought him rather unfriendly, but as my visits became more and more frequent I realized that he was just a little shy and quite possibly anxious about our ability to communicate properly, as he didn't speak English and my French was very limited.

'How many dogs do you have?' he asked on my second visit.

'Five,' I replied.

I visualized French franc signs whizzing round in his eyes like cherries on a fruit machine. But over the following years I came to rely totally on his generosity and tolerance, as our veterinary bills swallowed up our entire budget, and more. I was in debt to the practice continually, and as soon as we managed to reduce the balance another more expensive disaster would occur to boost it right up again.

A visit to the veterinary surgery was always interesting, because of the diversity of the clientele, and the medications and appliances on display. In such a rural district, the major proportion of the clients had originally been farmers, but now as household pets became more common the practice was divided between the two. There were two tariffs for treatment, as well. The rural tariff covered all farm animals and was quite a lot less expensive than the tariff for domestic pets. Neat ladies with trimmed poodles sat in the waiting room, and farmers in mucky rubber boots and muddy overalls came to collect powders for cattle with diarrhoea, treatments for sick rabbits, castration rings, and antibiotics for newborn livestock. The articles on display in the cabinets ranged from sinister metal instruments whose function I didn't want to think about, through jewelled collars and hygienic panties for dogs, to ingenious little gadgets designed to remove ticks complete with their heads. They were called Tic Tocs. Sometimes somebody came in with a creature in a cardboard box, maybe an ailing duck or rabbit that needed to be diagnosed in case it had some rampant disease that might affect all its companions. Once a man drove up and called M. Audoux outside to examine something in the boot of his car. It was a deer that had, so the driver claimed, jumped in front of the car. He wanted the vet to examine the carcass and pronounce it fit for eating, which he obligingly did. An old lady came in one day wearing her cardigan, flowery apron and carpet slippers. She was bent over at the waist at 90 degrees and walked with tremendous difficulty. To talk to anybody else she had to tilt her head to one side, as it couldn't lift upwards and backwards. Her fingers were terribly swollen and knotted, and ingrained with soil, not only around the nails but deeply in the skin. She sat down next to me and smiled cheerfully. 'It's my sheep,' she explained. 'I've only got the one, now. One of her feet has gone all soft, and she's lame. I need some of that blue spray; that'll heal it. Mind you, it's expensive, but all the same, we have to look after our animals.'

I always found the French attitude to animals ambivalent. Many hunting dogs spent their lives, apart from when they were out on a shoot, either locked in cages or tied on short chains, although their owners professed to worship them, and were certainly proud of them. Wildlife was trapped, poisoned, or shot. Farm animals could live their whole lives locked in dark barns. But I had sat beside a shabby old man who had bowed his head and was audibly weeping over his tottering and threadbare old dog, which was quite clearly making its final visit to the vet, and I knew many French people who were genuine animal lovers. In the queue at the supermarket one day was a big rough-looking man in grubby clothing whose trolley was entirely filled with tins of dog and cat food. I asked him how many animals he owned, and he said none. In the village where he lived, he said, there were several stray dogs and great numbers of cats, which nobody else fed. 'I can't stand to see an animal hungry,' he said. 'Nobody else cares about them, but *tant pis*. I buy them food every week and make sure none of them go hungry.' A farmer I was talking to one day told me he had a pet fox he had captured as a cub. 'Ah, what a fantastic pet he is. I really love that animal,' he said.

During one of my innumerable visits to the surgery, a distraught-looking woman with a cat box on her lap was sitting opposite me. Her straggly greying hair formed a sort of crazy halo round her face and she stared fixedly at me with unblinking eyes. I thought her behaviour was due to anxiety over her pet, so smiled at her and asked what was the matter with the animal.

She replied in English, in a broken, croaky voice, a bit like the bleat of a goat, that the cat was just there for a vaccination, and asked where I lived. I waved my hand vaguely, and then it was my turn to be seen by the vet.

About a fortnight later, the phone rang, and the bleaty-voiced lady announced that her name was Michelle, and that she had got my phone number from another English lady living nearby. She apologized profusely for disturbing me, and said that she desperately needed my help.

'I know you're an animal lover,' she began. 'You must know how cruel the French are to animals. I hate them. All they do is torture animals. There is a dog in my village that the woman owner tortures all the time.'

I was horrified.

'I'm ashamed to be French,' she continued. 'They're such hateful people. Because they know I care about animals they hate me too, and they want to poison me and my dogs.'

I asked what I could do to help.

'Well, you must help me rescue that terrible woman's poor dog. It's tied up with a huge chain, at the back of her house. You will have to keep her talking, and I will go round the back and take the dog.'

I didn't think so. 'I think it would be better if you report this to the police, and let them deal with it. You can't go around taking people's animals, and as a foreigner living here I definitely can't be involved in anything like that.'

'The police! They're the worst of the lot! They encourage people to hurt animals; they run them over deliberately. If you won't help me, please help me to find somebody who can.'

I said I'd do my best, and after she had given me her phone number several times and insisted that I repeated it twice to ensure I had it correctly, she hung up.

I phoned the woman who had given my number to this strange new acquaintance, and said I'd appreciate it if she wouldn't make a habit of it – who knew how many oddballs might be lurking in wait.

'Look, I'm terribly sorry, but she just wouldn't leave me alone! She rang me to say she'd met an English woman at the vet, who lived in this village, and that it was desperately urgent that she contact you. She was so persistent that I gave in.'

'How did she know you?'

'She started talking to me in the supermarket one day when she saw me buying cat food, and she seemed very friendly so I gave her my number. Then she kept phoning me because she wants me to rescue a dog.'

Ah.

Over the next few months I met more and more English people who knew Michelle. Everybody blanched when her name was mentioned.

'She's totally unreasonable. She rings at midnight, or even later, saying that kittens are being murdered, or horses killed, and tries to get you to go and take them away, or take photographs. The only way to get rid of

41

her is to find a new English person and dump her on them.'

Now I understood.

But I couldn't find anybody to pass her on to. Until some new and unsuspecting arrival turned up, I was stuck with her, and few weeks passed without a dramatic phone call with ghastly graphic descriptions of new atrocities. By now, we had two elderly horses, five dogs, two parrots and two cats to consider, plus numerous poultry, and at least one of them was generally swelling the vet's pension fund, and although I explained forcefully and frequently to Michelle that I simply wasn't in a position to take on any more, and asked her not to distress me with further heartbreaking stories, she continued regardless, ringing day and night, until I was forced to install a telephone answering machine to screen her calls.

Nothing daunted, she started driving round to our house, scrutinizing our menagerie closely to ensure I wasn't mistreating them, and pointing out that our neighbours were probably doing terrible things to animals that I couldn't see.

'They're all horrible people. I don't like being French, but I'm not like the rest of them. That's why they hate me.'

M. Meneteau saw her driving away one day, and asked what she was doing there. 'Be careful of her,' he warned.

I thought what she did was probably with the best of intentions, but every encounter with her left me feeling jumpy and depressed.

The local garden centre was a rather dilapidated affair of yellowing, crispy polythene, under the management of a fierce-looking lady. Nevertheless, she was friendly, obliging and knowledgeable, and the plants I bought there seemed invariably to outdo the more uniformly perfect specimens purchased from the classy garden centres in town at twice the price. Where the idea came from that the French don't garden I can't imagine, because the garden centres were always teeming with people pushing trolleys burgeoning with shrubs, trees, pot plants, bedding plants and packets of seeds, and I don't recall ever seeing an unkempt French garden anywhere.

In the town library there was a section devoted to books in English, and the friendly librarians were happy to try to get in any other books we asked for. The more I became accustomed to life there, the more it seemed to me that France was a most civilized place to live. The tap water was drinkable, the telephone worked, the roads were well surfaced, and the electric current could even navigate our archaic installation, which resembled a family tree. A single two-pin socket in the living room wall represented the top of the tree; into this we plugged a short cable that dangled down into a four-way socket connection on the floor; from each of these four sockets ran more cables, leading to more multiple sockets. The cables branched all over the floors and up the walls, and were expected to run fridge, kettle, TV, bedside lamps, washing machine, computer, aquarium, lawnmower, etc. etc. etc. To make things a little more complicated, some of these still had English plugs on them, and some had French. I learned that you could plug a two-pin round French plug into a three-pin square English socket if you first poke something into the third hole of the socket (being very careful to ensure that the thing you poke in isn't conductive, because if it is, of course, you'd probably electrocute yourself. Personally, I always used a twig). There isn't any way that you can get an English three-pin square plug into a French two-pin round socket, though. At least, I couldn't find one. There were times when it all went pfffffffft and nothing worked, but

43

it was usually just a matter of changing a fuse or re-arranging the family tree.

About the only thing I really did find exasperating was when people serving in shops answered the telephone whilst serving you, and dropped you like a hot coal; while you stood pointlessly, captive, with outstretched hand awaiting your change, they embarked on an impossibly lengthy conversation repeating the same thing dozens of times.

'Yes. A hundred and eighty-five francs, including tax. We'll have it on Wednesday afternoon. Yes, we're open from two fifteen to seven o'clock. Yes, that's right, in the afternoon. On Wednesday. Any time between two fifteen and seven. A hundred and eighty-five francs. No, it won't be here until Wednesday. It's a hundred and eighty-five francs, yes, that's right, including tax. No, we won't have it on Monday, it will be here Wednesday. No, the delivery doesn't come until after lunch . . .'

The frantic barking of the dogs heralded the arrival at the gate of a large, male person whose thinning hair gave him a rather threadbare appearance, so I mentally christened him Fred. Fred Bear.

'Are you Sue?' he called out.

'Susie.'

'Bill said you're an expert on horses.'

'No, I'm afraid not. I have a couple of retired horses of my own, but I'm far from being an expert.'

'Well, it's for my mate in Spain. He's a champion dressage rider, he wins all the cups, and he wants me to find him a new, top-class horse. Bill said you'd be the person to ask.'

Frankly, I thought it an extremely strange idea, asking a friend to locate a high-performance horse – much the same as delegating someone to track down a perfect wife – but being as naïve as I still was, and because I didn't want to seem either unfriendly or unhelpful, I said I'd do my best.

'Don't worry, dearie,' said the threadbare one, 'I'll pay for your phone calls.'

And so in good and quite misplaced faith, I embarked on a crusade to find a dressage horse for a man I didn't know who lived in Spain.

I spent several days phoning various people who referred me to various other people, and we were unamimous in agreeing it was a very bizarre way of trying to buy an expensive horse. Anyway, nobody had one, and with a phone bill reflecting calls that had started off local, and from there wended their way to national, international and inter-continental, I reported back to Fred that I hadn't been able to locate a suitable horse for his friend. I didn't like to mention the phone bill, and apparently neither did he, and I never did get re-imbursed.

Chapter Three

Our kitchen was slightly unconventional, because before Terry had left to return to England we had set it up 60 metres from the house, in the large open-fronted barn at the bottom of our garden. You might think this was a rather eccentric decision, but at the time it had made sense. There was no space within either of the two existing rooms in the house for the kitchen, and the rest of the building, the main barn area, had no electricity, the walls comprised pieces of rock and flint vaguely held in place by mud and manure, there was no ceiling and we could see daylight through the elderly tiles, and the floor had been the livestock's toilet for decades. Really no place for a kitchen. So we established it in the lower barn, which also had no electricity, no ceiling, and a dirt floor, and was accessible to whatever wildlife chose to roam around in it. In retrospect, I can't quite remember the logic, but anyway, there it was at the bottom of the garden, also 60 metres from the only source of running water on the premises, an outside tap attached to the wall of the house. Oh yes – the fridge/freezer was in the garage, 60 different metres away from the kitchen, and the only place with an accessible electric power point. We had bought and brought with us a malevolent second-hand gas cooker that the previous owners had earnestly assured us worked perfectly. If 'working perfectly' was defined as producing a flame on which you could cook, the owners had been truthful. But what they hadn't mentioned, or had maybe failed to notice, was that each time it was lit it shuddered violently, gave out a great bang and spat blue flames randomly from the joints on the casing. As it was our sole source of hot water and cooked food I had to live with it, but it was a relationship built upon fear and loathing. The washing machine stood outside the garage, sharing the power point with the fridge/freezer, connected by a piece of hose to the water tap 10 metres away, and discharging directly into the thirsty earth through a length of drainpipe.

Instead of a bathroom we had a plastic bucket that served as a basin/bath, and while the scorching weather lasted it was perfectly practicable. We installed a chemical loo in an old goat shed. All nice and simple, and it did away with the need for any tiresome housework.

That first summer it was almost indescribably hot. The tarmac melted and bubbled up through its own cracks. Flies were horrendous, a plague that was everywhere. Not content with going about their vile personal business, they swarmed at you and tried to get in your hair. Absolutely disgusting. It was a no-holds-barred fight to the death: swatter, aerosols, sticky fly papers and dishes of yellow granules containing, so the label said, flies' sex hormones (what a distasteful thought), which were meant to attract and then kill them, but didn't.

There was a wide variety of stinging and biting insects to get to know. They homed in on me, raising lumps of various sizes and degrees of irritation. Midges and mosquitoes, flies that bit, huge horseflies that *really* bit, horrible delta-shaped giant flies called *mouches plates* that almost ate you alive; wasps, bees, and a hateful little creature called *aoûtat* that bit my face, bringing it up

47

in hard red shiny lumps, which amalgamated so that I looked like a cricket ball.

During the fierce summer heat my feet expanded several sizes and wouldn't go into any of my shoes, so I bought a pair of plastic sandals whose soles were studded with hundreds of little plastic spikes. A label said that these massaged your feet and made you feel good. For three days they only made me feel good when I took them off. Wearing them was like walking on a bed of nails. But having invested the equivalent of two pounds in them, I couldn't afford to let them go to waste, so persevered, firstly with socks, and finally without. By the end of a week, if I'd had to leave a burning building with only one item, it would have been that pair of sandals. Once you were past the pain threshold, they were divine.

I simply could not glow as a lady should, or acquire a golden tan as everybody else seemed to be able to do. Couldn't even perspire like a gentleman. In the overwhelming heat, I sweated like a horse. My skin took on a livid scarlet radiance. One afternoon in August the thermometer registered 43°C. Just breathing was a struggle, like inhaling warm treacle. Being in a car, even with all the windows open, was the equivalent of being in a sauna with the heating on high. The plums and grapes were ripening, attracting swarms of wasps. The only sensible place to be was indoors, shutters closed, and doing nothing more energetic than reading.

Like the listless, dusty trees and the frizzled brown grass, I was absolutely exhausted by the heat, and I craved rain. Three weeks after we'd arrived the first and very welcome drops fell, preceded by several hours of cracking thunder. For two hours torrents of water from purple skies smashed into the baked ground, and hailstones the size of marbles bounced and ricocheted off the roofs. The rain just poured down; I stood out in it, enjoying its violence and silky warmth, although I could have got almost as wet indoors as it gushed down the chimney, through the broken window panes, under the door, through the ceiling and down the walls.

Because for so much of the time I was alone, and because it was so hot, and because I used the beastly oven as seldom as possible, I ate fairly simply, although sometimes rather strangely. A typical meal could have been something like a handful of bourbon biscuits and half a jar of pickled onions. On one of those sweltering days I sat reading peacefully and sipping a glass of wine (later, beseiged by company, I was glad I had taken advantage of my solitude when I could). While I read I absent-mindedly smeared a good runny Brie, carefully maintained at room temperature to allow it to mature nicely, onto some crackers. When it came time to turn over a page, I put down the plate to take a mouthful of wine, and noticed that there was movement round the rim. A handful of plump creamy maggots, no other word for them, were humping over the edge. My first optimistic hope was that they had fallen from a nearby bush, or come out of the biscuit tin, but then I saw some of their kith and kin emerging cautiously from the cheese. Yes, all those wary little maggot faces were peeping out to make sure that some great mouth wasn't going to bite them in half, or squash them on a cracker, like those of their brethren that had gone before them. Aieeeeeeeeeeee! For a vegetarian it was not a good moment. I gargled and swilled out my mouth with vodka, spat, then knocked back the rest of the wine bottle fast, and from that moment on kept all the cheese in the fridge, which never allowed it to reach that creamy stage of perfection, but did ensure that visible things didn't live in it. If you are vegetarian, too, or squeamish about eating maggots, do look carefully at cheese before you eat it. Don't worry, you'll see them if they're there – they're quite large. Really quite large.

In view of the amount of work that needed doing, I thought I should at least try to do some elementary repairs. Each time, I wished I hadn't. There was a patch of flaking paint in one corner of the living room. I peeled it off, and the surrounding paint broke into a crazed surface of flakes, which I peeled off likewise, leaving a large area of rough plaster with black stuff growing on it. The black stuff looked like some kind of mould, so I scraped at it. Huge chunks of plaster let go of the wall and tumbled into crumbly lumpy heaps on the floor, leaving behind inch-deep craters out of which trickled cascades of sand and dirt, exposing the stones and flints that formed the main substance of the wall. I prodded around and constructed more craters and cascades: there was something compulsive about this activity. I felt as if I could stay forever digging at the wall with my little chisel until I'd brought it all down onto the floor. But sense prevailed, and after sweeping up the part of the wall that now lay all around my feet, I went and bought a packet of filler and smeared it into the craters. This was easier said than done, as the loose sandy, dusty stuff in the craters did not accept the filler readily; nobody had mentioned that it needed wetting before the filler was applied, and I hadn't yet worked it out for myself. Just when I thought I'd got a nice smooth surface the whole thing would fall out in a sticky, gritty lump and I'd have to start all over again. After that I tended to ignore peeling paint or little patches of damp, and simply paint over them. It was quicker and safer.

Many of the beams had soft spongy patches that yielded rather pleasantly to the chisel. This too was hypnotic: it was so difficult to stop, so satisfying to whittle away the redundant material. The beams grew thinner and I finally abandoned them too before the whole house collapsed.

Every so often I started a 'home improvements' binge,

tackling some new project. With so much that needed doing, I never knew where to start. Garden? Unpacking? Cleaning? Painting? Knocking something down? Mending fences? The task seemed monumental. I started on the living room floor, and spent many painful hours on my knees with buckets of hot soapy water, gritty creams, and noxious foaming chemicals; when they were all used up the floor was no cleaner than when I started, so finally we borrowed a sander and managed to get to the wood beneath the grime that only decades could create, and it only took 16 hours on my hands and knees (not consecutively, but in several shifts over two days). Unfortunately the sander had lost the little bag that should fit on the side to collect the dust created by its efforts, so all of that was all over the newly painted walls. The floor looked rather nice though, apart from the parts that were collapsing round the edges, which I ignored.

Then I started on the ceiling, washing it down and applying three coats of varnish to wood that slurped it away invisibly. After a couple of weeks of this fun my lungs were full of sawdust, my hair was covered with high-gloss varnish, my clothes and shoes were decorated with sploshes of paint and plaster and I seemed to have permanently changed shape into a question mark. Never mind; I was becoming insensitive to pain.

A strange creature began following me wherever I went. Its clothes were totally uncoordinated, and most didn't fit properly. Its hair was a disaster, straggly and shapeless, and it wore a frazzled expression. It was either sprinkled with dust, or splashed with mud. I thought it was female, although the shapeless clothing made it difficult to tell. Mostly I saw it when glancing in shop windows. What a dreadful mess it was. I couldn't understand how anybody could let themselves go about looking like that.

*   *   *

To the front of our house were three vines, their trunks twisted and ragged with age. They straggled up to a height of about three metres and there branched laterally into festoons of bright green leaves and great hanks of grapes. Snuggled into a knot on one of these vines was a nest of flycatchers, well protected amongst the leaves. Three small avian hooligans hung over the edge of the nest with permanently gaping maws, urging their parents to hurry, hurry, hurry, shrieking rudely and bouncing up and down waving their small feathered arms. Their parents worked on the wing from dawn to dusk, snatching invisible morsels from the air and returning to prod them into their offspring's bottomless throats. The mother bird concentrated diligently upon her task, but her mate tended to be easily distracted. One evening I watched as he returned to the nest with a beakful of bugs for the babies, but just as he was on the point of distributing this feast a small butterfly bobbed past, and he dropped what was in his mouth and winged after that, leaving the infants shrieking angrily with disappointment.

The garden teemed with birds: robins, tits, blackbirds, sparrows, wrens in crevices, wagtails strutting bumptiously, redstarts and blackstarts, swallows, martins and clouds of goldfinches. Impossibly exotic-looking hoopoes dug insects from the lawn with their long curved beaks. Crows, jays, magpies and pigeons co-habited in the large oak; green woodpeckers and spotted woodpeckers gave themselves away by their high-speed rapping, their laughing call and telltale dolphin flight. Herons sailed past on their way to the stream, trailing their long legs behind them like craneflies. The cuckoo's song that had been such a noteworthy event in England became monotonous, sounding repetitively from early morning to last light.

I had a car, of a sort. Approaching her twentieth birth-day, Tinkerbelle was a pale blue Citroën 2CV. These little cars have been aptly described as looking like giant snails pieced together out of old biscuit tins. They were first conceived in the 1930s, intended as affordable transport for the masses, to seat four adults (wearing hats), carry 120 pounds of potatoes, and be capable of traversing a ploughed field with a basket of eggs without breaking one. The car's development was interrupted by the outbreak of the Second World War, and when it was eventually unveiled at the Paris Motor Show in 1948 it was greeted with hoots of laughter and clouds of waving chequebooks as customers queued to buy. Their owners loved them and the 2CV became a cult car that offered a level of comfort and performance that belied its eccentric design and tiny engine which looked more suited to driving a sewing machine. So much in demand were they at one time that there was a six-year waiting list, and used models cost more than new ones.

I dearly loved Tinkerbelle, whom we had bought for an extortionate price from a very nice man who had left her to fester in a basement garage until we turned up to waken her from retirement. All 2CVs came with a fabric roof encompassing a rear window; the whole roof could be folded back on summer days to give the little vehicles a very rakish appearance. These roofs tended not to share their bodies' durability, and Tinkerbelle's was torn and battered; replacements were available from various sources, but the only colour we had been able to find for Tinkerbelle was bright red which, married to her blue lower regions, gave her a most distinctive appearance and attracted stares of open-mouthed wonder.

For the first few weeks of my new life I catered for my food needs by walking to the village or using the mobile shop that called in the hamlet three times a week, just as it had been doing for decades. It came from the *boulangerie* in the village, and apart from selling bread offered an interesting and diverse range of other items: buttons; cotton for darning stockings; envelopes; tinned fruit, vegetables, fish and meat; soft drinks and cheap wine; biscuits and fresh cakes; sweets; greetings cards. In most accounts of life in France the local bakery produces mouth-watering, simply delicious crusty bread. At that time, ours didn't. What it manufactured was an assembly of large holes linked by a dry white material like polystyrene ceiling tiles, the whole encased in a thick and vicious crust that cut your gums and got jammed inextricably between your teeth. It wasn't even any use for toasting, as the network of tunnels provided a fast escape route for any butter or other spread. This was only my personal view: the local villagers liked this bread and were proud of their bakery, but I liked my bread to be soft and chewy with a fine crust that didn't have the texture of tree bark. Anyway, I digress.

There were two reasons I was tolerating the horrid bread. One was that I was not at all certain of finding my way either to or back from town, 10 kilometres away, through a landscape of boundless fields, winding lanes and stone-built pantile-roofed buildings, all looking just like innumerable other fields, lanes and buildings. Occasionally, instead of pantiles, some roofs were tiled with slate, giving them a much colder and less homely appearance, and I wondered what the reason was. Many of the buildings in Saint-Thomas-le-Petit had slate roofs. I asked a French gentleman why, and he explained: 'Look at the pitch of the roof. Tiles, which are basically held on simply by their own weight, can only maintain themselves on the roof if the angle is not too steep. Notice how all the churches have slate roofs. It's all to do with the angle.'

My second reason for not venturing out was that I

was terrified of taking to the road in Tinkerbelle and having to contend with a steering wheel on the left hand side, whilst driving on the right hand side of the road, a complete reversal of what I had been doing for the previous thirty years. And apart from that, much as I loved Tinkerbelle, to be very frank I didn't have a lot of confidence in her mechanical competence. Also, I never had any idea which gear I was in. Tinkerbelle's weird gearbox configuration required much simultaneous pulling, twisting and shoving to engage a gear, and was quite unlike any other gearbox I'd ever used. There was a helpful diagram etched onto the primitive dashboard that illustrated the location of the gears, but I failed to notice it until somebody pointed it out to me several months later. In the meantime each movement was unpredictable. I just moved the knob around every so often and waited to see what would happen. But in time things started falling into place and soon I was bowling and bumping backwards and forwards quite confidently, humming along with Tinkerbelle's soft growling, although it was many months before I was certain of my whereabouts at any given time.

Well-intentioned friends in England regularly cautioned me to be excessively careful when driving, 'because,' they said, 'you know how awful French drivers are.' I didn't, but conducted a small local survey, and here are the results.

More an irritation than a hazard were the botty-sniffers who, like newly introduced dogs, aimed to get their snouts as far up your vehicular backside as possible. They got so close, for reasons you could not understand, that you could smell their breath; they looked hurt and startled if you kept tapping your brakes, and even if you reduced your speed to walking pace they would not overtake, but clung determinedly to your bumpers until you pulled off the road and stopped completely, forcing them to pass, which they did with a sad and reproachful stare.

Then there were the boy/girl racers, whose sole aim was to driver faster than, and be ahead of, anybody else on the road. There always seemed to be a scarlet-finger-nailed soignée blonde in a dog-tooth check jacket driving a BMW or Mercedes a hair's breadth from Tinkerbelle's rear, glaring exasperation and contempt into my rear view mirror. They menaced you by riding on your rear quarter, scowling because you were ahead of them. I felt safer once I'd allowed them past and they were out of my orbit. I used to wonder what it was that drove them to such excess of speed, whether it was simply part of their nature or whether maybe they were caught in a crisis of some sort, but in any event I was always happy to let them overtake so that I could continue my leisurely exploration of the countryside.

In a rural area, agricultural machinery on the roads was an inevitability, from the ancient lovable little snub-nosed tractors with hard metal seats, trundling and bouncing contentedly along shedding clods of mud and farmyard sludge, to their larger, menacingly angular descendants fortified with steel spikes before and multiple rows of plough shares behind; hay wagons occupying the entire width of the lane and occasionally toppling great rolls of hay onto the road; and gargantuan combine harvesters as big as villas. Whilst crawling along behind them you had to remind yourself that the farmers were simply going about their agricultural business, and not purposely obstructing your path.

There were multitudes of elderly gentlemen, bless them, invariably plump, rosy-cheeked, twinkly-eyed and bereted, who mentally were still travelling in the age of the horse-drawn vehicle. The concept of crossroads, or right of way, was quite alien to them, and they wore a permanent smile of blissful satisfaction as they drove steadfastly across the paths of other motorists, oblivious of the fact that they had narrowly missed killing or being killed. They neither gave nor responded to signals, but progressed at their own modest speed, and totally unpredictably.

In an area where public transport did not exist, apart from the school bus, and many elderly ladies lived alone in scattered hamlets several kilometres from the nearest shops, the only way they could maintain their independence was to drive. They zigzagged and weaved, struggling to hold a course, and either had never discovered that the car had more than one forward gear (perhaps like me they'd not noticed the diagram), or had chosen to ignore any but first, and their rear view mirrors too. I was absolutely certain many of them couldn't have reversed a car under pain of death, and must have had to plan their journeys and parking accordingly.

It was down to those more fortunate drivers among us who still retained some of our faculties to make allowances for these elders, to try to predict their next move, or lack of, and thus help to ensure the safe continuance of their journeys. Maybe people would do the same for us one day.

The winding local roads were little more than one car's breadth, and passing another vehicle meant having one wheel almost in the ditch to avoid contact, but that didn't seem to deter many a driver from using the full width of the road as they hurtled round bends. By anticipating a hurtler at every blind corner, you could probably prolong your life expectancy. Along all the major roads, and many smaller ones too, bunches of colourful plastic flowers on top of poles stood by the roadside indicating that a fatal accident had taken place at that point. There were many of them, and sometimes several in the same place.

Anyway, whether or not the French were particularly

57

dreadful drivers, I couldn't say, and in any case, having driven for ten years in Kenya, particularly in Mombasa, I'd seen everything there was to see as far as driving goes.

Surprises popped up round each corner. A crowd of camels grazing on the banks of the Charente, and the nearby car park crowded with llamas, when a circus came to town; in an isolated village a colourful and noisy muster of peacocks strutting down a lane. Sometimes, driving into town, I passed the old lady goatherd, the last remaining one in our immediate area and a living illustration of a passing era. With her sly crouching dog, she pedalled her bicycle alongside her twenty or so caprine charges trotting haughtily on their neat cloven hooves, and ushered them through the lanes to fields of stubble, where they grazed while she sat on a folding chair, bent over her knitting. On wet days she shrouded herself in a waterproof cape and green rubber boots. Her goats were glossy and sleek, and when she steered them home bleating in the evening, their udders bulged with the milk that would be made into one of the regional specialities, goat's cheese. The old lady was bent almost double with age, but beneath her tight grey curls her weather-beaten face was tranquil. When I waved, or pulled over to let her past, she beamed hugely and raised one knobbly hand, and her eyes sparkled like sapphires. When she was gone nobody would replace her, and she would fade into history. There was no romance in modern goat-farming that kept the animals hock-deep in straw-filled barns, and unless they could organize an occasional breakout they never saw daylight or grass.

Fred Bear, instigator of the abortive horse-hunt, was a regular visitor, his arrival marked by either an angry discourse on how he had been cheated by somebody, or a triumphant crowing over a financial victory in some petty matter. He arrived one day beaming with triumph: he had found a pair of gold-rimmed bifocal spectacles that perfectly suited him, for five francs from a charity shop. The fact that they were women's spectacles and far too small for him didn't bother him at all; had they had purple plastic frames with *diamanté* wings he would doubtless have worn them with pride simply because they were so cheap.

At each visit, which ostensibly was just to see if I was all right, he asked 'just a little favour, dearie'. He didn't actually mean 'a', he meant 'some'. The required little favours were always in clusters. They didn't amount to much – a phone call, a letter translated, an envelope stamped and posted, a fax sent, a few more phone calls. An hour here, an hour there; few days passed without a visit. More than the irritation of these interminable impositions, which I could tolerate if I tried, was being called 'dearie', which I absolutely hated. And always I would be paid, but I never was. Often he came bearing little gifts, things that were of no use to him, or to me, like the food mixer that didn't have a lid, but which I accepted graciously rather than appearing rude. Then he'd remind me that I owed him something in return.

Occasionally rather aggressive, when he wanted something he became very docile, batting his eyelashes and calling me 'petal' or 'my little flower', which was even more horrible than 'dearie'. The innocent blue eyes met mine, the helpless, wheedling expression spread over the face as yet another 'little favour, dearie' was called. I stared back at my reflection in the spectacles, and was sure I could see letters written on my forehead. As I heard myself agreeing to the latest little-favour cluster, I watched the letters darken and form, quite distinctly, Ɔ-U-M.

Up until then he had owned a house some distance

north, but so convivial did he find our area that he decided to move there, and began house-hunting, supplying regular updates on his progress. Finally, after discarding many houses because the owners 'were bloody joking, the prices they were asking', he found the house of his dreams. Although it was going for a song, he had no intention of paying the full price. Fred couldn't speak French, so he appointed me as his interpreter, despite my still-embryonic mastery of the language.

'Ring the agent, dearie, and tell him I'll give him so much,' he mentioned a figure, 'and he can take it or leave it.'

I said, 'You're a fool. If it's what you say it is, it's already a bargain.'

'I know, dearie,' he leered, 'but I'm still going to beat them down.'

I dutifully phoned the agent, made the offer, and he said he would call me back once he had spoken to the owners.

He didn't phone for a week, and Fred was beside himself. 'What's the matter with these bloody people? Here's me offering them top price for the place, and they can't even be bothered to phone. Ring them for me, dearie, will you, and ask what the hell's going on.'

So I phoned the agent again, and he told me with some satisfaction that the house had been sold for the asking price several days previously. He cheerfully rejected Fred's offer to match that price, and Fred went into a great sulk.

But a few days later, he was stamping up to our gate waving a fragment of paper over his head, and whooping.

'We've found it! It's the best ever! Can't believe it, perfect for us, and only two kilometres from here. There's a board outside with a phone number. Ring them for me, dearie, and find out the price.' He thrust the fragment at me.

One of the numbers was in Paris, and the other a mobile phone. The first number didn't reply, but the mobile phone was answered and for the next ten minutes or so I was asking questions of the owner and translating the replies to Fred at my own expense. Eventually, I had arranged a meeting between them for a week hence at 2.30 p.m.

At midday on the agreed date Fred stamped into the house. 'You've given him the wrong bloody address, haven't you? He should have been here by now!'

I pointed out that it was midday and that the vendor wasn't due for another two and a half hours.

'But I'd have thought he'd want to get here early, being as I'm waving fistfuls of money at him. Give him a ring and find out what's happened.'

With Fred it was easier to just do what he asked rather than waste your time appealing to reason, because he didn't seem to have any.

The vendor was surprised but friendly when I called him.

'Yes,' he said, 'we're on our way to you. Shortly we will stop for lunch, and will meet you as arranged not later than two thirty.'

I apologized for disturbing him and hoped he'd have a nice lunch.

For the next two and a half hours Fred muttered and shouted and said he'd never known anything like it, people stopping to eat when he was sitting here waiting to give them money. I tried to pacify him by pointing out that he'd have his money that bit longer. Several times he tried to force me to phone again.

'Only if he isn't here by two thirty,' I said.

Which, of course, he was.

We all trooped off to the *notaire*'s office where Fred signed the *compromis*, and then the vendor invited us back to his house for coffee. Fred agreed to buy certain furnishings in the house, not, he said, because he needed them, but because they were too cheap to resist. It was 6.00 p.m. before I got home, having devoted six hours to Fred and his house.

About two months later the final papers were ready for signing. I'd had a horrible morning, because Fred had come armed with a bank draft that he wanted to cash, and the local bank was unable to oblige because he didn't have an account with them.

'Would you tell them, dearie, that in England I wouldn't have this problem.'

'You're not in England.'

'Just bloody tell them that they're a bunch of idiots.'

The lady we were dealing with, who had explained very politely and apologetically that she couldn't help, and whom I knew vaguely, spoke a certain amount of English, and our eyes met. I rolled mine upwards.

'I am not going to be rude to these people because they can't help you. It isn't their fault, and you should have organized the money sooner. Please stop shouting.'

He faced the polite lady and yelled: 'You bloody French need to learn how to run a bank properly!'

A man came out from an office and asked us to leave.

In the *notaire*'s office that afternoon the vendor was waiting with his wife and little girl. Fred and I sat beside them, facing the *notaire*, who waited politely and patiently whilst we exchanged greetings of handshakes and kisses, and enquired as to the traffic on the way. When we were settled, she started reading out the *Acte de Vente*, with me translating for the benefit of Fred. Once this was finished, the painful moment came when Fred must pay for his new purchase.

'Ask her how much it is, dearie.'

'Could you tell me the exact amount, please, madame?'

She gave a tiny figure that wouldn't buy a decent doll's house in England, and I translated it to Fred.

'She's bloody joking! Where the hell did she get that figure from?'

'Please,' I said, 'don't make a scene in here.'

'I want to know where she's got her bloody figure from!'

'I'm sorry, madame, but could you show this gentleman how the total is made up?'

'Of course. This is the amount for the purchase, less the deposit paid. And this represents our fees for the work carried out.'

I explained to Fred, who snorted and stamped his foot.

'I'm not paying her that much for a few hours' work! Tell her I don't appreciate being ripped off because I'm English and they're bloody frogs!'

'OK. I'm leaving.' I picked up my bag and stood up.

'Now wait a minute, don't you go walking out of here. Just tell her I'm not paying those fees. They're a rip-off.'

'That's fine. Don't pay the fees. You won't get your house. I really don't care. I'm not going to stay here while you make an exhibition of yourself in front of these people.'

'OK. But you just tell her that I know she's cheating me.'

'I'm telling her no such thing. You want to be rude, you learn to speak the language.'

The *notaire* met my look and turned up her eyes expressively. The vendors looked flabbergasted.

With much sighing and cursing, Fred extracted his carefully folded chequebook from his neatly buttoned wallet, and pushed it towards me.

'You write it out.'

I did so, and he signed it bad-temperedly.

The *notaire* took it, thanked Fred courteously, and stood up to indicate that the meeting was over.

Suddenly, Fred roared: 'Hang on a minute! There's something funny going on here!'

'What on earth is the matter now?'

'Look – this cheque stub's not been filled in! It's blank! Somebody's stolen one of my cheques!'

'Don't be ridiculous. How could anybody steal your cheques? You never let your wallet out of your sight.'

'Well, I'm telling you, someone's had one of my cheques, because the stub isn't filled in, and I want to know what's going on!'

We all sat down again.

'What is the problem?' the *notaire* asked.

I explained that there was an empty counterfoil in the chequebook, and she enquired with her eyebrows what it had to do with her.

'Look, we'll sort this out later, at home, shall we?' I suggested to Fred.

'I'm not leaving here until I know who's had my cheque. Tell her to give me back my cheque.'

The *notaire* handed him back his cheque, which corresponded with the stub he had just written, but the previous stub was still guiltily and inexplicably blank.

'Ask her what she thinks that cheque could have been for?'

'The gentleman wonders if you can suggest what the cheque could have been used for?'

'But how could I know? I have never met this man until an hour ago. I've no idea what he does with his chequebook!'

We seemed to have reached an impasse. Looking at the bewildered faces watching this drama, I was overcome by an attack of the giggles, and the more I wondered how I came to be sitting here in this predicament, the more I giggled.

Then I remembered. 'You drew cash from the bank

this morning. You cashed a cheque. That's what the cheque was for.'

Fred eventually conceded that the mystery of the blank stub had been solved, and once he had laboriously rectified the omission we went our separate ways, him waving merrily and promising to pop down to see me very soon, and probably daily now that we were close neighbours. I waved back with a feeble smile.

Indignant, panicky bird noise woke me early one morning. Sparsely wrapped in only a short, white and semi-transparent kimono, and wearing a pair of battered sandals, I set off to investigate the commotion, which was coming from the ragged hedge separating our garden from M. Meneteau's. It was a sad specimen of a hedge, a composite of brambles, ivy and rusting wire netting, and tangled in it was a young blackbird struggling to escape. Its anxious parents fluttered about on a nearby roof. I went and found a rake and started pulling away what debris I could, crouching down so I could see what I was doing and making sure I wasn't injuring the bird. After a few moments I became aware that I was not alone – M. Meneteau was squatting on the other side of the hedge, half-heartedly prodding around with a stick. Protecting what very little modesty I had left, I called out 'Good morning', and he stood up.

'What are you doing?' he asked.

'There's a bird trapped – I'm trying to get it out of the hedge.'

'Ah.' He jabbed with his stick and the bird fluttered free and flew off with its parents. I felt we were getting to know each other quite well. Intimately, almost.

I soon discovered that M. Meneteau was a magician. He hoed a little, scratched with a fork, turned over some soil, scraped out a few perfectly parallel ridges, sowed a handful of seeds, and very soon neat rows of obedient green seedlings appeared, to shoot up into cabbages, beans, lettuces, tomatoes, sweet peppers, artichokes, leeks, endives, spinach and asparagus, the lines of vegetables prettily divided by clumps of lilies and marguerites. He could tell you exactly the right moment to plant, and the effect of every drop of rain, breath of wind, or blast of sun. He knew precisely what every seed wanted and needed in order to grow into a healthy plant, and never had to look up anything in a book; and he pulled up stinging nettles with his bare hands.

During July and August the holiday season was in top gear, and instead of two cars on the road, there were four; the cafés spilled their tables and chairs onto the pavements, and there was a burst of antique fairs, horse fairs, cycle races, street painting competitions, and a display of performing tigers. All around the hamlet, both on the plains behind and on the gentle slopes in front, the land was splashed with geometric ranks of green maize spears, rustling silver-speckled in the sunlight, and outrageous sunflowers with huge golden faces frilled with yellow collars. By the middle of September the holiday activity was starting to melt gradually away, and the countryside returned to its dozy state. The wheat and barley were already reaped, and the harvesters moved in on the frivolous sunflowers, who were by then looking decidedly ashamed of themselves and hanging their withered heads in mortification; the maize that had been such a lush green just a few weeks ago was already turning to pinky-beige, and the blackberries were ripe for picking.

I sat and wrote out lists of all the books I had always wanted to read but had never had the time to. I scoured gardening books and magazines on home renovation, making plans, dreaming dreams and wondering whether, or how, we would ever have sufficient money to accomplish any of them. The future was rather hazy, but in my mind one thing was crystal clear: life here was going to be deliciously peaceful, punctuated by nothing more eventful than the transition of one season to the next.

It was the sort of place where it was not, I felt, at all unrealistic to expect to live an uneventful life.

Chapter Four

Because of the time Terry and I spent apart, living at
different paces, quite a lot of adjustment was required for
his visits to run smoothly. Terry occupied the fast lane,
always under pressure to earn and supply our needs. He
drove fast and lived in a country where rushing was the
normal pace, while I wallowed in the ambient lethargy of
our new home. Consequently the first few days of each
stay were speckled with admonitions from him for me
to for heaven's sake hurry up, and from me for him
to please stop rushing around. The unhurried queues
in the supermarket and the casual service in the shops
exasperated him; I found my non-routine upheaved by
having to produce meals three times a day, and saw red
when he commented on the things I hadn't done rather
than those I had. After a couple of days he'd slow down
and I'd speed up until we reached a mutually acceptable
pace and settled back into our normal married enjoyment. Terry attacked project after project. It seemed
there was no limit to his energy, which made me feel
rather guilty, as mine was distinctly restricted. Most of
the tasks assigned to me sounded fairly modest when we
discussed them, and generally defeated me in practice.

*   *   *

So there I was, settling in, getting to know my way around, and looking after our five dogs, two parrots and Sinbad. The weather was glorious, and every day I put all the birds out in the garden in their cages. Unlike our parrots' wheeled, moderately lightweight models, Sinbad's 5 foot high, 8 foot square wrought iron cage weighed about six hundred pounds, and the daily struggle to manoeuvre it in and out through the narrow doorway and over the small step developed muscles in my shoulders and arms that a Sumo wrestler might covet. Time passed. The few days grew into weeks, and there was no sign of Sinbad's going home.

Bill lived a nomadic sort of existence shuttling his furniture trucks between Spain and England, stopping off every so often to deliver loads of items and pick up other things to take away with him. His barn was crammed full of furniture, cartons, crates, tools, building materials, odd wheels, a few breeze-blocks, tins and bottles of stuff. Outside there were four or maybe five caravans in various states of repair, or disrepair, and speckled with moss and mould. I'll explain why.

What Bill called his house was at that time not a house at all (neither was it actually his, as I would learn much, much later). It was just a large barn with a corrugated iron roof and a few bits of wall, which as I mentioned earlier he intended to convert into three houses, doing most of the work himself – quite a substantial project for one man who was already running a business on his own, although he didn't seem at all worried by the size of the task. It didn't appear that he had made very much progress since he had bought the property two years earlier, or that he ever would at the rate he was going, but he loved the place with a passion. As there was no electricity, running water, floor, doors or windows, when Bill was staying up here he lived in one of the caravans in the back garden. The others were used variously for guest accommodation, an office, and dogs' quarters.

We enjoyed a symbiotic relationship – he couldn't speak any French apart from '*bonjour*' and '*merci*', which he pronounced 'mercy', so my smattering of words came in useful when he was trying to buy or locate things. He knew his way around the area, sort of, and had introduced me to builders' merchants and some extremely nice English people including a friendly young couple, Carole and Paul, with two little boys I thought were simply awful. The elder one, Christopher, had a passion for snails; he collected them and let them crawl all over his face and body, watching their slimy progress with wonderment. Sometimes he kissed them, pressing them fervently to his lips. His younger brother Joseph found them fascinating too; if when we were out walking he found a snail, or a slug, he'd crouch down beside it saying, 'Look, it's boodiful.' We'd all agree that it was indeed boodiful, and Joseph would stay behind despite all our urging to catch up with us. After spending a long time crooning to the boody of the gastropod, he would grind it into the ground with his little boot and stand looking at the sticky patch with a huge grin of satisfaction on his face. When Carole laboriously sanded and varnished their old oak staircase, her children ran and got handfuls of dust and grit, and dropped it into the wet varnish from the landing. When she painted her hallway pastel blue, the kids sloshed a pot of black paint all over it with a thick brush. The cream leather suite was the background for a kaleidoscopic design in felt-tip, and if you left your car parked where you couldn't see it the boys would rummage around in their father's toolbox and start reorganizing the bodywork. Carole had a pile of winning scratch cards put to one side for collecting. The children had been instructed that in no circumstances were they to touch the cards, or scratch off the bottom

70

panel, because that would invalidate the winnings. You don't need me to tell you what happened, or what happened when their father bought Carole's Christmas present when he had Christopher with him. It was of course to be a big secret, in order not to spoil Mummy's surprise on Christmas Day, so not a word to her about the present. She hadn't even got out of her car before Christopher bellowed: 'Dad's bought you a circular saw for Christmas!' (She preferred things like that to toiletries).

There were other things too, but better left untold.

Because I had another friend also called Carole, to avoid confusion I nicknamed the first Carole 'Red', because of her beautiful copper hair. We quickly became firm friends, despite how I felt about her kids. A generation behind me, Red took me under her dynamic wing shortly after I arrived, and guided me along the path of righteousness and away from a clan of dubious expatriate characters who preyed on the unwary. Once I remarked vaguely that I dreamed of one day being able to soak in a full bathtub of water, as the plastic bucket in the garden did have its limitations. 'Come round and have a bite with us tonight,' said Red. When I arrived, the bath was run, piles of warm fluffy towels were heaped on a chair, and the radiator was turned on. I spent a blissful hour submerged in fragrant, steaming bubbles before sitting down to a perfectly cooked hot meal, served at a table standing on a proper floor. It seemed a long time since I'd done anything similar.

Of all the favours Bill did me, these introductions were the most valuable. Apart from himself, who was hardly ever here, I knew no other English people, but through these new acquaintances I set up a chain of contacts and the basis for much of my future social life. Far from being the only English person in the area, I found there were dozens of us, all looking for a new beginning.

71

Bill had many virtues, but reliability was not one of them. If he said he would be back on Tuesday evening, it was more likely he would turn up the following Sunday morning, or not at all for several weeks. I don't recall him ever being where he should have been when he said he would. Periodically he stopped by for a day or so to rearrange the clutter of junk that surrounded his place, because his wife Gloria was coming up from Spain for a visit. She had not yet seen the property, and Bill was very much hoping that she would decide to move there permanently. He talked a great deal about her, and I was looking forward to meeting her.

In the furnace heat of August, she arrived, petite and sunbrowned with a crown of heaped blonde hair, heavy eye make-up, a radiant smile, the most exquisitely elegant feet I'd ever seen, large daisy earrings and a taste for exotic and colourful clothes; a cocky little sparrow dressed as a bird of paradise. She brought with her two enormous Great Danes and one small terrier. Her first view of what Bill hoped might become her new home didn't seem to impress her overmuch (I couldn't say I was surprised), but she was funny and cheerful and I thought we'd get along quite well.

She had a wacky sense of humour and a very positive outlook on life, assets which must have been indispensable in her shambolic existence with Bill. Picking her way through the jumble of stuff lying round the outside, framed by some thriving nettles that had valiantly withstood the drought, she rolled her eyes and waved her hands as the panorama of mess unrolled before her.

'Look at it, just look at it!' she exclaimed, running a hand through her hair. 'Have you ever seen anything like it?'

I hadn't.

'Never mind,' she smiled, 'give me a couple of days and

72

I'll have it looking nice.' I thought she was being wildly optimistic.

She unloaded dozens of pots of plants from the truck she had arrived in, and distributed them around the outside of the building. She didn't know what most of them were called.

'What's this one?' I asked, pointing to a few withered sticks poking out from a clump of baked mud.

'Oh, it's nice, that one. Sort of feathery leaves. It just needs a drop of water. That one over there has big shiny leaves, and this one smells wonderful at night. I'll have to get some petunias.'

I suspected she liked petunias not only for their long-lasting displays but because they were one of the very few plants whose name she knew. She barked a stream of orders at Bill, who dug into the truck and pulled out some garden furniture, two swinging sofas, and a few large garden umbrellas.

'Put it there,' commanded Gloria, pointing vaguely. 'No! Not *there, there*!'

Bill patiently moved all the bits and pieces around until Gloria was satisfied.

'There you go,' she said cheerfully, surveying her new home. The two huge dogs staggered around in the waist-high dead grass and weeds, and the terrier chewed frantically on a plastic frog that squeaked loudly until it was fatally punctured.

At this stage Gloria hadn't seen inside the 'house' part, and I decided not to be there when she did. As I hadn't been anywhere other than the vet's and the local supermarkets since my arrival, I took myself off to the threshing festival at a nearby rural museum dedicated to the farming life of bygone days.

Outside the museum a procession was assembling itself. Men dressed in traditional farming costumes of black smocks and trousers, red neckerchiefs and black hats were accompanied by their ladies in long full black skirts with white aprons, black triangular shawls, and narrow cylindrical lace hats half a metre high. The purpose of the latter was beyond my imagination, and how their wearers managed to keep them perched on top of their heads, and why, a total mystery.

A long cavalcade of mules, venerable ox-wagons laden with children dressed in clothes of long ago, babies pushed in antiquated prams, heavy horses and tractors of all sizes and ages, some steam-driven, wended its way through the village, followed by an aged fire-engine and a band of drums and bagpipes. For about a kilometre we spectators followed on foot until we reached a field, where using ancient implements the men cut the ripe wheat by hand, wrapped it neatly in stooks tied with a length of stalk, and stacked the stooks to await threshing by a very elderly tractor-driven contraption. We stood round the edges of the field beside the carts and live-stock, and a lady produced a fiddle on which she played lively jigs. It was a captivating glimpse of local farming life before mechanization came along and spoiled it all. I picked up a handful of the cut wheat and made my way home, passing some French people who were going towards the field. Seeing the wheat in my hand, one of them said, 'Taking the wheat brings bad luck,' or possibly: 'We're too late to see the wheat being cut, what bad luck.' My French wasn't good enough to understand exactly what they were saying, but it stayed in my mind.

When I got home, Gloria trotted across.

'Come round this evening and have a drink with us. An estate agent we're in business with is coming over.'

I asked what sort of business they were involved in.

Bill explained that he knew many English people in Spain who were interested in moving to France, and he was going to introduce a steady stream of purchasers to the agent.

'He's a bit mad,' they warned me. 'If you come round you can help us to entertain him.'

I was proud and flattered to be invited to help entertain a mad person.

Whether or not he was clinically mad I couldn't say, but he was definitely a bit weird, and somewhat florid in a vulgar Hawaiian shirt and dark glasses. He spoke fairly fluent English with an alcoholic slur, and announced uninhibitedly that he was completely bisexual and, leering, that he had learned his perfect English in bed with English girls.

Bill and the estate agent were meant to be a partnership, but it seemed to me that neither side trusted the other, nobody quite knew what anybody else was meant to be doing, and that it was a relationship doomed to end in failure. A potential client was on her way up from Spain and they all awaited her arrival with excitement, because she had sold her mobile home there and was coming to France with the definite intention of settling. She looked certain to become the consortium's first lucrative client. One of her predecessors had succumbed to a heart attack a few minutes before signing the purchase contract, and the second had changed his mind at roughly the same time. All their hopes were resting on the impending arrival, and we drank a toast to her swift and safe advent.

She materialized the next day, in the form of a simply gigantic 76-year-old lady of Polish origin, called Mrs Malucha, with a Teutonic haircut and an alarming habit of erupting unexpectedly, and for no apparent reason, into thunderous guffaws of laughter. She was disembarked, with the help of three men, from the furniture wagon in which she had migrated from Spain, and established in a garden chair that immediately began to

75

transmogrify beneath her invincible buttocks. Entrusting her to my involuntary care, Bill and Gloria drove away to find her a suitable house. Despite her age and size, it seemed to me that Mrs Malucha was rather green around the edges. She had sold her mobile home in Spain at a loss because of 'something to do with currency', and had put herself into Bill's hands in order to get herself established in France, a country she had never visited and knew absolutely nothing about. I asked her what had attracted her here, and she replied that it was the weather. Spain was unbearably hot, and England was far too cold, but she understood that the climate in France would suit her very well indeed. I didn't want to burst her bubble by telling her that in summer France can be pretty nearly as hot as Spain, and in winter sometimes even colder than England. I had a feeling she was going to have enough to contend with.

Three hours later Bill and Gloria returned with the joyful tidings that they had found a dear little house that would suit Mrs Malucha perfectly. An appointment had been made for her with the *notaire* the following day, where she would sign the preliminary contract and pay a deposit. She could stop and have a look at the property on the way to the *notaire*'s office.

Delighted with her good fortune, Mrs Malucha sat squash-buttocked in the shape-shifting garden chair, chain-smoking, bursting into nerve-racking paroxysms of wild laughter, and asking what time we were going to eat. Not only was she a chain-smoker, but she appeared to be a chain-eater, too.

She was thrilled that the ideal house had been found so quickly, and looked forward to moving in, despite the fact that she didn't know anything about it or its location and hadn't even seen a photograph of it. I asked Bill how long he thought it would be before Mrs Malucha could take possession of her new home.

'Monday,' he replied. It was Thursday then.

'Are you sure? It usually takes several weeks to complete a purchase.'

'Oh no, it's all been taken care of by the estate agent. She'll be given the keys when she pays the deposit.'

I was very glad for Mrs Malucha's sake, and impressed at the speed with which the transaction seemed to be taking place. But then Bill mentioned casually that there was no electricity in the house, but he would install a generator, and no bathroom, but he would build one. She plainly wasn't going to be able to live there until the work was done. Luckily, the estate agent owned a house in a small village which was at the disposal of any potential buyers arriving from Spain, and therefore available for Mrs Malucha until her own house was ready. It was also at the disposal, Bill believed, of himself and Gloria, and so off they hied and installed themselves there with their 10-year-old grandson, who'd come out from England for a holiday on one of Bill's recent trips, plus Mrs Malucha, the two truck drivers who'd delivered her from Spain, and the three dogs.

Carole and Norrie, more friends to whom Bill had introduced me, and who were ever on hand in times of need, went with Mrs Malucha to translate the proceedings for her at the *notaire*'s office. En route they stopped for coffee, and Mrs Malucha complained that she was hungry, breakfast being almost an hour behind her. Unlike their English equivalents, French cafés seldom serve food, just coffee and alcohol, but Mrs Malucha was not convinced until she had questioned the contents of every visible container on the shelves and satisfied herself that there was nothing edible within them.

'I'll just have coffee, then, if there's no food,' she replied dejectedly to Norrie's enquiry.

'Well, I'm having a *pastis*. Anybody else fancy one?'

'Yes,' roared Mrs Malucha, brightening up, 'get me one as well.'

'What, as well as coffee, or instead?'

'No, both, coffee and *pastis*.'

Norrie returned with a tray, and placed a coffee and a glass of *pastis* on the table in front of her.

'What's this,' she asked, pointing at the cloudy yellow drink.

'That's the *pastis* you asked for,' said Norrie.

Mrs Malucha was utterly crestfallen. 'Oh, but I thought you were talking about Cornish pasties,' she said.

After signing the initial contract, Mrs Malucha learnt that her house, which she had yet to see, was about twenty-five kilometres away from our hamlet, and one kilometre from the nearest shops. There was no public transport, and Mrs Malucha couldn't drive and could hardly walk, but she didn't seem worried.

'I expect I'll find somebody to run me around,' she said, beaming meaningfully in my direction.

In honour of Mrs Malucha's successful purchase, Gloria prepared a celebratory lunch at the estate agent's house, to which I was invited, as were a couple of cranky old English people whom Bill knew. They declined, which turned out to be a good thing because, just as we were clearing away the main course in preparation for the dessert, the estate agent screeched his car to a halt, leapt into our midst with his claret-face, and started screaming abuse at us all. The gist of it was that none of us had any right to be there except Mrs Malucha, and we had ten minutes to vanish without trace or he would start shooting. We scraped up bowls of food, dirty dishes, glasses and bottles, piled into an assortment of vehicles and hightailed it back to Bill's barn, leaving the poor Polish lady to fend for herself.

Back at home we were hardly out of the cars when another bunch of people arrived. Gloria's friend from

Spain, Elsa, had come to stay with her teenage daughter and her daughter's nubile friend. You had to feel sorry for Bill. He had four caravans, two of which were completely uninhabitable, and a huge open barn with no internal walls and no sanitary or cooking facilities, and in one fell swoop he had to provide accommodation for all these people.

Hats off to him, he got a shower rigged up and working very quickly, but it still left something lacking in the sleeping and toilet arrangements. Elsa would share one caravan with Gloria. Bill and their grandson would occupy the other caravan, the hired drivers could sleep in the wagon, and the two girls bedded down in a tent I lent them.

Elsa and Gloria took it in turns to stay awake, as the two drivers were hell-bent on getting into the tent with the two girls, one of whom made no attempt at all to discourage them.

The phone rang the following morning. It was the estate agent, and he was shouting and spluttering and not at all apologetic for his manic behaviour the previous day.

'You're bloody well going to have to talk to Bill,' he bellowed down the phone without any preamble.

'Talk to him what about?'

'I'm a very important businessman in the community. When I took Mrs Malucha to the *notaire* to sign the contract, Bill turned up in jeans with his arse hanging out of the back, and Gloria was nekkid! Whatever are people going to think of me?'

Curiosity got the better of my impulse to put the phone down.

'How do you mean, Gloria was naked?'

'She was just wearing a thin piece of cotton wrapped round her body. Everybody could see her knickers. She wore nothing underneath. It was absolutely *disgraceful*.'

Gloria did favour exotic costumes that were a little unusual in the staid villages of rural central France.

Relishing the mental image, I said: 'Look, this has absolutely nothing to do with me. If you don't like the way they dress, you'll have to tell them yourself.' I replaced the receiver.

In the afternoon I crashed out behind closed shutters hoping to catch a few hours' sleep. The metallic clang of the gate, some loud whispers, the rattle of the latch and the squeaking of the ancient door on its hinges jerked me from the pre-drop-off zone. I opened one reluctant eye to see the nubile girl glaring down at me.

'I want a proper toilet,' she snapped. 'We're meant to use a Porta-Potti behind a curtain in Bill's barn!'

I could sympathize with her: it was pretty distressing. It wasn't much fun using our own chemical toilet, which rocked playfully from side to side on the uneven cobbles of a redundant goat shed, threatening to topple over during use, but it did offer at least a degree of privacy and a delightful view of a flowering cherry tree through a hole in the wall.

'So do I. But I'm afraid I don't have a proper toilet, either.'

'You *must* have one!' she yelled.

'Yes, I know I must, but in the meantime I'm afraid I don't. I'm really sorry.'

She glared at me disbelievingly, and flounced away, banging the old door behind her.

A piercing whistle from the grandson roused all the dogs, who had until then been sleeping quietly and contentedly, and they all started milling around and jumping up and down. The boy threw stones and sticks for them and chased them around whooping like a Red Indian, and I abandoned all thought of the siesta.

Sinbad was still with me, too, and I was getting pretty fed up with forcing the great cage backwards and forwards each day, but in view of Bill's beleagured circumstances I didn't like to mention it.

The strange old English couple who hadn't come to the disrupted celebratory lunch lived nearby and Gloria took me to meet them. The husband was a gentle, vague soul, who seemed to do most of the domestic chores. He volunteered to make tea, and returned ten minutes later with a tray beautifully set with cups, saucers, spoons, small plates, a large plate of very hard sweet biscuits that scratched your teeth, a bowl of sugar, a jug of milk, and a teapot filled with scalding water. Gloria disappeared into the kitchen and discreetly dropped some teabags into the pot. The aged pair explained that they didn't have a car, because of the pollution it would cause (and also, he confided once, because he had been quite unable to master the technique of driving the thing), so they were totally dependent upon taxis and friends. I thought the wife was a real tyrant who bullied the old man mercilessly. His gentle defence was to remove his hearing aid, tapping and reinserting it several times before giving an apologetic little smile, shaking his head sadly from side to side and saying the device would have to go back to be repaired. It seemed to spend quite a lot of time being repaired.

The old woman needed delivering to and collecting from a physiotherapy clinic in a nearby town several days running, and Bill announced that as he was off to Spain that evening he had volunteered my services to run her backwards and forwards. I said I wasn't confident about carrying a passenger because Tinkerbelle had been misbehaving recently, making sinister clanging and thumping noises interspersed with screeches. Bill brushed aside my concerns.

'No, those old puddle-jumpers all make noises like that,' he explained. 'It's perfectly normal. Don't worry.'

So I picked up the old biddy on day one, drove her to

town, mooched around for a couple of hours waiting for her, and stowed her back into the car. We'd progressed about two kilometres when Tinkerbelle gave a terrible grinding noise and emitted a cloud of pungent black smoke from beneath her bonnet. As my passenger could barely walk, I decided to try to get us to the nearest telephone box, which was another 2 kilometres away, and call for help. Miraculously Tinkerbelle summoned up her reserves and suddenly surged forward, roaring throatily back to life. We cheered with relief, and reached the call box just as the car became unnaturally silent. Suddenly further clouds of smoke emanated from the engine and engulfed us, at which point Tinkerbelle stopped dead and wouldn't move another inch. Somehow, I wasn't at all surprised, but at least she had delivered us to a place where I could send out a distress call before we waited in comfort in a nearby café.

Gloria came and collected us. My passenger paid me fifty francs for fuel, and I was left with a car which was immobilized 10 kilometres from home and no longer any use whatsoever. Still, said Gloria, Bill and his friend would be back the next day, and since they both knew all there was to know about 2CVs they would have her back in peak condition in no time at all. I wasn't to worry. In those days I was still achingly naïve, and fully believed that Tinkerbelle would be back in action in a couple of days. True, the two experts did arrive the following day and diagnosed a terminal disorder of the gearbox. There was no way we could afford a new one, but Bill said he could easily pick up a cheap second-hand one in Spain on his next trip. Tinkerbelle sat despondently for many long weeks waiting in vain for a gearbox that never materialized, and I'd lost my only means of transport.

Not only was Tinkerbelle out of action, but I'd had several other mishaps and four visits to the vet in the space of ten days. My mind kept going back to the

French people at the threshing festival, and I was convinced that taking the wheat from the field had brought down the wrath of some harvest god upon me, so when Terry arrived on a visit we drove back to the field and reverently placed the wheat back where it had come from.

I'd only been here five weeks, and the tranquil and gloriously solitary life I had envisaged was already in a state of disarray, but this was only the beginning. It was going to get much, much worse.

Chapter Five

The motley crowd round the corner seemed to settle into some sort of domesticity, and over the next few days life lapsed into a pleasantly tranquil pattern. Apart from regular assaults from the grandson and the younger girl wanting to play with the dogs, the comings and goings at Bill's didn't much affect me. Yet.

Terry arrived with his car crammed as usual with tools, paint pots, items of furniture; anything that could be useful to us. He was always delighted to see the dogs sprawled dozily in the garden and to notice such small improvements as I'd been able to make, and he never seemed at all overwhelmed by the magnitude of the work that lay ahead. It was just another challenge to be met.

He remarked on the encampment round the corner. I tried to explain the events that had been taking place over the preceeding week, and he said, 'You shouldn't get involved in all that sort of thing.' Easier said than done, thought I.

The empty loft space above our living room was only accessible from the barn via a prehistoric and very worm-eaten ladder with a penchant for snapping its rungs when you least expected it. Somehow or other we had managed with Bill's help to winch up this thing, and through the low doorway, a 6 foot wide bed and mattress and an enormous mahogany chest of drawers. I dared not use the ladder when I was on my own, for fear of injuring myself and lying broken-boned until somebody stumbled upon me, but when Terry was here we used the loft as a bedroom, which was infinitely more comfortable than the fungal little room downstairs that I used when I was on my own.

Coincidentally with Terry's arrival, Bill and Gloria's visitors were preparing to depart. They were only awaiting the arrival of Elsa's brother and his family from England, who would spent one night with them (heaven knew exactly where), before they set off together for Spain. Elsa had driven to Paris to meet her brother, but on the return run they had become separated and by nightfall there was no sign of him. Nobody seemed inclined to go and search, so it was left to him to find his own way.

At just after one o'clock in the morning, our telephone began ringing. Our phone lived downstairs, down the ladder. What was more, you had to descend the ladder into the barn, exit the barn, walk round the garden to the front door, and get through that and the door to the small room where the telephone was. It took several rings to wake us, and many more for us to actually reach the instrument, whereupon it stopped ringing. We stood around for five minutes to see if it would re-ring, which it didn't. Not, that is, until we had retraced our steps to the bedroom. I think I forget to mention that there was no electricity in either the barn or the bedroom, so all nocturnal navigation had to be done by torchlight. Once more we fumbled for the torch, climbed down the ladder, crossed the barn, scrambled round the corner and in through the front door, then negotiated the second door into the small room. The phone stopped ringing once again. After the third fruitless mission, we gave up and spent the rest of the night worrying what sort of emergency had befallen whom. Other than ringing all those nearest and dearest to us, at what was now nearly three o'clock in the morning, we could only hope that whatever had prompted these night-time calls would have sorted itself out by morning.

A few minutes after six o'clock, off went the phone again, and unhampered by the torch Terry managed to reach it.

'It's me,' said a male voice. 'Can you come and get us?'

'Who are you?'

'Are you Bill?'

'No, I'm not Bill. Who are you?'

'But that's Bill's phone, isn't it?'

'No, it isn't Bill's phone. Who are you, and what do you want?'

'I'm Elsa's brother. We got lost. I'm in the village. We've been sleeping in the car park all night. I kept ringing but you didn't answer. Can you come and get us?'

Terry said, 'I'll go and tell Bill to come down for you.'

He replaced the receiver, raised his eyebrows expressively, and went round to tell Bill there was someone in the village who wanted to be got.

'How is it,' he asked me, 'that that person has our phone number? Why didn't he ring Bill's number?'

'Bill doesn't have a phone.'

'You're joking. Why doesn't he?'

'Well,' I explained, 'apparently somebody else ran up a huge bill on his phone, and it was cut off and he can't get it put back on unless he pays the outstanding bill, which he can't.'

'So you mean he uses our phone?'

'Yes, but he's going to pay me for any calls he makes. I time them and write them down, and he won't give our number to anybody except for emergencies.'

'I really don't think that's a very good idea,' Terry said.

Well, neither did I, but somehow it had happened and

86

I couldn't see a way out of it until Bill got his own phone sorted out.

Sometime later that day Gloria came round, her usual cheerful self.

'He's a drug addict,' she chirruped.

'Who is?'

'The brother, that one who ended up in the car park last night. He's with his wife and they've got three little ones with them. They're all very pale.'

We digested this information.

'How do you know he's one?'

'He told us. He's got needles, and some sort of prescription.'

Terry rolled his eyes at me, and we went out for the day, away from the squealing pubescent girls, the hyperactive little boy, the randy drivers, the drug addict and any other odds or sods who might turn up. We didn't get back home until nightfall, when we learned that the travellers had broken camp and were en route for Spain.

The next day we'd designated for blocking up the hedges to try to prevent the dogs from escaping. Quite soon the novelty of having trees to bark up, mole hills to investigate and dark mysterious corners to explore had worn off, and once they'd tired of their own acre and a half they set out to explore further afield, terrifying the neighbours. I trotted along behind them as they peeled off in opposing directions, waving my arms wildly and shrieking, 'It's OK! They're very friendly. Biscuits! Dinner! Walkies!' The neighbours were unconvinced and the dogs less interested in promises than in exploring new horizons. I'd built barricades from old doors, rolls of wire, pieces of rope, a giant roll of polythene, part of a gate, anything I could find that might keep them in, but nothing was a match for their ingenuity for long. During the sizzling heat of the day they mostly sprawled out in whatever patch of shade they could find, or snuffled about in the cluster of dilapidated buildings that made up their new home. In the relative cool of the evenings we went into our little field where they raced and chased each other in noisy circuits. I loved walking here, where there were occasional glimpses of 18-inch long green lizards scuttling for cover through the grasses, the wild mint and thyme scented the air as we trod, and marguerites, huge hairy-leafed mullein, spindlethrift and dozens of other wild plants whose names I didn't know studded the ground. At dusk the dogs amused themselves, and me, by trying to catch the swallows and bats that swooped tauntingly low over their heads, in a futile exercise of which they never tired. But if I took my eyes off them for more than a few minutes, Vulcan and Wizzy found a new escape route and vanished.

I spent hours driving around fields and lanes hooting Tinkerbelle's croaky horn, or wandering through fields of sunflowers and maize, following streams, rattling tins of biscuits, shouting 'Dinner!' and asking everybody I saw if they had spotted two large brown dogs. Nobody ever had, but they could all give me some advice. Either the dogs had been stolen for vivisection, caught by the *gendarmes* and taken to the pound, poisoned by eating bait in traps, killed by a car, or shot for chasing sheep, or else they were so far from home, and so completely lost, that there was no chance of ever seeing them again. Frantic with worry and having phoned every *gendarmerie, mairie*, and vet in the area, I would simply have to sit and wait. The first time this happened I went to lie sleeplessly and a bit tearfully on the bed just before midnight, wondering what fate had overtaken our errant boys. Just after 3.30 a.m. all the dogs in the hamlet went off suddenly, barking and yowling. Carrying my trusty torch, and wearing nothing but a quickly snatched-up hand towel and a pair of slippers, I sprinted to the end of the lane and found them, coated with mud, skinny as toast-racks, red-eyed and footsore, but evidently extremely satisfied with their expedition.

Sometimes they vanished for days on end, but were always found, safe and well, being sheltered and fed on one neighbouring farm or another.

These escapades were becoming ever more frequent, and we knew it wouldn't be long before something serious happened to one of the dogs, so the fence-blocking project took priority over all other outstanding matters, like getting running water in the house, or making a proper kitchen.

Armed with rolls of wire, hammers, sticks and nails, we had just set off towards the meadow when the phone rang. I trotted back to answer it.

It was Elsa, calling from Spain. 'Have you heard from my brother?' she asked.

'No. Should I have?'

'I've lost him at the border. Let Gloria know, and tell her I'll ring back later. If he turns up back there, tell him to stay put until I phone. Cheerio.'

Staring down the phone at the dialling tone, I couldn't believe what was happening. There, in a tiny hamlet in the middle of nowhere, in less than a month I was already involved with dope fiends.

Obediently I went round to let Gloria know the addict was lost, and that Elsa would phone later.

Terry was absolutely furious with these intrusions into what was intended to be our peaceful life, and even more so at the prospect of having drug addicts in our midst, so I'm afraid I took the phone off the hook for the day, and what became of the lost man and his white-faced family I never heard.

Terry left the following morning, and Gloria arrived to say she was going to visit Mrs Malucha who, don't forget, had been stuck for several days in the middle of nowhere in the beastly estate agent's house, with no transport and no telephone and no way of communicating with the outside world. Gloria wondered whether I'd like to go along to keep her company. Why not?

The great lady herself was sitting at a primitive trestle table, on a wooden chair, which with a single gas ring, a tiny refrigerator and a small bed made up the entire furnishings of the house.

Quite understandably, Mrs Malucha was not in good spirits. Ignoring Gloria completely, she hollered: 'Sue, phone the American!'

'Susie,' I corrected. 'Who is the American?'

'Phone him and tell him what they've done to me. Look at me, left here like an animal! I've been frozen.'

In the blistering heat of August I couldn't imagine how, but I did feel sorry for the poor old soul in her spartan surroundings.

'What do you want us to do?' asked Gloria.

'Get me out of here, Sue,' she said, still pointedly ignoring Gloria. She heaved herself up from the chair, which expelled a wooden sigh of relief, and, dragging a battered suitcase behind her, made for the door.

Gloria shrugged and we trotted behind her and jammed her and the suitcase into the car.

'Where do you want to go?' enquired Gloria.

'I don't care, just get me away from here. Leaving me here like an animal. Wait till the American hears about this. You'll phone him, Sue, won't you?'

'Susie,' I corrected.

After a tripartite discussion we installed Mrs Malucha in a small hotel nearby, to her total satisfaction and my heartfelt relief. I need not now worry about phoning the American, she said kindly, because the hotel was perfectly comfortable and she would be happy there. Searching questions on my part hadn't uncovered any clues about what was happening with the formalities for her property purchase which didn't seem to be making any progress, and it concerned me that she was going to have to foot hotel bills for an unknown period as I knew she didn't have a great deal of money, but as she didn't seem at all worried as long as the food was good, and the helpings generous, it wasn't my business. Maybe now I could get on with my new life.

A few days later I was enjoying a few hours of respite when Bill, briefly back from England, came round to announce that he was off again for four days.

'Gloria's not well,' he said. Gloria suffered very badly with asthma. 'Would you keep an eye on her? I'll not have her getting upset.' He gave me a deep and meaningful look that I understood to imply that the responsibility for Gloria's emotional and physical well-being rested solely upon my shoulders during his absence. With that, he was gone.

No sooner had he vanished in a cloud of vehicular farts than my phone rang. It was the hotel where Mrs Malucha had been so happily ensconced for the last week. The hotel was very sorry, but Mrs Malucha had to leave and would we please come and collect her staight away. According to the manager, there was some mysterious law that prohibited ladies of Mrs Malucha's age from staying in their hotel for longer than one week. I didn't believe that for one minute and suspected the real reason was concern over whether Mrs Malucha's account would be paid, but I said we would go and collect her.

Off went Gloria and I, debating what could be done to accommodate Mrs Malucha until the purchase of her house was completed; there was still no indication whatsoever of how long this might take.

Mrs Malucha was quite delighted to see us.

'Hello, Sue!' she yelled merrily.

'Susie,' I corrected.

The hotel was wonderful, she announced. The rooms were warm, the food was excellent, and the proprietor was in love with her. This was normal: since she was a young girl men had found her irresistible. She batted her enormous lashless eyelids. Gloria and I smiled politely. She was sorry to be leaving, but she understood that rules were rules.

We brought her back to the hamlet, and while Gloria cooked a meal for her guest, and Mrs Malucha sat wedged in a plastic chair, we discussed her options.

She couldn't stay at that hotel. She refused to return to the estate agent's house. She was not going to stay in one of Gloria's caravans.

'Can't I come and live with you?' she enquired plaintively.

'No,' I said.

'Well, you'll have to drive me back to Spain. I don't think I'm going to like France after all.'

The prospect of conveying this yelling, chain-smoking, eternally hungry giantess several hundred miles over the Pyrenees in Tinkerbelle, who had great rust-holes in her lower regions allowing unimpeded views of the passing tarmac, was intoxicating, but I managed to resist, and while Mrs Malucha tucked into another meal Gloria prepared a caravan for her, as we hadn't managed to come up with any alternative means of housing the unfortunate lady.

With very bad grace, she allowed us to usher her up the steps into the mouldy caravan, where she locked the door, drew the curtains and turned on her radio full blast.

As I walked back to the house, the phone was ringing. It was the American Mrs Malucha had mentioned and about whom I knew absolutely nothing, calling from Spain, and wanting to speak to Mrs Malucha *right now* and he didn't want *any excuses* or else I was going to be in *real trouble*.

Leaving the receiver dangling in mid-air, I watered the pot plants on the window sill and then strolled back to

Mrs Malucha's caravan and tapped on the window. I had to tap several times before she snorted: 'Go away!'

'Mrs Malucha, the American wants to speak to you. He's on the phone. Can you come over?'

The caravan shook and rolled and groaned, and after a couple of minutes the door opened.

'Help me down, Sue,' she said.

'Susie,' I replied mechanically, bracing myself as she extruded herself through the doorway.

'It's no good, Sue, I can't walk to your house. You'll have to bring the phone here.'

'Mrs Malucha, the phone will not reach here. Just hold on to me, take your time and walk very slowly.'

She applied her weight to my proffered arm and almost succeeded in dragging me to the ground, and we made satisfyingly slow progress back to the phone and the rude American who by now had spent quite a lot of pesetas listening to the sound of silence.

Propped into a valiant garden chair, Mrs Malucha bawled down the phone, assuring the American that Sue was the only decent person here. She wanted to go back to Spain immediately, if not sooner than that. She would not travel by train or coach, her leg wouldn't allow it. The American agreed to make the 1,600-mile journey and collect her. In the meantime he urged Mrs Malucha to be of stout heart and keep her spirits up, and make sure that I looked after her.

'Don't worry, Sue's here, she's taking care of me. Nothing's too much trouble for her.'

I gave her a long cold drink, answered her request for some cake or biscuits quite truthfully by saying I didn't have any, and steered her back to the caravan.

The August heat was blistering, and what it must have been like inside the caravan, with all the windows closed, I couldn't imagine. However, Mrs Malucha complained that she was cold. She had a heavy sleeping bag and one woollen blanket, plus her own very substantial insulation, but she was cold, very cold, and risking pneumonia, if not something worse. She needed more blankets. All I had was a large pile of dog blankets in a box, so I washed them and tumbled them dry. Although they looked rather hairy, they were clean and smelt fresh. She accepted them noncommittally and locked herself back in.

An hour later she opened the top half of the caravan door to howl that the toilet in the caravan was too low; she couldn't bend sufficiently to reach it. So Gloria rounded up some concrete blocks and we constructed a sort of throne, hoping that the combined weight of the blocks and Mrs Malucha wouldn't plunge them through the floor.

Gloria tried frequent food offerings – trays of salads, cold meats, cheese and bread, cakes and cups of tea – but Mrs Malucha steadfastly refused to communicate. The food lay untouched and desiccating in the sun on the steps of the caravan, like tributes to an Eastern deity. Mrs Malucha on hunger strike was a serious matter. Gloria was distressed and starting to wheeze ominously, and I remembered Bill's parting words and wondered what I was meant to do about everything, particularly as I had not worked out how my involvement had come about in the first place.

Gloria arrived looking exasperated.

'She wants you.'

I trudged round to the caravan.

'Now look here, Sue,' began Mrs Malucha.

'Susie,' I replied uselessly.

'I can't stay here. It's too cold. Freezing. Like an ice-box. I'm not staying in here tonight, and that's it.'

'OK, then, I'll try to find another hotel room for you.'

'No, that's no good. I don't want to go to a hotel. Why can't I come and live with you?'

94

I could have given a dozen reasons – there was no bedroom, no bathroom, no running water or satisfactory electricity in the house. The floorboards such as they were would not bear her weight. I didn't want her to stay with me, and certainly couldn't afford to stoke her enormous appetite. Because she chain-smoked her clothes smelt horrible, and she was absolutely nothing to do with me. But I simply replied: 'Because you can't.'

'Well then, how about your friends? Have you got some friends I can go and stay with?'

'No.'

'Then you're going to have to drive me back to Spain!'

'I've already told you, Mrs Malucha, I can't do that. The best I can do is try to find you a nice hotel room.'

'But I don't want to stay in a hotel!'

'Then you'll have to sort yourself out,' I snapped. 'I really can't do any more.' I started to walk away.

'Wait, Sue,' she screamed. 'I'll go to the hotel.'

So I phoned a hotel and booked her a room, and Gloria and I squished her once again into the car with her bags and bundles. It was a very pretty hotel with a flowery courtyard filled with tubs of geraniums and covered in leafy vines, and Mrs Malucha didn't like it one little bit. She couldn't come up with a reason, she just knew it was not a good hotel. Politely ignoring her tantrums, the proprietor led the way to a steep and narrow staircase.

'Aha!' crowed Mrs Malucha triumphantly. 'There you are! I knew it! I can't get up those stairs with my bad leg!'

'Oh yes you can!' Gloria and I cried stereophonically, and with the help of the proprietor heaved her upwards and into a very pleasant room overlooking the pretty courtyard. She might have been slow-moving, but Mrs Malucha was swift to note the deficiencies in her new accommodation.

'It's going to be too cold. There aren't enough

blankets. The bed is too small. There's no armchair, no telephone, no light switch near the bed. What do you think I'm going to sit on all day?'

I asked the proprietor, who was still politely smiling, whether she could supply an armchair and more blankets.

'Just one blanket?'

'Could you manage four?'

She blinked and twitched an elegant eyebrow, but went away and returned with a great pile of blankets, and eyeing Mrs Malucha's bulk rather doubtfully said she would try to find a suitable armchair. There was nothing she could do about the light switch, nor the telephone, for which I was supremely grateful, but she would ask someone to come up regularly to check on Mrs Malucha's needs.

'I won't be able to go down for meals,' threatened Mrs Malucha with satisfaction.

'We can bring your meals up for you,' replied the patient proprietor.

Temporarily defeated, Mrs Malucha crashed down onto the bed.

'Well, we'll leave you to settle in,' said Gloria cheerily, and the three of us headed for the door.

As we trotted down the corridor, Mrs Malucha's voice boomed: 'Hey! What about my cigarettes? I've no cigarettes. You'll have to go and get me some.'

When I returned with a hundred cigarettes, she was plugged into her radio and feeling rather sorry for herself.

'I don't know what's going to become of me, Sue. I don't want to stay in France. Did you know the people here don't speak English?'

'Yes, I had begun to suspect something of the sort. But never mind, the American will be here on Tuesday to take you back to Spain.'

96

'But I don't want to be in Spain. It's too hot.'

'Have you thought of going back to England?'

'Oh no, I couldn't live in England. They don't let you sing there,' she added mysteriously.

Well, having ruled out Spain, England and France, where she had paid a deposit and signed a binding contract to buy a house, I had run out of suggestions and took my leave, promising to return the next day to see how she was getting on. Mrs Malucha had now taken up several complete days of my life.

Gloria was going down with flu, and I was contemplating whether I could squeeze in a quick nervous breakdown before something else arrived to occupy my time. The American phoned to find out where Mrs Malucha was, and the hotel rang with a message from Mrs Malucha that I was to go to the caravan and find her brown shoes and take them to her the next day.

Predictably the American didn't turn up, and neither did Bill. Ensconced in the smoky fug of her hotel room Mrs Malucha became more manageable, asking nothing more than a wholesale supply of cigarettes and batteries for her radio, and regular large meals, with wine, to keep her happy.

With Bill absent and Mrs Malucha tucked away, once Gloria had recovered she and I went off for an afternoon to visit a nearby stud farm where trotting horses were bred and trained. We spent three delightful hours following a group of people around whilst one of the staff explained enthusiastically the pedigree, personal habits and triumphs of each of the rather angular horses. The stock varied greatly in size and shape and bore little resemblance to the English thoroughbred racehorses we know. It would of course be a rather bizarre sight to see an English thoroughbred flying along at an exaggeratedly extended trot whilst dragging behind it a bouncing little man on a flimsy chariot. Even more peculiar, perhaps the weirdest equine sport devised by man is the ridden trotting race, when the little men bob up and down impossibly quickly on the horses' backs, looking really rather silly. Neither Gloria nor myself understood a word of the three-hour commentary, but it was a nice sunny afternoon with pleasant smells and one horse that laughed if you tickled its top lip.

After the tour we followed everybody else to a nearby building and enjoyed quite delicious local biscuits and wine, and then trailed after our tour leader by car to a nearby lake and sports area, into a tent filled with more biscuits and wine, where the mayor gave a short speech which we also didn't understand. Although we came home very little wiser, it was a welcome break from the demands of drug addicts, displaced persons, and phone calls to our phone that were not for me.

Gloria flew south with the swallows for a visit to Spain, leaving the dogs and the care of her plants to Bill.

'Try to keep an eye on the plants, will you?' she asked me. 'Just remind him to water them a bit, but not too much.'

I said I would.

Each time I went across to check the plants, they were drier and browner than the time before, and each time I suggested that if Bill didn't have time to water them I could do it.

'No, no, I'm just about to do it. I've not forgotten.'

He even went so far as to find a kettle to put some water in. But still the plants wasted away into withered twigs and wilted stems. Poor things. About two days before Gloria was due to return, Bill said: 'Do you think the plants are looking OK?'

'No, they're dead,' I replied.

'But if I give them some water now, they'll be fine, won't they?'

'Bill, the plants are dead. Giving them water cannot make them be alive.'

'Oh, that's a shame.' He went back to whatever he was doing.

When Gloria returned, she ranted and raved for a few minutes, then collected all her pots of dead plants and stood them outside, and gave them a drop of water.

'What are you doing that for?' I asked. 'They're stone dead. Absolutely, completely dead.'

She laughed. 'No, they'll be all right. They just need a bit of time to recover from *him*,' she said, glowering in Bill's direction.

Astonishingly, most of the plants, after a long rest, did start to sprout new growth. Then Gloria nursed them to full health, and when she went away Bill murdered them once more. It was a continuous cycle of death and rebirth; they must have been very confused.

Mrs Malucha was still wedged into the hotel room waiting for somebody to do something with her. I was quite fond of her in an exasperated sort of way, and concerned that she was running up a large bill in the hotel, where she had been enjoying full board and room service for nearly a month, and there was no mention of the house she was meant to be buying. But there wasn't anything I could do for her, other than to urge Bill to go and see her and sort her out, which he seemed strangely unwilling to do. In the interim, he had seriously fallen out with the estate agent, who had tried to punch him, had also tried to injure our friend Norrie by running him down in his car, and was being hunted by the police. Ultimately, the agent was forced to return Mrs Malucha's deposit and pay compensation to her. On the sale price of the property of 40,000 francs, he had been charging her 60,000 francs in fees.

Chapter Six

Now that Gloria had gone back to Spain and Mrs Malucha was out of circulation, life was a little more organized. Early each morning, and again at dusk, an elderly lady fed her chickens in the small field which backed onto ours, and, feeling that it was time I introduced myself to some more of our new neighbours, I went down to talk to her one morning. Mme Grimaud was a widow whose bent back and smiling, lined face were in their mid-seventies, but her sparkling blue eyes were only twenty.

'What do you have there?' I asked, pointing to a small bowl in her hand.

'Chicken soup,' she beamed, putting it down in front of her hens. 'They love it!' I wondered if they realized where it came from.

'Those chickens there,' I pointed, 'they're the ones called *cul nu*, aren't they?'

She giggled and ducked her head. '*Cou nu*,' she corrected, laughing. Bare neck, not bare arse, as I had suggested in my muddled-up French. Strange-looking things, they were, those tall chickens, with no feathers on their long necks. They looked as if they were moulting, or suffering from some unpleasant disease.

Mme Grimaud's beautiful Christian name was

Eglantine, meaning wild rose. She'd lived in the hamlet for 50 years, and could paint a vivid picture of how life had changed in those decades. Over coffee in her tidy little kitchen she pointed to her smart gas cooker, and the neat row of enamelled saucepans hanging from hooks, all of which were relatively recent acquisitions that had replaced the original open fire and the cast iron pot suspended over it for cooking the daily soup, and the small coal-heated tripod used for making omelettes.

Just outside her house stood the communal bread oven that had once served her end of the hamlet. On baking days they made enough to last for two to three weeks, and stored it on a rack hanging from the ceiling, where it collected dust and got hard, and was shared with those mice ingenious enough to reach it. There was a small brick-built stove in her garden, which had been used for cooking the pig food, and a very large old stone container with a drain hole at the bottom that had served as a primitive washing machine. The dirty linen went into the pot, and water was boiled on the stove and tipped over it, together with the ash that was used as a cleanser before the days of washing powder. Then they hauled the wet laundry down to the stream to rinse it. The people from Saint-Thomas came to use the stream too, in the days before there was any running water in the village.

But they didn't do the laundry too often, said Mme Grimaud – the sheets only got washed about once a month.

I'm not surprised.

She was a gentle and merry soul and when she talked she had a most appealing way of bending her head and looking at me sideways, smiling and flashing those lively eyes, and I could see her as a beautiful and flirtatious young girl. She was always happy to pass the time, and describe how life had been for her as a young woman – hard work and simple pleasures.

Her days had started at 5.00 a.m., milking the goats, by hand, and then taking them out to the fields to graze. The goats needed milking three times a day. Water had to be carried in buckets from the stream, two buckets at a time, and when the stream dried up, as it sometimes did for long periods, it meant walking to the well on the other side of the hamlet and laboriously drawing up the water.

The villagers produced most of their own food, even their own oil made from poppy seeds and walnuts. There was very little money, and they paid the travelling butcher, fishmonger and grocer partly in eggs for the few things they couldn't produce themselves, like salt, sugar and coffee.

During the war life had been even harder. There was nothing in the shops, not even soap, so they made their own. And sometimes the Germans came to the hamlet, and she would go with the other women and children to hide fearfully in the woods while the German soldiers searched their houses for the hunting guns they had ordered the men to surrender.

The nearest thing they had to a holiday was a day's visit to relatives – not only was there no money, but their animals needed constant attention.

Young girls cycled to the village fêtes to dance and meet the eligible young men from the neighbouring villages – but always in the company of their parents, because at that time unmarried girls were not allowed out without some form of chaperon. It was at one of these revels that Mme Grimaud had met her future husband.

Her father-in-law, she told me in a lowered voice, had hanged himself. He'd lived with them and been very ill for a long time, and one day he'd sent her husband to do something with the cattle, and her to do something else, which would keep them out of the way for a while. When one of his nephews came to visit him, he found him hanging from a walnut tree in the garden. They'd cut the tree down, afterwards.

One day she took out from a cupboard a tin box containing printed menus from village festivities decades ago, some old photos and certificates, and a card with a beautiful and poignant French poem printed on it, recounting the story of a young man from a neighbouring hamlet, less than a mile away, who had died fighting with the Resistance during the war.

In that box of souvenirs, I felt, was the story of Mme Grimaud's life.

Watching Mme Grimaud with her chickens, I thought it would be rather a good idea for us to have some too. Tinkerbelle was still off the road, but Bill was always very willing to help out and drive me anywhere I wanted to go, and I was completely at ease in his company; his manners were faultless.

We went off together to a nearby market, where I planned to buy a couple of happy hens. Twice a month the market took over the whole town centre, and you could buy just about anything there: saddlery, tractors, piglets, plants, fresh fruit, vegetables, fish, meat, cheese, bread, pig-coloured corsetry complete with little rubber suspenders and circular-stitched bras with sharply pointed cone-shaped cups, kitchen equipment, sweet roasted peanuts, fishing tackle, jewellery. A small scruffy tent dispensed plastic cups of red wine to gangs of elderly farmers, and eels grilled to charred fragrance over a coal brazier. The livestock area was rather harrowing, with rabbits and poultry crammed into tiny cages, or tied to each other by their feet in piles on the ground.

I had in mind a couple of big fat motherly hens, but was seduced by a pair of Silkies, with their soft white fur-like feathers, and two bantam hens, twice as many as I had intended and none of them either big or fat.

'I wouldn't mind a couple of hens,' Bill murmured, 'but I don't want more than two, because Gloria's allergic to eggs, so it'll just be for me. Do you think I should get the black ones, the white ones, or the brown ones with no feathers on their necks?'

I said I had no preference, so he bought, to my amazement, two of each.

'You're going to have an awful lot of eggs, Bill. What are you going to do with them?'

He muttered something incomprehensible, and pointed. 'What are those grey things?'

'They're guinea fowl. Terribly noisy creatures. For heaven's sake don't buy one of those.'

Bill didn't buy one. He bought two.

Then he bought two white turkeys. There was no stopping him now. He'd developed poultry mania, and I tramped round with him as he built up his flock. We accumulated a large stack of cardboard boxes tied with string, emitting rustles and squawks.

Then Bill saw the geese.

'Ee, I've got to have one of those. I do like a nice goose egg. But it's got to be a female.' Well, yes.

There were three geese in a pen, and I asked their villainous-looking owner whether amongst them was a female. He subjected them each in turn to an intimate and undignified gynaecological examination which they all fought spiritedly. The first two were rejected as males, but it seemed we'd hit the jackpot with the third. This was a female, we were assured. She was inserted indignantly into a cardboard box to join the stack.

With the boxes and their feathery occupants piled into the back of Bill's car, we headed homewards.

'I'll be off to Spain next week,' said Bill casually.

'But who's going to look after all these birds?' I asked stupidly, already knowing the answer.

'I'll only be gone a couple of days,' he assured me.

When they were released at home, my Silkies and one of the bantams behaved impeccably, and after a brief exploration of their run snuggled into the rickety coop I'd built for them. As soon as she was out of her box, however, the other bantam flew up to the barn roof, where she stayed wobbling on the ridge until nightfall, when she flew into M. Meneteau's plum tree and settled down for the night. Nothing I could do would dislodge her from where she sat on a branch 3 metres above my head, looking down on my efforts with a smugly triumphant expression that I suspect poultry seldom have the opportunity to exercise.

The terrestrial bantam, whom I named Lizzie, was a pretty black-feathered creature, with a golden lacy veil over her head and back, black legs and little silver toenails. She was the first of the three girls to lay an egg, and announced the event with the pomp and circumstance befitting a royal birth. She yelled her head off for an hour, describing how she had done it, what it looked like, and where it was, whilst the other birds stood around her in a semi-circle listening raptly. The arboreal bantam, Sandra, was beige with black speckles, rather like a small pheasant. With their snowy white plumage, turquoise wattles and brilliant red combs, the Silkies were absolutely enchanting.

Although Sandra persisted in roosting in the plum tree, she descended daily to dutifully lay one small egg, like her more down-to-earth companion. The Silky hen, on the other hand, was a bit slow to get going on egg production. For several weeks she did nothing but wander around scratching in the garden and eating, while the cockerel kept offering her fragments of leaf or pieces of dried grass, which she took and stamped upon. He also tried enacting a little war dance on one leg to impress her, without success, and leaping on her when she wasn't expecting it, all to no effect. It seemed that the secret lay in bellowing 'cocorico' very loudly and repeatedly into her ear, because after a day of that she finally started laying.

In turn the hens went broody and started producing more and more babies. The chicks were adorable, little bigger than bumblebees. Their mother, aunts and father were very attentive to them, making sure the dogs didn't get too close, rooting up insects for them and teaching them how to scratch and dig. Each night Sandra flew back to her home in the plum tree, abandoning her young to fend for themselves; they were lucky to have a diligent father who scraped them up under his paternal wing.

Whilst the shed I'd contrived for our poultry was primitive, at least they had somewhere safe to sleep. Bill's didn't have anywhere. One section of his barn was used for the safe storage of clients' furniture, and contained a cornucopia of wardrobes, mattresses, tables, chests, boxes of clothes, pictures, gardening tools, plant pots, leather chairs – you could name just about anything and find it there. He moved in his newly acquired birds, and they took to their new quarters with enthusiasm, perching on top of wardrobes, scraping nests into armchairs with their lethal claws, and shitting all over everything as only poultry can. We constructed a sort of pen in one corner, out of people's furniture, and at my insistence installed an overhead light to supply some heat for one of the little white turkeys who was looking very fragile indeed.

M. Meneteau wandered down to enjoy the game, and said he didn't give good odds on the turkeys' surviving.

'White turkeys,' he spat. 'They're useless. They all die.'

But not if I can help it, I thought.

Forward planning wasn't Bill's strongest point. Although it should have been more than obvious that the birds couldn't continue living on his clients' furniture indefinitely, he had made no provision, or provision for making provision, for their accommodation. Time slid by, and in another two days Bill would have flown the coop leaving me with not only Sinbad, who was still in residence, but eleven other assorted birds, in various states of health, and with nowhere safe to live. I also had a worrying suspicion that he was going to try to leave the two Great Danes with me, and here I was definitely going to draw the line. Gentle and affectionate as they were, they were both chronically ill with a disease contracted in Spain, the canine equivalent of AIDS. They also suffered from permanent diarrhoea. With five dogs of our own and assorted poultry, and remembering how the 'couple of days' I was to look after Sinbad had turned into 10 weeks, I didn't want any more responsibility or mess to clear up.

'Bill, the birds must have a proper place where they can be locked up. I'm not taking the responsibility for them otherwise. It's only a matter of time before a fox gets them.'

He assured me he'd get a poultry run built before he left, and asked whether he could use the telephone to call Gloria in Spain.

While he did so I sat in the adjacent room keeping a record of how long the call lasted, because he was a bit of a chatterbox and I was getting quite worried about my phone bill.

The conversation went like this: 'Yes, I'm leaving here on Thursday. Oh, you don't want me to bring the dogs with me? Yes, but I can't leave them here on their own. No, I don't really think so. Not very. No. Well, I'm coming down in the car; I'll have to put them in the back. Do you think they'll be OK in the back, all that way? Will they have enough room? You don't think they'll suffer, the two of them, being so big and having to squash into the back of the car for such a long journey? They're big dogs to have to travel so far in such a small car. Do you think it will harm them? No, of course I won't forget to give them water. Yes, it's a real pity we can't find someone here to keep an eye on them, but I wouldn't dream of asking Susie; she's got more than enough to do with all the . . . I mean, her own dogs.' He went on in this way, while I pretended I was reading a book. Finally I heard him say: 'OK then, love, I'll see you on Friday. And don't worry, I'm sure they'll survive.'

I feigned such deep interest in the book that I hadn't heard him finish his call, and smiled innocently when he came into the room and said: 'Right, thanks a lot. By the way, I forgot to say, but don't mention anything about the birds to Gloria, will you? She might not understand.'

I was almost certain she wouldn't understand why her husband had bought 11 birds that were of no practical use to him, which he was not going to be here to care for, and which had nowhere yet to live. I didn't understand it, and probably neither did he.

Anyway, the birds were now a *fait accompli*, and the following day, with the help of our ever-obliging friends Carole and Norrie, we fashioned a rustic enclosure from pieces of angle iron and chicken wire dragged out from amongst Bill's mess. Norrie even managed to build a two-storey roosting area complete with a neat little ladder to give easy access for the birds.

Despite their unamimous and multi-directional resistance, the four of us managed to round up the poultry in no more than a few hours, and install them in their new dwelling.

It was time for Bill to leave for Spain and I could hear him telling Norrie how worried he was about having to take the two huge dogs all the way to Spain in the back of the little car. Norrie looked politely non-committal, and finally Bill loaded the animals into the vehicle and drove off, with very poor grace and a big black frown on his face, saying he'd see me in a couple of days.

The smaller of the two turkeys didn't look at all well, standing hunched up and trembling, and it was touching to see that the goose, the other turkey and the white chickens seemed to be trying to mother it. They stood close to it, and fetched it morsels of food which it pecked at despondently. Bill hadn't left any food for his birds, seemingly under the impression that they fended for themselves.

His poultry found myriad and multiple ways of escaping from the laboriously built pen, meandering around the hamlet pecking at plants and scratching in flower-beds, and disappearing daily. Most evenings, as the sun was going down, M. Meneteau would appear on the lane, shepherding a diminishing bunch of poultry in front of him. 'They were right over the other side, in the maize field,' he would say, apparently not at all bothered at finding himself in the role of chicken-herder.

The smaller turkey was blind in one eye, and never seemed to grow. As I was still without transport of my own, Bill had kindly left a car which I was welcome to use. Although the brakes, steering and tyres were all defective, it was at least insured, and I wasn't in any position to be choosy. I went one day to stock up on food, including some for his poultry, and when I returned found that the birds had staged another mass break-out. I rounded them all up apart from the small white turkey, whose pathetic cheepings led to the discovery that it had fallen into the 3-metre deep hole that might one day accommodate Bill's septic tank. There was half a metre of water in the bottom, but the turkey had managed to get itself onto a dry ledge, where it peeped mournfully and waited for someone to rescue it. Ever-helpful M. Meneteau obliged, leaving his lunch uneaten, fetching a ladder, climbing down into the pit and hauling the bedraggled bird out. Later that afternoon it went missing again, and after climbing over the old bikes, washing machines, mattresses, rolls of barbed wire and flower pots that decorated Bill's garden, I finally found it tucked into the rim of an old tractor tyre.

Each night, when the birds – or what was left of them, because two of the six hens and one guinea fowl had disappeared never to be seen again – had been tracked down and rounded up into their enclosure, the goose shepherded them into a corner and wedged herself up against them protectively.

Bill's flock dwindled to the goose, 1 guinea fowl, the 2 white turkeys, and 2 hens. All the rest vanished. The little white turkey continued to ail. I took it to the vet in a cardboard box tied up with string; M. Audoux diagnosed a blocked sinus, and flushed it out. Can you imagine anything more bizarre for a turkey to have? Anyway, its sinuses were unblocked and I was given a supply of needles and syringes and a large bottle of some slimy stuff to inject it with twice daily. Mme Meneteau came up trumps when I told her that I couldn't manage injections, and she came round cheerfully morning and evening for five days to puncture the bird while I held it tightly and looked the other way. Little did I know that the time was looming when I'd have to become very proficient with the needle.

As Bill had hardly been around for several months, and seemed to have totally lost interest in the poultry, and as I'd seemingly inherited sole responsibility for their nutrition and welfare, including the intensive nursing of the small white turkey, it seemed a logical step to move them all into our garden, which I did one afternoon, driving them along the lane with the aid of a small stick. There was a hay barn which they settled into quite contentedly, apart from the little turkey which insisted on taking up residence with the bantam hens, one of whom snuggled up to it closely at night, in a rather endearing

110

way, as if she was sheltering it. She seemed not to notice it was four times her size. Then a friend told me that hens and turkeys can't be successfully kept together, because apparently the turkeys get a disease that the hens carry, but by then it was too late to do anything about it, except curse Bill mildly for having got the birds in the first place and adding a further burden to our vet's bill and animal food bill. I gave his two surviving hens to M. Meneteau, as I had more than enough of my own, and a few days later he explained why none of the six hens Bill had originally bought had ever produced a single egg. They had all been cockerels, and were sold for their flesh, not for laying.

On one of his brief visits, Bill made faint rumblings about a plan to install an old transport vehicle in his field and colonize it with pheasants, which he was under the impression would fend for themselves as far as feeding, watering, cleaning and security were concerned, so I wouldn't have to worry about that. But I did, oh yes, I worried day and night about the possibility of finding myself mother to a flock of pheasants. And then when he started rubbing his hands together and saying he was going to get a piggy, I really panicked. Now I just adore piggies, but I didn't want to have to look after one. If I had, I would have saved up in a piggy bank for one of my own. I phoned Gloria in Spain to share my fears with her.

'Oh God,' she said, 'if he had a brain he'd be dangerous. Don't worry, leave it to me.'

I never heard Bill mention the piggy again.

Despite all I could do for him, the little turkey didn't make it. But the other one just grew and grew. Now they were officially part of the family I christened them: the goose was Alice; the guinea fowl Blue; and the surviving turkey Toby. They had formed a very strong alliance which Terry and I named collectively the Gang of Three. They were always together exploring, and their explorations led them right into the house, which was not difficult as we only had a tattered plastic sheet where we had taken down the huge barn door. (I'll explain later.)

Terry had come out for a visit for a few days, and we'd started to try to make a bathroom, first by laying a concrete base for the floor, and then fitting the bath, bidet, loo and washbasin that Terry had bought in England and somehow managed to fit into a Citroën AX to bring out with him. The Gang of Three watched intently while we mixed cement, plastered and tiled, as if they were hoping to learn how to do it themselves. Toby and Alice were huge, and started challenging the dogs for their food. Alice trained Toby to chase the dogs, who ran more in confusion than fear from the two great white birds. A large white turkey, fully inflated, galloping after five dogs who are scattering before it, is quite a sight. But outside mealtimes they all lived in harmony with each other.

When I sat reading in the garden on those occasions when I was not in demand, they lay at my feet with the dogs, although the guinea fowl was a very restless creature and could only keep still for a couple of minutes before turning its attention to my shoes and trying to eat them, or wandering round the perimeter of the fence very slowly, with its beak touching the ground, like Sherlock Holmes seeking a clue. Despite its ungainly body it was surprisingly nimble, and would sometimes, without any apparent stimulus, break into a fast run and, leaping into the air, turn a complete somersault. If I hadn't seen this happen with my own eyes I wouldn't have believed it possible – guinea fowl are simply not aerodynamically designed. But Blue turned somersaults, and when she landed just carried right on with whatever she had been doing before this original idea popped into her little mind. Or, for a bit of variety, still with her beak to the ground, she would run frantically in circles at top speed for two or three minutes, and then continue her strange slow walk. She took a great fancy to our chicks and appointed herself as their nanny. Daily she shepherded them round the field, and once they had conquered their initial terror they took to her and accepted the little morsels she kept offering them.

Then Alice started making amorous advances to Toby, and it finally became evident that Alice was no more a goose than I was a shooting star. Alice was a gander, and the target of his affections was a turkey stag (that's what male turkeys are called, don't ask me why). Now, when a turkey gets angry, it's quite an awe-inspiring sight. Toby was getting decidedly angry, and he was very, very large. In the centre of his chest was one black feather, a little coarser than the white feathers around it, and above his beak was a red wobbly thing that dangled rather pointlessly. When Toby's dander was aroused, the wobbly thing extended itself several inches, and turned crimson; at the same time he puffed out his feathers to make himself look twice his already impressive size; he made a roaring sound, and he stamped his foot, making the ground shake. And Alice, rejected, became angry too. The two birds faced each other, Toby stamping and Alice screaming with rage. Then they launched themselves upon each other. Alice shrieked, Toby bellowed, the dogs gathered to watch and started barking manically. Alice tugged out great clumps of feathers from Toby's angry chest, and Toby kicked out hard with his sturdy toes. I had to wade in with wellington boots and a yard broom to separate them. Toby wandered off straight away to look for food, having retracted the crimson wobbler, but Alice was mortally offended, with a dragging wing, and crept into a corner and refused to move or eat for two days.

Both birds seemed very depressed by this change in

their friendship, and every so often the terrible combat broke out again. It couldn't continue, so my next project was finding a 'good home' for one of them, and I decided it would be Toby. I was adamant that he was not going to be killed, and numerous phone calls finally located a gentleman who was starting a small turkey-breeding set-up and wanted a good healthy turkey stag. I had his solemn oath that Toby would live out his natural life in comfort, and we made a rendezvous for Toby's new owner to come and collect him.

Two gentlemen drove up in a small van. One was short and round, dressed in the typical blue overalls of French country-folk, and with a beaming ear-to-ear smile stretching across his polished rosy cheeks. His companion was a tall man with dark curly hair and a spectacular handlebar moustache. The shorter gentleman clutched a one-and-a-half-litre bottle of clear fluid in his hand, and the other man a rather small wooden crate, the sort of crate an average-sized chicken could fit into.

'Madame,' beamed the short gentleman, 'have no fear! I promise you, your little turkey is going to a good home, with lots of ladies to enjoy. He will be well cared for. You have my word.'

I thanked him profusely, because believe me, finding a good home for a turkey in an area of France that is almost entirely populated by farmers and carnivores is not at all an easy task. He proffered the bottle, assuring me that it was the best *eau-de-vie* I would ever taste.

Toby hove into view at that moment, and the two gentlemen stared at him in astonishment.

'That is your turkey?'

'Yes. Is there a problem?'

'But he's *magnificent*! What a splendid turkey! We were not expecting such a big, fine bird – what do you feed him on?'

I explained that Toby, of his own volition, lived mainly

on dog food, and shaking their heads in wonder they proceeded to try to get the turkey into the little crate. It took a lot of folding and holding while Toby put up a heroic fight, but finally he was secured, and extremely angry.

'Don't worry, my son,' the short gentleman told him. 'You'll be home very soon and wait until you see your wives! You are going to be a very happy turkey!'

With many handshakes and promises, they drove away, leaving me with a bottle of fire water and a gander called Alice, who started entertaining himself playing with the doormat, or maybe trying to kill it, or mate with it. The guinea fowl began roosting on the sofa next to our very old dog, Natalia.

On one of those days when I didn't have any visitors or commitments, I sprawled on the sun-lounger listening to music hits of the Sixties, remembering hula-hoops, bobby sox and stiff net petticoats. The dogs stretched out on the grass, which, despite a drought that had lasted several weeks, was surprisingly lush and strewn with daisies thanks to a small underground spring which kept that part of the garden permanently moist. Alice settled himself under the garden table in the shade, and Blue squawked and yelped her way round the perimeter of the garden. The sky was the palest blue; the fruit trees were in blossom, and the oak and lindens in full leaf. The wind was warm and gusty, and the horizon that had been brown for several months had suddenly become flushed with green as new crops started to emerge. I watched the big glossy rat who lived in the barn emerge from his den in the stone wall to help himself to the chicken food, looking left, right, and left once more before running out, grabbing a mouthful and flashing back into the wall again. The parrots sang along with the wild birds, the chaffinches called their repetitive 'pleased to meet you, pleased to meet you'. The swallows twittered noisily, and

Alice tilted his beautiful elegant head on one side and observed them with a bright blue eye, rather questioningly, as if wondering either how they could fly so fast, or why they bothered when they could be sitting comfortably on a cool lawn surrounded by daisies. I had a broom at hand to fend him off if he tried lavishing any more affection on me – the bruises from his last show of tenderness were just starting to fade.

Then an egg apppeared on the middle of the lawn where Blue had been sitting. One minute it wasn't there, then it was, like a rabbit from a magician's hat. It was a little bigger than a hen's egg, and rock-hard. I mean, the shell was all but unbreakable: you could throw it like a ball down the garden, and it would bounce. Wizzy, our largest dog, retrieved it enthusiastically for several minutes before giving it a hard, experimental bite, when it broke with a loud crack. Having discovered the secret of this novel missile, he started waiting each day for the egg to appear. At first Blue laid haphazardly wherever she happened to be at the critical moment; but once she started to get the hang of the process she settled down on a pile of straw in one of the barns, and sat for about half an hour with a blank unblinking stare to produce another egg which Wizzy immediately devoured. As time went by, he would settle down beside her on the straw and wait with an expression of delighted anticipation until the arrival of the egg. This daily ritual moved into another phase as he became more and more impatient; now he sat beside the vacant-looking bird and poked his snout under her rear end every few minutes to see whether the egg had arrived, tipping her onto her beak where she would remain motionless until he removed his nose and allowed her to settle back and get on with the business in hand. He tracked the bird daily as it meandered on its noisy way round the garden, waiting for the first sign that the magic egg performance was imminent, wagging his tail ever faster as Blue settled down on her pile of hay.

Next Alice, whom we renamed Alex, fell in love with Hecate, our younger bitch, and followed her everywhere, ferociously attacking anybody or any other animal who came near her. Hecate totally and disdainfully ignored Alex's affectionate attention, going about her daily affairs with the gander trotting along beside her. When Hecate sunbathed, Alex sunbathed. When Hecate drank, Alex drank. And when Hecate curled up on her cushion and went to sleep, Alex curled up right next to her and kept one eye open to ensure no harm came to her. While this was initially both amusing and endearing, it seemed unfair to the bird, and so I set out to locate a mate for him. Geese are notoriously difficult to sex, which maybe was why Bill had ended up with a gander in the first place. M. Meneteau said sometimes the females had narrower beaks; somebody else said you could tell them apart by the width between their legs. Eventually I found somebody who was prepared to sell what he believed, but could not guarantee, to be a female goose. Off I went and met a gentleman in a car park carrying a very beautiful but absolutely enraged bird encased in a brown paper bag up to her neck, where the bag was held in place with a piece of string. An awful lot of money I couldn't afford changed hands, but, certain I had done the right thing, I took Lucy-Goose home, helped her out of the soggy bag and introduced her to Alex. For four long days and nights he harried her. He bit her, chased her, bashed her with his wings, tried to drown her, drove her from her food, hissed and generally terrorized her in every way he could devise. On the fifth day I decided to take her back to where she had come from, as she was so tired and bedraggled.

And then, to my – and no doubt Lucy's – delight, Alex's hateful shriek changed all of a sudden to a gentle

117

croaking, and he led her lovingly to the plastic paddling pool that served as their pond. He ushered her in and from that moment on they became inseparable. Alex attacked anything or anybody who came near Lucy – dogs, horses, people, everything except for Blue, who like a faithful attendant shuffled along behind them wherever they went. Visitors cringed outside the gates and would only come into the garden after assurances that Alex wasn't in the vicinity. If he appeared, they climbed onto tables or ran for the house.

Blue learned to sing. A guinea fowl's song is a simply appalling racket, a noise that was a combination of shriek, groan, screech and honk, uttered rhythmically from first light until total darkness had fallen. It was the sort of noise I imagined could be heard from a shipyard when a liner was under construction.

In volume she got probably as far as a guinea fowl can go, but her melody did not improve, and her grating honk-shriek-screech-groan outweighed the benefit of the daily egg, so I decided she would simply have to go. Her other vice was suddenly and unexpectedly running full tilt at unsuspecting people and pecking them hard on the shins. Very luckily for Blue, the first person I approached said she would be glad to take the bird, but she would have to get her brother to do the killing, as although she herself could kill rabbits and chickens, guinea fowl were notoriously difficult to despatch. Much as I wanted to be rid of Blue, I could not condemn her to a painful death. However, nobody seemed prepared to take her except as a meal, so I embarked on a hunt to find her a kind home. A few phone calls to bird welfare organizations led to an introduction to a very large sanctuary, le Marais aux Oiseaux on the Île d'Oleron, about a hundred and eighty kilometres away. Primarily and originally a haven for migratory birds in distress, they also accepted other creatures, like unwanted pet

118

rabbits, tortoises, and domestic poultry, all of which live in a large area of woods and marshland. They were happy to welcome Blue, so Terry and I packed her into a cardboard box and drove her, still bawling, to the sanctuary. There, to our common delight, we found a healthy flock of similarly noisy birds, into whose bosom Blue was welcomed. Without pausing for breath she melded into the crowd and became immediately indistinguishable from the rest.

Despite Alex's wedded happiness, his temper was no better. He seemed to hate everybody and everything, and attacked horses, dogs, chickens, people: anyone but Lucy. M. Meneteau mentioned that Lucy would start laying soon, and that I should expect Alex to become very belligerent. It was almost impossible to imagine how much more belligerent he could conceivably be. I could hardly wait. But where Lucy was concerned he was a model of gallantry and tenderness, shepherding her round the garden, croaking some sort of goose-talk to her. They shared a very happy life for nearly two years until one night Alex lost a battle with something stronger than him. Lucy was devastated and went into a state of depression, and I was afraid she would die of her grief, so I popped her in the car and drove her to join Blue in the sanctuary on the Île d'Oleron, where there were other geese to keep her company. That was the end of the saga of Bill's birds.

Chapter Seven

Fred Bear was an almost daily visitor. He didn't have a telephone, because, as he rationalized, he only spent a few months each year there. During the winter he and his wife rented property in Spain, coming back to France to enjoy the summer weather. Why should he, he asked, pay telephone line charges for the time he wasn't in residence? Absolutely no point at all; he just gave everybody our number, and thus it was that I started receiving calls from more strangers, asking me to pass a message to Fred. That was no problem; I merely had to drive the 2 kilometres to his house to relay the message. And 2 kilometres back again, of course.

To his great credit, he did drive himself to the nearest call-box, approximately four kilometres away, to make outgoing calls. Even taking into account the fuel and depreciation on his car, he was probably winning until I dug my toes in and decommissioned myself from the telephonist's post. Reluctantly he asked me to arrange an installation at his house, with much cursing and muttering about the iniquitous charges of the 'bloody French bastards'. I began to dread the sight of his car pulling up in the drive.

Really, it was a great pity because on the rare, very rare, occasions when Fred was not talking about money, he could be quite charming and amusing, and his wife was the dearest little lady you could ever meet. If they invited you for a meal at their house no expense was spared. You were fed royally and started thinking what a nice old boy Fred was. And then he'd go and spoil it yet again over a few pennies. Under his mantle of meanness I saw there was a heart of gold, but he could not let it beat. He spent hours strimming our grass for me when our mower was broken, then told me I owed him a favour. He would insist on loaning me money when I was in extreme financial difficulty, but panicked when he got the idea into his head that I wasn't going to pay it back. He asked me to caretake money for him when he was away, then telephoned in a rage because he thought I might be stealing it. If I mentioned the phone calls and fuel I had expended on his behalf, he was offended and belligerent.

Attached to his new house was an outbuilding that would give him valuable potential to extend his house and handsomely increase its value. The outbuilding belonged to one of his neighbours, a local farmer, and Fred asked whether he could borrow my services to translate for him. Although he did make quite an effort to socialize with his neighbours he wasn't up to wheeling and dealing in French, which is where my limited talents came in. I rang the gentleman concerned, explained the purpose of my call, and arranged a meeting with him. The farmer and his wife welcomed Fred and myself with smiles, handshakes, and a choice of wine or coffee at their handsome pine kitchen table.

'Right.' Fred opened the negotiations in his inimitable fashion. 'Tell him, dearie, that I'll give him eight thousand francs and not a penny more. Tell him I'm no fool.' ('plum pudding' was the term he actually used, but you might not have understood that, and the farmer definitely wouldn't) 'and that I'm not going to be ripped off by him.'

121

I smiled at the farmer, who was looking curiously at Fred's rapidly reddening face. Keeping my voice completely neutral, and looking at him very directly and meaningfully, I said: 'This gentleman would like to thank you for inviting us here this afternoon. I am here only to translate between you, and I want you to know that I am not responsible in any way for anything he says. So please understand my position.'

He nodded gravely. 'Of course, madame, I understand.'

'The gentleman is offering you eight thousand francs for the ancient outbuilding attached to his house.'

'That's not nearly enough. Its value is fifteen thousand francs, and that is what I'm asking for it.'

'What's he saying?' demanded Fred.

'He says he wants fifteen thousand francs for it.'

'Tell him he's a bloody thief. Eight thousand francs is my final offer. Tell him to take it or leave it.'

'The gentleman is still offering eight thousand francs,' I translated, aware that the farmer had a very good idea of what Fred had actually said. He smiled, and shook his head.

'He'll leave it.'

'Well, that's it. Tell him he can bloody keep it, and I don't want to see him round near my house. Tell him.'

'The gentleman says he'll think about it, and maybe talk to you again later. Thank you very much for your time and hospitality.'

We shook hands and I trotted after Fred who was stamping up the road, shouting to his wife, poor little lady that she was, that the bloody French are all robbers and bastards.

With the arrival of the poultry, our rodent population flourished. An expanding dynasty of rats set up home under the chicken house, and however hard I tried I couldn't help finding them endearing. They were glossy, bright-eyed and cunning as the devil. I watched them help themselves to food and water, with a weather-eye always open for danger. I was an interested observer as they trained their young, teaching them to look carefully in both directions before venturing onto open land. The mice thrived too; a regular battalion of four came up through the floorboards in the evening and shinned effortlessly up the legs of the parrots' cages, helping themselves to sunflower seeds while I sat a few feet away reading. While three of them concentrated on stocking their larder, the fourth trundled around collecting fallen feathers and manoeuvring them, with quite some difficulty, back to the nest. Their home must have been something rather special, decorated with bright red, bright green, dark blue and grey feathers. I found a mouse sitting comfortably on my bed one morning, and they quite often scampered over my head during the night. One regularly sat on the lid of a particular saucepan to perform its ablutions. When I picked up a bunch of grapes I'd left on the table and found a field mouse clinging to them, I kept very still, and after staring at me for some time and twitching its whiskers, it ate its way through a whole grape whilst sitting on my hand. The dogs spent patient hours staring at spaces and gaps hoping for a sighting. Sometimes their patience was rewarded. A very tiny mouse appeared right in front of Wizzy where he had been standing motionless all morning. The dog's tail wagged very slowly as he watched the mouse scurrying around for a few moments about eighteen inches from his nose, and then it shot out of sight and he resumed his static vigil.

Neither mice nor rats troubled me unduly, although I did appreciate that ideally they would be more acceptable if they weren't living in our house; I wasn't afraid of them and didn't understand how they could strike panic into the hearts of some people when they were so small and furry. But spiders – now that's something quite different. The greater French farmhouse spider is a terrible creature, with a 3-metre wingspan, maniacal ruby red eyes, and muscles the size of tennis balls on its uncountable legs. They growl like tigers, deep in their throats, trap you with webs stronger and thicker than steel hawsers, and hang you by your ankles while they chew your ears off. Do not mess with these creatures.

If the rodents could have been content to live in the various outbuildings, rather than moving into the house in great numbers, I would have left them alone. For heaven's sake, there was more than enough space for everybody; they didn't need to crowd us out of the house. Reluctantly I realized that we couldn't go on sharing our life so intimately with them. I used poison once, and seeing the results was determined to find a more humane solution, so I started looking for a cat. We had a very lovely friend called May who lived in a hamlet about nine kilometres away; she was a passionate animal lover, and absolutely cat-ridden, because her neighbours' myriad and unneutered cats were constantly propagating, and their resulting offspring usually migrated to May's house where they were sure of getting a better meal than at their own. She had varying numbers from about a minimum of four up to, I think at one point, fourteen. I rang and asked if she knew of any kittens needing homes.

'Oh, yes! Our neighbours have three gorgeous kittens, about six months old, and they're due to be killed very soon.'

'Killed? Why?'

'Well, they let their cat have kittens every year, and leave them to live for a few months, then when the next lot are born they shoot the older ones. They think it's kind to let them live for a while.'

I didn't think we could have three cats, and when I

124

went to see the kittens decided I'd take the first one to come to me. A grey and white one galloped up, with strange markings on his face that made him look like the Phantom of the Opera, and I instantly fell in love with him: that's how we acquired Beau, who did a sterling job in controlling the rats and mice. One night after a distressingly noisy fight, he laboriously dragged a rat almost as big as himself into the bedroom and began crunching it up with audible relish. It is not a nice thing to lie in bed and hear a cat eating a rat, so I chased him out with it and closed the door on his rather hurt and indignant face. The next morning, there was not a trace of the rat.

A while later May rang to say she had another cat that needed a home, a black thing with huge round green eyes, that her other cats simply would not tolerate. They chased it every time it came to the house, where it sat on the window ledge tapping on the glass with one hopeful paw.

'Honestly,' she said, 'it's just heart-breaking to see his poor little face at the window. I've made him a bed in one of the rabbit hutches, and put a duck-down duvet in there for him, but he's desperate for affection.'

And that's how Louis joined the family. He did not have the same eating habits as Beau, who finished off every scrap of whatever he caught. Louis was something of an epicure and only downed those parts that particularly appealed to him, so it was quite common to find a little set of clawed feet, a disembodied head, a backside and tail, or just a heap of shiny bits under our bare feet in the morning.

We had left our two very old horses in England with our friend Sandra, who had offered to let them live out their lives on her farm. The more I thought about those dark, wet English winter days, the more I felt it was unfair to

125

ask her to take on the muddy and time-consuming chores that horses demand in winter; she already had at least a dozen horses of her own, most of which she had rescued; and anyway, I missed them. Some people thought that travelling such a long distance would prove too much for the old ladies, and that it would be kinder to have them destroyed, but I thought that given the choice themselves they would unanimously opt for risking the long journey.

Terry, our daughter Julie, her husband Steve and their beautiful daughter Catherine brought them over in a giant transporter, once the formalities at the English end had been completed. After a long but uneventful journey (apart from when the transporter rolled backwards and demolished somebody's horsebox and Sandra's lawn-mower and garden wall as it pulled out of the stable yard), they arrived shortly before midnight on a warm September night and stepped down the ramp of the transporter, gazing about them and surveying their new home with the regal air of a pair of duchesses arriving at a state banquet. They stood for a moment in the dark, and then wandered off beneath the stars and started tearing at the lush grass. A little later I proudly led them into the small barn that I had lovingly spent four days preparing for their accommodation. I'd pulled down the rotting boards of the ceiling, dug out the dried manure and scraped it off the walls, shudderingly unfestooned the giant spider's webs from the beams, disinfected the floor and laid down a thick bed of fresh straw. They went in obediently enough and chewed politely on the hay nets I'd put up for them. In the morning they kicked down the door and took off out to the field, and from then on steadfastly refused to ever again go into that barn.

When we'd completed the purchase of the house, we'd asked the English estate agent we dealt with for his advice on heating, and his reply was: 'Don't waste your money. It doesn't get cold here in the winter, apart from a few days here and there. You won't need heating.' I can still remember the look of delight Terry and I exchanged, like a pair of simpletons, at these glad tidings. We couldn't have afforded heating anyway.

As it was now mid-September, and winter was approaching – even though apparently it was going to be deliciously mild – it seemed prudent to move the kitchen from the bottom of the garden and bring it into the house, especially as the horses had free access to it and had started knocking over the pots and pans; so Terry and Steve moved the units and the homicidal cooker and set them up on the uneven dirt floor of the barn part of the house. Terry also installed a rudimentary plumbing system that meant we had running water coming out through taps, and draining away from a sink. The problem was light – there were no windows and no electricity in the barn, and the 9 square metre opening 10 metres away at the far end was filled with an elderly oak door which only allowed in such illumination as could squeeze through its cracks, so we decided to take the door off. Remember, it didn't get cold here.

We removed the door and tacked up some sheets of plastic with drawing pins, in case it got a bit breezy.

Coupled with the delight of the horses' arrival was the enormous pleasure of having some of our family here for the first time, and we all managed to happily survive the primitive living conditions. They left after five days, and at 4.51 a.m. on the morning following their departure the sound of madly barking dogs and whinnying horses woke me from a warm and comfortable sleep. Lying still and hoping did not stop the racket, so with enormous reluctance I pulled on a dressing gown, a pair of socks and a woolly hat, jammed my feet into wellington boots,

127

and managed, surprisingly, to find a torch that still produced a faint glimmer of light. Outside it was quite chilly and pitch dark. I waved the fading torchlight around until it illuminated two large shaggy figures. Behind them lay an acre of pleasant meadowland, and a large weatherproof barn filled with hay and buckets of fresh water. So there really had been no need for them to force themselves over two strands of barbed wire and a fallen elder tree, to land up in a neglected area of about thirty square metres, where there was nothing but weeds and rolls of discarded chicken wire in which they were caught up. Having discovered for themselves that theirs was a wasted mission, they were unable to extricate themselves from the entanglement around them and had panicked. Cindy had got her tail caught in a roll of chicken wire, which was holding her back and getting further tangled in the undergrowth, creating ever more alarm in her equine breast. Leila had tried to step back over the barbed wire and had both hind legs trapped between two strands that tightened every time she moved.

I ran back to the kitchen to find a strong pair of scissors, and jamming the almost extinct torch between my cold knees succeeded in cutting away Cindy's tail from the chicken wire, turning her and leading her over the fallen tree and barbed wire to freedom. The barbed wire was attached to a fence post, which by lifting and twisting I could free from where it in turn was trapped under more wire, which released the tension and allowed Leila to wander off into the darkness. The torchlight died, and I returned to my now cold bed. When I got up again at 8.00 a.m. to feed everything, both horses were again trapped in the same area, from where they gazed at me mournfully as if they had been transported there entirely against their will. I released them once again, reflecting that there is no understanding the mind of a horse.

It was the first time in 37 years of owning horses that I had had sole responsibility for them; previously we'd kept them in places where there was always somebody experienced to ask for advice. I hoped I was going to be capable of caring properly for these two large and utterly dependent animals. Being able to see them from the bedroom window, standing in a field we owned, was a joy beyond description. Mme Grimaud, feeding her chickens, beckoned me down to the fence.

'What a pleasure to see horses here again! At one time we saw them all the time, working the fields. Then the tractors came.' She wagged her head ruefully. 'Times are changing.'

They were none the worse for their long journey; in fact they were thriving. Old as they were, their coats shone and they seemed to have regained their youth. The bigger mare, Leila, herded Cindy around, deciding just where and for how long she could stay in any one place. Cindy, ever placid, co-operated. Despite the frailty of the various lengths of fencing and hedging, they seemed content to stay in their allocated space. Just for the time being.

Between our house and Bill's barn was an empty cottage, with a pretty little orchard, whose owner, a plump old lady, had died just before our arrival. Because we didn't own sufficient grazing to support two horses, I telephoned the old lady's son to ask if I could rent the orchard, and we struck a deal. A few weeks later Daniel Guillot called, ostensibly to collect the derisible rent we'd agreed, but more I think just to chat. He was a sociable and interesting man, and took me in to look at his mother's cottage. I'd only ever seen the old lady once, when we first found our house. She'd been sitting on a wooden bench outside her front door, facing and soaking up the afternoon sun, as she had been doing for decades.

She was 93 when she died, and her simple cottage was absolutely spotless. The oak parquet floors and great old flagstones were all polished like mirrors. The wallpaper was typically French and floral, and a door from her bedroom downstairs led directly into a pretty little sun-trap garden. There was a large empty loft upstairs with stunning exposed timbers, and it was the only house in the village with a west-facing front door.

Daniel told me how during the war the Germans had installed themselves in the village of Saint-Thomas-le-Petit. The Guillots then owned a black German shepherd dog that never barked except when it heard Germans coming, and it could hear them from a kilometre away. Daniel's father had a radio on which he listened to the latest news about the progress of the war, but as soon as the dog barked the radio was hidden.

The German soldiers used to come to the house and ask Mme Guillot, who had a reputation as a great cook, to prepare a meal for them. When she had cooked the meal and set it before them, they would thank her politely and ask her to just taste a little herself 'to make sure it was good'. Daniel said that the soldiers were invariably well mannered and pleasant, until the day when, having heard on the news that the tide was turning against them, M. Guillot had been reckless enough to say: 'Allemagne, kaput!' which had earned him a severe beating.

When they'd first arrived the Germans had been quartered in the village school, leaving the children to take their lessons seated under the trees in the courtyard; but later the soldiers had built a barracks. After the war, the whole building was dismantled by the villagers and moved a few hundred metres down the road, where it became the present village hall.

Daniel's wife, Marcelle, was a very small girl when the war ended. A group of German soldiers had surrendered to the local French militia, who were marching them in convoy through the village where Marcelle lived. As the locals were standing watching the soldiers passing through, an Allied aeroplane suddenly appeared and began strafing the village, mistakenly believing the soldiers to be a still-active unit. With bullets flying everywhere, everybody threw themselves to the ground or took shelter where they could. Marcelle said that it took many, many years for her to recover from the terror of this, and to stop running for cover whenever she heard an aircraft noise. She still looked up automatically at the sound of an overhead engine.

In October the maize harvest began; looking at the fields of withered brown stalks it was hard to believe that there was anything there to reap, but the harvesters worked round the clock, glaring-eyed dragons rumbling backwards and forwards through the fields, reducing the stalks to stubble and filling trailer after trailer with the golden nuggets of corn. Autumn settled into its stride, and great wedges of geese hauled their way southwards, honking to each other over the susurration of their wings; the leaves from the walnut tree turned gold and yellow and dropped, and I collected them and put them in the chicken house to make warm bedding for the poultry, because despite the estate agent's assurance it seemed to me that the weather was becoming distinctly chilly. As winter advanced, the migrating cranes followed in the path of the geese, their croaking calls drawing attention to their V-shaped formations in the sky directly above our heads.

We didn't have any form of heating whatsoever in the house. As the temperature during November plunged down to zero, and kept slipping ever lower, I was very seriously discomfited. The animals were fine, the poultry in their leaf and straw-lined coop, the horses with their shaggy coats, the dogs in a deep nest of straw and blankets and the two parrots' cages covered in a duvet, but on the sofa-bed with its thin mattress through which I could feel the springs, covered by a skinny duvet and one blanket, I was colder than I believed it possible to be and still breathe. The house was very damp; the north-east wind shredded the silly plastic sheeting we had so optimistically pinned over the gaping doorway in the barn, and in came the rain, hail and snow to join what had fallen through the cracked roof tiles. It was too cold to cook there, so I put an electric kettle in the living room, which wasn't a great deal warmer, and lived on hot drinks, cider and packets of biscuits. The small room that in the summer was a cool haven became, as the days shortened and the north wind started to bite, visibly damp and terribly cold. Despite the paint and polish I splashed all over, it was fungusy and mildewy in no time at all, with new colonies of mushrooms popping up on the walls. Most of the floor had entirely collapsed onto the richly pungent earth below, and as I lay in the dark I was aware of things substantial enough to be heard nibbling and scuttling about around me. Once I'd tugged on the string that caused the light bulb to go off I was usually asleep in seconds, to awaken later to the sounds of scraping, munching and scampering. More than once, light, fast bodies with cool feet ran over the bed, tittering as they went. I burrowed further under the covers. It wasn't an ideal bedroom, and I looked forward to getting a staircase into the loft space so I could sleep up there even when I was on my own.

Minimum daywear was at least one thermal vest and pants, tights, two pairs of long socks, jeans, T-shirt, jumper, scarf, gloves, woolly hat, sheepskin-lined denim coat. My nightwear had changed from its normal Chanel No. 5 (only kidding, I don't wear scent at night) and was the same as my daywear: I slept fully dressed. And I was still cold. In the morning I lay in the small room until the dogs' barking became so persistent that I had to go and feed them. Then I spent the day wandering around banging my arms against my sides and stamping my feet, or sat huddled in a chair with a blanket wrapped around myself, feeling like Babushka in Siberia while I ticked away the hours waiting for the first signs of evening when I could feed everything again and put them to bed, so that I could burrow back into my uncomfortable little nest. Terry brought out an electric blanket from England and the nights took on a less arctic quality, but conversely made getting out of bed in the morning even more of an ordeal.

One morning I awoke to an unusual sound. It was the sound of a stream burbling merrily close by; almost, by the sound of it, in the garden. I clambered out of bed and into wellington boots, and stuck my head outside the front door, to see a brisk brown brook swishing its way down the lawn. The two things that immediately struck me as strange were, first of all, that we had not had a brook running through the garden when I last looked, and second that there had been no rain during the night.

With an uneasy feeling I followed the brook upstream to its source, which was located in the provisional kitchen that no longer stood on a dirt floor, but in a spreading, chuckling ocean of mud. The copper pipes that delivered water to the sink had transformed themselves into ingenious water features, gushing thin, high-pressure fountains from eight separate locations. The mud was ankle-deep and rising.

· I sploshed to the phone and called Terry to announce this alarming development. 'I'm going to have to get a plumber in here quickly.'

'No, don't do that. We can't afford a plumber.'

That was true.

'You can sort it out yourself.'

I snorted. 'Don't be so ridiculous! You've absolutely no idea what's happening here – the water's flowing through the barn and right down the garden! It isn't a little no-account trickle, it's rushing about all over the place, and there's mud and water everywhere!'

'OK. Listen. Go and find the toolbox, and the blow-lamp. And turn off the stopcock.'

'Where is the stopcock? What does it look like?'

'It's a red-topped tap, and it's somewhere beneath the basin.'

I found it just above the waterline, and stopped the multiple little squirts.

Over the next two hours Terry gave me an elementary plumbing course via the telephone; he instructed patiently, and I did exactly what he said, cutting through pipes with a hacksaw, manipulating little brass rings nonsensically called olives, and soldering splits, all the time slithering and sliding about in the slimy residue left by the receding stream. Finally the last crack was sealed. I was colder than ever, soaked and filthy, and we still only had the plastic bucket to wash in.

The contents of the refrigerator were frozen: butter, milk, eggs, fruit, cheese and bread were all solid. The washing up liquid had turned to crystals and if shaken made a noise like a pair of maracas. The jams and sauces in the jars were frozen solid. All our houseplants were dead, a limp green mush. During the night the temperature had plummeted to minus 18°C.

A week later there were 10 centimetres of snow on the ground in the morning. All the taps were frozen again, but intact. There was no way of getting water for the horses, so I slid round collecting snow in rubber buckets, but it wouldn't melt. After four and a half hours in the living room, they were still buckets of snow. I stood them in front of a small electric fan heater that I borrowed, and that did the trick. In about ten minutes it was all melted, including the buckets which were buckled and no longer bucket-shaped. In the end I went and got some water from Mme Meneteau, whose house was heated and pipes were lagged, and whose water consequently flowed sensibly through her taps regardless of the external temperature. I thought it was a little ironic that Terry and I had almost certainly made, over the preceding years, more money than all the inhabitants of the hamlet had jointly earned in their entire lives; and yet while they were all cosily comfortable in their houses, thanks to their wood-burning cooking stoves that also provided heating, we were plainly freezing.

I wondered what the estate agent regarded as cold, and from where came the misconception that anywhere south of the Loire is always warm and sunny. During that first winter, the weather suffered violent mood swings. It could be bright and sunny one day, and the next bitterly cold, with thick ice on the horses' water buckets. Two days later it might pour with rain, and the following day out would come the sun again. The horses were particularly perplexed; used as they were to the monotony of cold wet English autumns and winters they didn't understand why the seasons changed here with such rapidity.

My friend Red offered me a job as a part-time secretary in her company, which undertook the transport and delivery of mobile homes to campsites throughout France. I would work the afternoon shift and the other Carole, who had helped build Bill's poultry palace and translated for Mrs Malucha, did the mornings. The job was a tremendous boon to me, because it meant that I could become a part of the French social security and medical system, and although the pay was minimal, every little helped. Not so long before, the pound had bought 10 francs; by now you were lucky to get 7.3 – our money had devalued by 27 per cent in just a few months.

135

Anybody whose income derived from England, such as English people retiring to France on pensions, was having a very hard time making ends meet. Terry and I agreed that as soon as I'd accumulated enough from my new employment, we'd buy a good, solid wood-burning stove.

Terry had found and fitted a new gearbox for Tinkerbelle, so I was independent once more. A group of French ladies were learning English at a technical school in a town not far away, and I'd been asked if I would spend one afternoon a week talking English with them. They were a jolly crowd. One of them was very generously built with an ultra-voluptuous bosom ('*il y a du monde au balcon*,' as the French say – the balcony's crowded). She had stepped out of her car the previous week and broken her leg, and seemed to find the fact that she was encased in plaster from toe to thigh utterly hilarious. She collected things – beer mats, matchboxes, thimbles, phone cards, wine corks; the list was endless. She also collected biscuit tins and had 1,800 of them. She told me that an early Huntley and Palmer tin, which unfortunately she didn't own, was worth £4,000; which knowledge somehow appalled me when I thought of the millions who died of starvation or curable diseases simply because there wasn't the money to buy the medication they needed. It seemed obscene that a piece of cheap metal could be worth so much. Another lady collected straw hats.

Being France, it wasn't long before we were on the subject of food. The straw-hat lady asked as diplomatically as she could whether beef cooked with pineapple, with cauliflower in cheese sauce, which she had twice been served when dining with English friends, was a typical English dish. I assured her that it wasn't. Sounded absolutely disgusting. Christmas wasn't far away, and the ladies wanted to know if, in England, we had the same sort of Christmas meal as they do in France, with plenty of oysters and *foie gras*.

I tried to describe a traditional English Christmas meal.

'The first course varies. It could be anything – soup, asparagus, whatever. But the main course is almost always a roast turkey, with two different kinds of stuffing, one in the neck, another in the body cavity. It's served with roast potatoes and mashed potatoes, roast parsnips, brussels sprouts, fried bacon rolls, miniature sausages, carrots, peas, bread sauce, cranberry sauce and gravy. Sometimes there is roast beef, too, and Yorkshire pudding.'

'*Mon Dieu!*' They looked aghast and asked what bread sauce was. As I told them how it was prepared they stared hard at me as if trying to see whether or not I was joking; their lips turned down unanimously and they made retching noises. They were not prepared to believe that it is quite delicious, or that cold it makes a great breakfast.

'And you eat all that together?' they asked in disbelief.

'Yes. Then we have Christmas pudding, which is set on fire, and served with brandy butter, cream and custard. Then mince pies.' I listed the ingredients of the pudding and pies to my audience, who were politely trying not to look horrified. 'And after that people sit and crack nuts, and eat fruit and chocolates.'

'And then you don't want anything more to eat for a week!' cried one.

'Oh, no. We've not finished. Later in the day we have Christmas cake, made with similar ingredients to the pudding and pies, coated in almond paste and sugar icing. And cold meat and cheese and salad.'

'Why do you have to eat so much?' asked one lady.

'Well, because it's Christmas.'

'And you don't eat any oysters?'

'No, I don't think they'd mix very well.'

'But you do have wine, of course?'

'Oh yes, we have lots of wine.'

'Ah well, at least that's something!' laughed the big-bosomed lady.

'Will you have all that, here in France on Christmas Day?' asked someone.

'No – we don't eat meat at all. We'll probably have some fish, something quite simple, and some good wine.'

'Bravo!' cried someone else. 'That sounds *much* nicer.'

When our first Christmas did come round, Terry and I spent most of Christmas Day rendering the walls of what was going to be our bathroom. We mixed loads of cement and wheelbarrowed it through the mud and rubble, whilst at the same time I tried to produce a meal befitting the occasion in the makeshift kitchen in the dirt-floored barn. As that was before we had a door knocked through between there and the living room, I had to scamper over heaps of rock and debris, through a brisk drizzle, to deliver the meal. In the event it was quite successful; we'd decided that before the end of the year we were going to have one really good meal in our new home, and so tucked into a modest array of oysters, caviar with sour cream on blinis, and a little lobster each, and plenty of good wine.

Terry managed to impale his hand on the oyster knife, and so put a stop to any further rendering that afternoon.

Chapter Eight

Although I had come with schoolgirl French and a few books and tapes, I thought the best way I was going to learn French was by talking and listening to French people, so I took every opportunity to do so. I knew how to construct a sentence in the correct order, but my vocabulary, while full of *plumes de ma tante* and *frères Jacques*, was not very helpful for day to day conversation. When I couldn't find the word I needed, I created one that sounded vaguely as if it might be correct, and threw it into the conversation.

There was a sticky moment in the very early days, following a night of tremendous crashing storms. Mme Meneteau asked whether I'd been frightened of the noise.

'Oh no,' I thought I replied breezily, 'I love . . .' Now, whatever was the French word for 'storm'? Probably something like '*rage*'. I tacked it onto the end of the sentence.

She shrank back from me slightly, smiled a little nervously, and said she had to go and pick some cabbages for her sheep. I suspected I had got things a bit wrong, so I dug out the dictionary and looked up '*rage*'. It means rabies. A storm is an '*orage*'. Oh well, I knew next time. I never missed a chance to talk to French

139

people, and was soon making little jokes. They always laughed, but whether at the content, or at some ghastly mistake I was making, I was never quite sure.

The insurance agent arrived to check the measurements of the property to ensure that it was adequately insured. Quite why this was necessary I didn't understand, as he had been insuring the same land for the previous owner for a decade during which time the dimensions hadn't changed, but anyway, he said he had to check for himself. He came wearing wellington boots, as it had been raining non-stop for two weeks. We chatted away for half an hour; I assured him I was blissfully happy living here in our ramshackle kingdom, and he looked politely disbelieving. The more we chatted and laughed, the less certain I became of what he was saying, and the more I doubted he understood what I was saying. But we continued chatting and laughing while he measured each building by the simple method of striding up and down in his boots. One step equalled one metre. No need for theodolites or laser levels: the insurance premium was calculated by his stride.

Talking with M. Meneteau, our next-door neighbour, was an education in itself, not least because he had a very noticeable accent and spoke in the local patois. His 'j' was pronounced 'h'. So *jardin* became *hardin*. I had asked him the best local market to visit and was told Hançay. Failing to find it in any map or atlas, I asked him to point it out on the map, and found that it was actually called Gençay. We discussed matters medical, horticultural, philosophical, and ecclesiastical; the other neighbours; the latest English immigrants and anybody local who had recently died. He was beautifully polite and acted as if I spoke the language perfectly. When I failed, or mispronounced a word, he just gently added it into the conversation without any comment.

While we were talking over the hedge one morning, he

gave a sudden small triumphant shout, vanished momentarily and reappeared waving a trap and a very tiny mouse by its dead tail.

'Look at the monster!' It was about the tiniest rodent I'd ever seen and I felt the epithet he gave it was a little exaggerated.

'It's been eating my endives,' he said bitterly, stamping on it. Endives, you will of course know, are what in English are known as chicory. *Chicorée* is what we English call endives.

The French language is such a delicious minefield: it's full of words with double meanings that have no apparent way of distinguishing themselves. '*Baiser*' is one such word. If somebody says they want to do this to you, you don't know whether you're meant to proffer a cheek, or lie on your back. It is also frequently confused with '*baisser*', meaning to lower, thus offering another opportunity to make a frightful fool of yourself and entertain the natives. Another notorious verbal trap is the word '*préservatif*', which in anglophone countries is something that keeps food from deteriorating. In France a *préservatif* is most commonly a condom. There may not be a single market in the whole country where the local people have not been astounded and delighted to hear an English person enquire whether the jams or juices contain any condoms. Introducing somebody as '*mon ami*' leaves the other party at liberty to decide whether it's a friend, or a lover. It could be either. You think you've learned to form the feminine of many words by adding to the masculine the final letter plus an 'e'. So *chat* = cat, *chatte* = female cat; *chien* = dog, *chienne* = female dog; *chiot* = puppy, *chiotte* = lavatory. See what I mean?

I joined a French class, as much for the pleasure of the company of my classmates, five English ladies, and our charming teacher, Amelia, as for learning the language.

Under Amelia's expert and highly entertaining tuition the mysteries of the French language started to unfurl themselves, so that conversations with French people became less of a hit and miss affair and more of a pleasure than a pain. There was so much to learn, not only in terms of vocabulary and grammar, but also about the simple use of words. We learned that '*mal au coeur*' does not mean a bad heart, or that somebody is having a cardiac arrest. It simply means that the afflicted person wants to be sick. To telephone an ambulance and announce that your spouse has '*mal au coeur*' will probably elicit a shrug as they wonder why you thought they might be interested in such a trivial matter. The French for a heart attack is '*crise cardiaque*'.

I bought a small television, hoping it would help to improve my understanding of the language, and discovered that there was a hole in reception in the hamlet: the inbuilt aerial couldn't pick up a signal, and I needed a far more powerful one. The model I was shown cost more than the television and more than I had in the bank, so the man in the shop very kindly dug out an old used one that I could just afford. He said it would work perfectly in the loft, as there was no way I'd be able to fix it up on the roof by myself. I suspended it from a piece of string, with other pieces of string and some coat hangers anchoring it to a stepladder to keep it at the correct angle. This took innumerable nerve racking trips up and down the decaying loft ladder, until I could get a decent picture on four channels. Several times a week I sat staring at the screen, trying to make out from the high-speed babble exactly who was saying what to whom. Once I thought I had understood a film right up to the very last seconds, and when the *dénouement* arrived I realized that I hadn't actually understood it at all.

One aspect of my job with Red was applying for and

chasing up the necessary permits to allow the extra-wide loads transit through France. This was a bureaucratic nightmare, as each load required a separate permit from each of the *départements* it traversed, which could be as many as six or seven. The application forms had been designed to be as unfathomable as possible, and in more than one *département* the issuing authorities showed a definite antagonism, whether towards foreign transporters, transporters in general, or Red in particular, I didn't know, but they made the whole process incredibly difficult and protracted. Having to telephone these people and try to get them to return the permits in time was a terrible experience. If the vehicles were moved without the permit, the transporter faced heavy fines. During the 'low' season, which was most of the summer, when the mobile homes had been delivered to site for the enjoyment of holidaymakers, we tried to keep Red's fleet of trucks moving by sub-contracting from other hauliers, so I had to telephone French haulage firms and persuade them to give us some work. I floundered very badly, but learned more about the French language during that period than at any other time. Without being able to resort to diagrams, dictionaries or gesticulations, I was forced to listen properly to what the people at the other end were saying, and to make myself understood by them.

As a change from struggling with a foreign language, I learned how to struggle with my own. Valérie had introduced me to a lady from Sri Lanka, or somewhere near there, married to a Frenchman, who lived just outside Saint-Thomas-le-Petit. Although she spoke excellent English, she had embarked on a correspondence course in the English language, for a reason she couldn't explain. And she couldn't do the course, either, so once a week she descended unannounced upon me, with books and paper, and insisted that I should do her homework.

That was the first time I had ever experienced any difficulty with the English language: it was totally unfathomable, the questions so obscure that they might as well have been written in Aramaic. I couldn't imagine that the course had been designed by a bona fide organization, nor could I see how anybody would ever be able to learn English from it. Although I explained this to her, she was convinced I was just trying to duck my involuntary obligation to help her, and would sit determinedly until I had written out at least a couple of pages of gibberish, which she would take home, copy out neatly and post off hopefully, to receive it back a couple of weeks later with scathing remarks about her lack of progress and inability to understand simple questions. I clutched at the straw that this might lead her to find an alternative slave, but she still kept coming back and urging me to try harder. Sometimes she brought her sons with her, two very handsome little boys, hyperactive and noisy, who rushed through the house and garden, slamming doors so the fragile glass shook, skidding up and down the wooden floors I had so laboriously waxed, trying to catapult each other into the air via an old rocking chair, dragging furniture around and rummaging in drawers and cupboards, tipping the contents all over the place, while their mother apparently didn't notice. I hoped that a drink might pacify them, and poured them what I thought was a shandy. Far from calming them, it had the opposite effect and being in the room with them was like being in the eye of a hurricane. After they'd gone home I collected up the empty bottles, and found that it wasn't shandy, but very strong beer.

She was a nice girl, and after she decided to abandon the English course and take up the clarinet instead, she came to thank me for all my help, and brought me half a dozen jars of jam made by her mother-in-law. The jars were thick with cobwebs and the jam had green fuzz growing all over it, but it was a kind thought and I recycled the jars.

As my French started to improve, I was more confident talking to the neighbours, and able to learn from them a great deal more about local history.

Just above the tiny stream at the bottom of the lane lived the hamlet's youngest resident, a charming man named Jean-Luc, who owned a large acreage which he rented out to a local farmer. He actually spoke English a great deal better than I spoke French. Listening to him, I realized for the first time, with rather a shock, that the peace and quiet and wide open spaces that so many of us love represent, for these small rural communities, the closing of a page in their history, and the loss of a way of life that had lasted for generations.

In the old days, the hamlet had been full of life: there were four small farms, and two big ones, one of which belonged to Jean-Luc's family, and the other to M. Meneteau's, and there was a constant movement of people, tractors and animals. During the summer, harvesting contractors went from village to village to thresh the wheat that the farmers had cut and stacked in the fields. Everybody worked to help with the harvesting, and they all ate together outdoors, up to thirty people, at long tables laid with salads, bread, charcuterie, cheeses, and *mijé*, the local traditional mixture of red wine, sugar, bread and iced water. All the farmers used to deliver their wheat to the bakery in the village, and were given bread in return. Our hamlet's remaining bread oven hadn't been in use for decades, except during the Second World War when it had been brought out of retirement because there was nowhere to buy bread.

Every hamlet and village had its own fête once a year, with live music and dancing in marquees. All the people from the neighbouring areas went to each fête, to dance and socialize with their neighbours. In those days everybody travelled by foot, or the better off by bicycle. Jean-Luc's grandfather was the first person in the hamlet to own a car, even though he didn't have a driving licence. He wasn't a rich man, but he wanted to have a car so that he appeared wealthy; Jean-Luc thought he'd probably sold some cattle so that he could afford the car. Jean-Luc's father passed his driving test when he was 18, but he didn't like using the old man's car. He was embarrassed to be seen in it, and preferred to travel by bicycle.

During the 1960s, when Jean-Luc was a child, there was an epidemic of brucellosis, and Jean-Luc's father decided to keep goats instead of cattle. However, he waited until his father had died, because the old man was very fond of his cows.

Jean-Luc also pointed out the *communaux*, the small parcels of land that every village in France is required to set aside by a law introduced by Napoleon so that the poorest inhabitants would have somewhere to graze their livestock or grow food.

'You can use it,' he told me kindly.

His father had been a local councillor, and had struggled for 20 years to implement *remembrement* in the commune. As a result of the way in which property was divided between the surviving children of landowners, a mosaic of odd-shaped little pockets of land had been created that made working them difficult. *Remembrement* was the regrouping of these parcels into a more regular outline, for the benefit of everybody who owned and worked them.

But there was a lot of resistance at the time; people didn't want anything to change, and Jean-Luc's father became very frustrated and eventually withdrew from local politics. It was only in 1992 that *remembrement* did come about here, but that was after his father's death.

Jean-Luc produced an old map and pointed out ragged-edged fields with little bits and pieces bitten out of them. 'This was how it was before.'

Now all the fields have neat edges, but there are very few small farmers left.

Above Jean-Luc's bungalow stretched a neat row of three old cottages. The one on the far end was seldom occupied, but belonged, according to M. Meneteau, to Jehovah's Witnesses, no better than Satanists and cannibals, his tone implied. I never saw them.

Next door lived a large gentleman, M. St Martin, with a buxom wife and a small and very overweight miniature Pinscher, a little gasping balloon on legs. M. St Martin walked the tiny inflated animal through the hamlet twice a day. His wife, who always walked slightly behind her spouse, was more sociable than he. With his straight back, stern expression and close-cropped hair, a spiked helmet would have suited him perfectly, and mentally I called him the Prussian. The nearest he got to a smile was a brusque inclination of his head, and his lips did not move at all from the horizontal. And yet when one of our horses let itself out of the field, as they so often did, and he found it ambling around on the side of the road, he returned it safely home, only mentioning the matter to me a few days later. And I noticed in his neat garden pink roses blooming in December. They were still flourishing in January, and their splendour was undiminished in February. I managed to catch him on one of his canine perambulations one day, and asked how on earth he managed it. For a fraction of a moment it looked as if he might smile, but he checked himself just in time. '*Plastique*,' he announced. '*Pourquoi pas? C'est agréable voir les roses dans l'hiver.*'

Pourquoi pas, indeed?

Mme Grimaud lived immediately next door to them, and about fifty metres uphill from her cottage the single-track tarmac road turned at right angles. On the interior of the angle, next to a stone well bedecked with pots of plants, was the home of M. Royer, the rotund bachelor with the enchantingly shy smile whose family originally owned what had become our house, and in whose kitchen we had signed the *compromis*. His house and garden were immaculate, and no matter what the season there were always flowers of some sort blooming round his garden gate. Stacked neatly by the fence was a great quantity of firewood, 10 cords at least (in those parts a cord equalled 3 cubic metres), and he kept half a dozen bantam chickens and a few sheep. Dolly, his beagle bitch lived on a chain in the garden and barn, and seemed happy with her lot. During the hunting season, M. Royer roamed slowly through the fields in his green jacket, wellies and flat cap, sometimes with Dolly, with a shotgun slung over his shoulder. In the years I lived there, for all the many times I passed him, I never saw him with anything he had bagged. Usually, he would say he had seen pigeons, but they were too far away. I think he simply liked wandering around.

French cockerels crow in French. They cry: 'Cocorico.' M. Royer had a younger cockerel that had only got as far as 'Cocori', at which point it tapered off into a sort of gulp. It practiced for hours on end, until I felt like shaking the final syllable out of it.

On the corner opposite M. Royer lived the family I called the Roly-Polys. The exterior of their house was unsightly, a collection of building materials and car parts, overflowing rubbish bins and bags, and washing in a uniform shade of grey pinned to their gate. House-keeping didn't seem to be Mme Roly-Poly's forte. I couldn't criticize – it wasn't mine, either. The two ladies of the household, Mme Roly-Poly and her daughter, were immensely round, and very short. Quite seriously, these ladies measured far more around than from top to bottom. M. Roly-Poly was thin and wiry, with missing teeth. They had numerous cats and dogs, and poultry, and when I first arrived had a tame magpie that lived on their roof and talked. Mme Roly-Poly had a passion for birds, and she was always willing and pleased to care for any that were in need, like the young blue tit I found bumping around in a deserted barn; she tucked it tenderly into the bottomless cleft of her bosom, and crooned to it and fed it with an extraordinary gentleness. On a scorching August day I was driving past a field bleached pale beige by the sun, where a tractor was harrowing the baked earth into a dusty cloud. A lone crow stood motionless, and for some reason I couldn't explain it didn't look right. There was nothing particular about it, except that it simply seemed to me it shouldn't be standing there so still, with the tractor no distance away. Returning fifteen minutes later, I saw it was still there, directly in the path of the tractor about a hundred metres off. I braked Tinkerbelle to a rocking halt, and scampered across the flints and dust to where the black avian sat like a stuffed toy. It looked up at me with some interest and no apparent fear, and allowed me to pick it up, carry it to the car and sit it on my lap, where it stayed perfectly relaxed as I drove home.

In the house I put it in a large cardboard box on a bed of straw, in the cool of the living room, with a small bowl of water. There was no sign of injury, and I thought it was simply suffering from heat and dehydration. Leaving it to recover, I lay down on the bed in the corner and drew a cotton sheet over myself. My eyes closed, and in the box the crow rustled and scrabbled. It rustled and scrabbled increasingly noisily, and I opened my eyes and lay watching as it hauled itself to the top of the box and perched there rockily for a few seconds before hopping onto the floor. Without any hesitation it strutted towards the bed, and using its beak and claws dragged itself up the cotton sheet and onto my leg, where it sat and studied me. We regarded each other amicably for a moment, and then I pulled the sheet over my face. I felt its clawed feet march up my body until it was on my chest; the sheet twitched, and was pulled back so that I could see the obsidian eyes of the bird staring at me, its head cocked to one side. I covered my face again with the sheet; old black eyes tugged it off. We played this game for ten minutes. I was astonished by the instant, fearless friendliness of the creature.

I left it exploring the living room for a couple of hours, and then as the sun collapsed over the horizon I took it out to the field to see if it would fly. But it sat there looking up at me in puzzlement, and when I turned to walk away, it bounced along happily beside me like a small, feathered puppy. I couldn't keep it, not with five gundogs, and so I carted it down the lane to Mme Roly-Poly. In her gigantically rotund way, she was charmed and her small eyes, almost swallowed up by her cheeks, glowed. A podgy paw stroked the composed bird where it sat on my hand. Yes, she would be happy to take it. Her cousins had always wanted a tame crow. I was alarmed. There wasn't any way this creature was going to live in a cage, I told her. She laughed, stroking the black feathers.

'But no! They want a crow or magpie like the one we had, that lived on our roof. We would never keep it in a cage.' She gave me her solemn oath, and I handed over my new friend into her care.

A week later I asked how the crow was faring.

'Ah, the cousins are delighted! It is very happy there, living in their garden, coming into the house, and even though it's stripped all the fruit from their cherry tree, they love it.' It stayed with them for several years, before flying away one day.

The Roly-Polys were relative newcomers in the village.

They were not a farming family and did not mix much with the other hamlet dwellers, most of whom had lived here for generations; but they had their own large social circle and during the summer months they often ate out of doors with their friends, playing music at a considerately low volume. I found them friendly, although a little shy, and they always had a kind word for our dogs. The only thing about them that disturbed me was that every so often they killed things in the pathway. Sometimes it was a pig, sometimes a goat, occasionally a goose. If on a Saturday morning a number of cars appeared and parked on the lane, it was my signal to disappear and stay away for a few hours. When I came back, there would be ominous galvanized buckets outside their house, and magenta rivers running down the lane. Sometimes the dogs appeared with gory stringy lumps in their mouths, and guilty expressions. On other occasions there might be a great pile of white feathers, signalling that the Roly-Polys had one live goose less. Once they had two beautiful baby goats, like real live Bambis, who lived in a dark shed where they could just peep over the top of the door. One day they had gone, and in their place were two snowy white skins and eight tiny hooves hanging from a cord. I couldn't look. They were not cruel people: it was simply their way.

As dusk was falling one evening I called the dogs to put them in their sleeping accommodation, and locked them in. The phone rang. It was Jean-Luc.

'Susie, do you have your dogs with you?'

'Yes, why?'

'Well, there is a dog like yours injured on the road.'

I ran to count the dogs and sure enough Vulcan was missing.

'One of them is missing.'

'Please come to our house. We will help you.'

I charged down the lane, hearing anguished yelping

and seeing a cluster of cars grouped on the road. My heart sinking, I headed for the scene.

There were five cars blocking the road to prevent any traffic going through, and about eight people standing round Vulcan, who lay on the side of the road, crying and lifting his head. Mr Roly-Poly was there stroking him, and he reassured me: 'Don't worry, madame, he isn't badly hurt. He'll be OK.'

'Can he walk?' I asked.

'No, he doesn't seem able to, but we're certain he is only shocked.'

I galloped back up the hill to get Tinkerbelle and a blanket, with which we lifted the dog into the back of the car. Then I thanked the crowd for their help, and the driver of the car that had hit Vulcan started earnestly explaining himself. I thought he was apologizing, and assured him that there was no need; I quite saw that he couldn't have avoided it. But he didn't seem reassured, and kept saying something I couldn't understand.

'What's he saying?' I asked Jean-Luc.

'He says your dog has damaged his car, and he wants you to pay for it.'

I stared at the dilapidated jalopy, which was a mass of dents and bodywork panels in varying colours, and I stared at the driver.

'Is this man, who has injured my dog, asking me to pay for damage to this?' I pointed at the vehicle.

The crowd started murmuring.

'Where is the damage?' Mr Roly-Poly asked the driver, who pointed to a small dent, one of many, on the leading edge of the bonnet.

Mr Roly-Poly lifted the bonnet, gave a push, and let the bonnet drop.

'There you are, the damage is repaired,' he told the driver.

'Bravo!' called someone from the crowd.

Then we all shook hands and I drove back home to see how badly Vulcan was hurt. It was no more than a collection of superficial cuts, but he was shaken and feeling extremely sorry for himself, so I gave him half an aspirin and a bowl of sweetened milk and he settled down on my bed for the night. The following morning he was his bouncy self once more, and spent the day trying to find a way to get back down to the road.

In contrast with the Roly-Polys, whose garden was enhanced by supermarket trolleys, maggoty bones and overflowing dusbins, next door M. and Mme Meneteau's house and garden were as neat as a new pin. No matter what the season, Mme Meneteau, like her brother M. Royer, always had something in bloom; her step was swept, the flower beds weeded, the car polished.

Mme Meneteau was about the same height as her husband, which wasn't very high at all, and wore a permanent smile; she had a strong face, but a very kind one, and a charming way of tilting her head to one side as she talked. Behind their white-painted and blue-shuttered house was a large barn filled with firewood, neatly cut and stacked. In the grassy courtyard were pens of rabbits, hens, ducklings, guinea fowl and pigeons, all destined for the table, and half a dozen sheep whose lambs delighted us in the spring, when they bounded and wobbled around, bouncing into the air on all four legs, climbing woodpiles, chasing each other pell mell, and then suddenly collapsing in tired woolly piles. M. Meneteau grew all their own vegetables in neat, hoed rows, and their fruit trees yielded cherries, apples, apricots, pears and figs. They often passed bowls or bags of fruit and vegetables over the hedge to me.

Mme Meneteau had been born in our living room, and had grown up there with her siblings and her farming parents. She talked of the work the women had to do in those days: how only a couple of days before her baby was due she had been out in the field harvesting the maize. Being enormously pregnant didn't spare you from hard work. At harvest time, everybody had to help. There were no machines then, and the cobs were chopped from the stalks by hand, the grains then beaten off the cobs with a piece of wood. And the women had to prepare meals for all the workers, too. It was also the women's work to hand-shear the sheep, to laboriously wash the greasy fleeces in hot water, and then to tease and spin the wool and knit it into socks and waistcoats. They were sociable times, before the advent of television. In the afternoon and evening the ladies sat together by the pond, knitting and chatting, and the men entertained themselves by playing cards in the village cafés on Sundays.

There were no clothes shops; people bought fabric and had it made up for them by tailors and dressmakers. Healers, who had their own strange methods of dealing with injuries and disease, complemented the local doctor's services. It was more usual for the healer than the doctor to cure burns, which Mme Meneteau said they did simply by touching the victim. Skin complaints like ringworm, eczema and impetigo were rampant, often transmitted by cattle to humans; the healers dealt with these by cutting a small piece of the patient's hair, dabbing something on it and then applying it to the affected area. M. Meneteau, earthier than his wife, said. 'Piss. We used our own urine to cure skin problems.'

Between the Meneteaus' and Bill's domains was a sizeable barn and a small abandoned house smothered by a neglected but vigorous vine, a firebreak for the Meneteaus between their neat and tidy property and the overwhelming chaos that was Bill's. This little house and the barn also belonged, like the empty cottage on the other side of Bill, to the Guillot family.

The lane continued for another 20 metres before it ran

out at the gates which we had erected, somewhat futilely, to try to contain our dogs. And that was the full extent of the hamlet. It was generally utterly peaceful, apart from the demands of the visitors, the quiet broken only by the day-long call of the cuckoo in early spring, a sporadic tractor trundling up the track behind the hamlet to the great fields of sunflowers and maize there, the triumphant yells of chickens fresh from laying, and at night, beneath the beauty of the moon and stars, the croaking of frogs and crickets, the nightingales' divine chorale, and sometimes the hoots and screeches of owls.

Chapter Nine

That first year the winter was mercifully short, and spring came in with violets in hues from almost black to almost white, not at all shy or modest, but great big things mugging the roadsides and studding the lanes; buttercups too, and celandines, daisies and those little blue flowers with the white hearts whose names I can never remember. The swallows and the cuckoo arrived together on 21 March, and the hoopoes soon after.

For about a week huge machines had been rumbling on the fields that our garden overlooked, and I was sad to see that they were gouging up the copses and hedgerows. M. Meneteau was more than sad, he was incensed.

'Fools,' he shouted across the hedge, 'they don't know what they're doing. Look at them, tearing everything up. People don't know anything about farming these days. They're spoiling everything. Pouf! Our fathers planted when it was the right time to plant, and so did we. We knew when it was mild enough, wet enough, when the time was right. Now they have men with computers who analyse the soil and twiddle knobs on their machines, and that tells them what to plant, and when, and where. And they fill the land with chemicals. Bah! We used animal manure. And the food tasted better.'

He spat on the ground and stamped away.

I knew that some local farmers were still actually using animal manure, for when I walked the dogs in the fields in early spring, tractors appeared towing great tankers filled with the delicious green-brown sludge scraped out from the floors of the sheds where the cattle over-wintered, and they sprayed this gorgeous aromatic gloop over the ground and the dogs all rolled in it.

Bill hadn't been around for several months, but he had taken Sinbad back to Spain with him, so there was a little more space in our living room. Gloria hadn't made up her mind whether to stay in Spain, or move to France, and I hadn't seen her since the previous summer. Bill turned up in April with a new project: selling second-hand furniture, of which he had great heaps. An English lady published a small magazine locally in English, and he placed two advertisements in it: one for his furniture removal service, and the other announcing that he had a stock of quality used items of furniture for sale. Not having a telephone did threaten to jeopardize the success of this venture, so it was agreed that our phone number would be used and I would relay messages to Bill. Terry didn't think this was a particularly good idea, but Bill did us a lot of favours and I was happy to be able to reciprocate in some way.

Now the telephone started ringing with calls from people interested in wardrobes, pianos, bicycles and beds. I'd explain politely that Bill was absent just at the moment, but would call them as soon as he returned, and then scamper round to pass the messages to Bill, urging him to return the calls, which he seldom did. Callers became angry and indignant when they didn't hear from Bill, complaining of my inefficiency and asking whether my boss was aware that I wasn't doing my job properly.

A rather haughty woman rang to enquire about a piano that Bill had advertised. It was actually a rather lovely-looking thing, with an inlaid picture of a peacock on the front. The woman was very keen indeed and wanted to view it immediately, so I sped round to Bill's house and suggested that we get it under cover, as it had been sitting, rather lopsidedly, in his driveway, exposed to the elements, for several weeks. We couldn't put it in Bill's house, because he didn't have one, so we humped it onto a sort of trolley, dragged it into our living room and gave it a good polish. Bill rang the interested lady.

He explained it was an old family piano, and that all his children had learned to play on it. Yes, it was rosewood.

'Walnut,' I hissed.

'Walnut.'

The woman asked what make it was, and whether its frame was wood or iron. Bill hesitated, and said he'd just have a quick look. She lost interest, and it was a fortnight before the piano went back to Bill's driveway.

Eventually, as he didn't seem to care whether or not he actually sold anything, I told any enquirers that whatever they wanted, we didn't have it.

There were also frequent phone calls at all times of the day and night, from men saying, without any preamble, 'Run and get Bill for me, will you, love.' This really did enrage me, especially as we had agreed that our number wouldn't be given to all and sundry, so I would tell these callers that they must have the wrong number, and not to ring it again. Strangers who had somehow acquired our phone number would call asking if I had rooms to let, knew anybody who did, could find them property to buy, or knew where Bill was.

I didn't, because he'd disappeared again.

The cranky old people from the village had gone to Spain for a holiday. I had always thought the husband was the milder half of the couple, so I was considerably surprised when he rang one day, announced himself, and said, 'Would you mind switching on your fax machine – we're selling the house and want to fax you the inventory. You'll have to collect the keys from the *notaire* so you can show people round.' I'd only met them twice, and I found it quite astonishing that people took it for granted that a virtual stranger was sitting waiting to be given tasks to do for them.

Despite his little eccentricities, Bill was a very helpful and friendly person. Nothing was too much trouble for him. He mended things for me like the lawnmower, the Hoover, the strimmer – anything in fact that was in need of mending – provided transport, and, greatly appreciated, used his digger to excavate the necessary trenches and pit so we could get a septic tank installed. He did nearly knock down the house in the process, but that was an accident. He was also an exceptionally clean person, forever washing himself, his clothes, his caravans, his pots and pans, and his cooker. In fact most times when I went looking for him, he would be cleaning something or other. Once we planned a joint trip to town, leaving at 11.00 a.m. I presented myself at Bill's on the hour, and by the time he had washed his trainers, changed the hose on his washing machine, cleaned the cooker, changed his socks and brushed and washed the doormats of his caravan, it was 2.45 p.m. What was so strange was that his passion for cleanliness didn't extend to the outside of his property, which was simply littered with decaying machinery, abandoned tools, and fly-infested pools of fluid dog shit ('Turd Hall,' he sometimes laughed). Several times I tried diplomatically, or once or twice quite bluntly, to suggest that something be done to tidy up the property, and Bill would always say, gazing into middle distance, that he was going to get it all sorted out. But he never did. His zeal for hygiene only seemed to extend to his person and an aura of about two metres around it.

M. Meneteau came round one day. 'It's summer,' he pointed out. I agreed. 'The countryside looks beautiful. The flowers are all out. The sky is blue. But look at this mess!' He waved his arm at Bill's cluttered empire.

Three mouldy caravans were gathered round the entrance to the building. There was a wheelbarrow full of rusty metal and water, weeds everywhere, a great roll of water pipe, some blown-over garden chairs. It looked horrible.

'Would you ask him if he could put the caravans and all this stuff,' he indicated the piles of junk, 'round the back of his house, where we couldn't see it, or in his barn? It's such a shame to see our little village in such a mess.'

I said I'd speak to Bill when he returned, but although I left friendly notes on his door, they went unheeded. I even managed to catch him on one very brief visit, and expressed the neighbours' distress. That faraway look assumed itself on his face, and he said: 'I must do some-thing about getting this cleared up nicely.' But he never did.

During the wet weather he always parked his truck in the quagmire that formed outside his house, where it bedded down comfortably into the mud, and required the services of M. Meneteau and his tractor to haul it free. After several minutes of wheel-spinning and mud-spattering, he would trot off to ask M. Meneteau, in a loud voice, stressing each syllable carefully: 'Poss-i-ble trac-tor you?' pointing at the embedded vehicle. His obliging neighbour would cheerfully bring the tractor round, couple the truck to it with a chain, and release it from its muddy prison. Then he would indicate, with sign language, that in times of mud it would make sense to park the vehicle on the hard surface. 'Mercy, mercy,' Bill would mutter, and tuck a bottle of whisky into M. Meneteau's pocket. Fairly soon afterwards, the truck would be back stuck in the mud once more.

With the advent of the summer evenings, large winged creatures, striped yellow and brown, began marching into the living room under the crack in the door, and then blundering noisily around the electric light bulb, from where they fell to the ground, and whirled around on their backs trying to regain their feet. I scooped them up on a piece of card and tenderly ejected them through the door; it was a time-consuming procedure because they kept crawling back in again.

One morning M. Meneteau came round to warn me about the *frelons*, which he said were very dangerous, and of which there were a great number about.

'Be careful. They give a very bad sting – it can kill a child, or a sick person, or a dog. And it could make you very ill.'

I hadn't any idea what a *frelon* was, so asked him to describe it.

'A large winged creature, striped yellow and brown.'

I nodded. They sounded familiar. I looked up *frelon* in the dictionary. 'Hornet', it said. Taking his advice to heart I decided to take a firmer hand with them, and blocked up the bottom of the door to stop them getting in. They fluttered angrily at the windows and buzzed menacingly, but I stuck to my guns and kept them at bay.

Terry, who was learning to do all kinds of tasks like plumbing, carpentry and electrics, had bought and fitted a solid staircase to replace the wormy ladder leading to the bedroom and installed an electricity supply, so that I could sleep up there as a more sanitary alternative to the fungussy room downstairs. But having light and a staircase didn't necessarily mean that life was a bed of roses. This is why.

To see my way upstairs, I had to switch on the light in the kitchen (a bulb hanging from a piece of string). As soon as I did that, in came the hornets through the sheet

161

of plastic where we still didn't have a door. That wasn't really a problem; they just flapped around banging into the bulb and dropping to the ground. The difficulty was that once the bedroom light was on, I had to come back down and switch off the kitchen light, leaving the bedroom door open so that I could see my way across to the bulb on a string and back up the stairs again. As soon as the bulb downstairs was switched off, the hornets made a dash for the upstairs one, so that by the time I'd got back to the bedroom they were swarming around in large numbers. I started by trying to knock them out of the door with a magazine, but as they came in herds of about twenty, by the time I'd knocked the third one out the first two were back in again. There was only one thing for it, and that was a mercifully swift whack with the fly swatter before I pushed out all the poor little corpses through the door. The following evening there were more. There were always more, until I found one day that they were actually living in the chimney. I lit a roaring fire and filled the living room with smoke and hornets that were very very angry indeed and I had to barricade myself in the little room next door until they'd settled down. When I went back three hours later they'd all disappeared, so the following evening, armed with a toxic aerosol, I repeated the fire and finished them off with the spray. They didn't come back, but one of our neighbours had a thriving colony living in his roof the following summer.

After I'd been living there for over a year, and had started to get to know people, it occasionally crossed my mind that I had not once been a target of male advances, and this began to bother me. Not that I wanted anybody to harass me sexually, you understand, but it worried me that nobody had tried to do so. Women will understand this much more readily than men. I was after all a woman living for the most part alone, and the most common question people asked me was whether I was continually fighting off amorous advances; it was rather humiliating to have to keep admitting that I wasn't, ever. In a contrarily female way, I both wanted and didn't want to be the target of some lecherous approach that I could rebuff. Just when I was beginning to wonder whether it would be necessary to deliberately provoke an attempt so that I could indignantly repulse it, it happened.

An Englishman who'd been introduced to us by Red was undertaking some small jobs around the house, putting up fences and laying a concrete floor. His initial formality had started to wear a little thin, and he was calling me 'love' and 'dearie' and telling slightly risqué jokes. It is customary in France for people to kiss or shake hands each time they meet, and when they part: in an office everybody kisses or shakes hands with their colleagues until everyone has been kissed or had their hand shaken by everyone else, which is why quite often it takes a long time for the telephone to be answered early in the morning. A step further towards intimacy between people who know each other reasonably well occurs when hand-shaking is replaced by a peck on the cheek; sometimes two pecks, or three, or even four. M. Meneteau told me that when he was a child this casual kissing was limited to relatives, and one peck per relative; then the custom was extended to two pecks, and to friends; now, he said, everybody kissed everybody, and the two pecks had become four, and heaven knew where it would all lead. It's a practice which had been adopted by the English too, and the difficulty was in knowing how many pecks were expected – miscalculation could easily lead to a peck planted in mid-air, or a proffered cheek being slighted.

Anyway, the builder, who was starting to settle himself a little too much into my life for my liking, spending longer and longer intervals sipping tea and recounting the tragic breakdown of his marriage, had always followed the hand-shaking custom. Then one morning he unexpectedly lurched at my cheek. As I was brought up to be polite I accepted the peck without flinching, which was obviously a mistake, because the next morning I got pecked twice, and from then on it became the norm. The peck as a polite greeting should be carried out without any other form of bodily contact, but his pecks were starting to be accompanied by a hand that tried to slip round my back, which I evaded with a nimble little manoeuvre that a sensitive person would have recognized as a rejection. But my man persisted, until the morning he tried a full frontal assault and asked me what I would do if he kissed me properly. I was educated mostly in convents, and courtesy had been instilled into me from a very early age, so I looked him straight between the eyes and said sweetly, with a friendly smile: 'Kick your balls right out through the back of your neck.' Our relationship deteriorated quite rapidly after this exchange and very soon I found myself looking for another builder.

However, it seemed as if he had opened the floodgates, because now a torrent of suitors started swirling around me. Hot on his heels was a local Frenchman who was very helpful and friendly, who had piercing and expressive blue eyes and a rather ferocious wife. It only took one brief look to distinguish this person as the sort of chap not to be satisfied with a chaste peck. He was going to try for all he could get, and frequently did, having an unerring instinct for finding me alone (although this was a condition becoming less and less frequent as the days passed). His approaches were always of a verbal rather than a tactile nature, and I could field his more ribald suggestions by pretending a failure to understand what he was saying. By some cruel coincidence it seemed that whenever he showed up, one of the cats would be sitting on my lap, a fact that gave him endless opportunity for innuendo. I devised a cunning plan to parry his offensives: I kept a handbag hanging beside the front door, and every time I saw his car approaching I grabbed the bag and trotted towards my car, calling merrily: 'Ah! How are you? What a shame, I've got an appointment at the doctor/dentist/vet whatever: I have to dash.' He seemed to get the message eventually and stopped his uninvited visits.

The next contender, who arrived at the gate not long afterwards, was someone to whom I'd recently been vaguely introduced, together with his very nice wife, at a friend's house. He was a notorious womanizer, and I was most surprised to see him as we'd only exchanged about a dozen words; he lived about twenty-five kilometres away and I hadn't even mentioned where I lived, but he had somehow tracked me down and come to make his play. Luckily I had invited some friends round for coffee, and I was able to use them as a shield. After an hour of enduring his Gallic charm, I sent him on his way unfulfilled, and I was really quite astonished when he subsequently reported back to our mutual friends, who relayed the message to me, that I was a '*chaud-lapin*'. A hot rabbit, in case you haven't guessed, means a sex maniac. Interestingly, there is no feminine form of this condition in French dictionaries.

By now my ego was satisfied by all this attention. But there was more to come.

The ancient cow-dung that held together the stones and flints making up the walls of our house was falling out in lumps and chunks and we needed to get it sorted out before the whole building came down. Wherever possible Terry did what needed doing because of our limited financial means, but some jobs were too time-consuming and we were delighted to meet an elderly

Frenchman who was a genius with trowel and cement. Although in retirement he was happy to undertake a few jobs now and again, and after satisfying himself that we were decent folk he agreed to come and give our walls the cosmetic treatment they so badly needed, and at a price we could afford.

He arrived punctually each morning, on his scooter, with a degenerate little home-made cigarette clamped between his lips, which were often blue with cold. After shaking hands politely, in the true tradition of a French artisan he refused offered cups of coffee through the morning, and worked quickly and skilfully until exactly 12.30 when he presented himself, hands and face washed, for his lunch. Ignoring the knife I laid on the table, he drew his own folding knife and used that to slice the bread and cut his food. Once the main course was finished, he would enquire whether there was any cheese, which of course there was, because what meal in France is complete without cheese? All this was washed down with beer, followed by a small cup of strong coffee, and at precisely 2.00 p.m. he was back at work, continuing until 5.00 p.m. when he swaddled himself in jacket and helmet, inserted another odious little cigarette into his mouth, and, having worked his hands into the furry gauntlets that were an extension to the handlebars of his scooter, kicked the latter into spluttering life and set off for home, with one hand raised in salute.

Thus we went for the first week. On the Saturday afternoon he arrived unexpectedly, and much to my surprise. He had just come to enquire whether his work was satisfactory, and to deliver a brown paper bag full of gladiolus corms. I assured him that it was, thanked him profusely although gladioli are not on my list of favourite flowers, and offered him beer or coffee. He chose the former. After about fifteen minutes he rose from the table and instead of offering me his hand planted a beery kiss on my cheek. I didn't really want this – he wasn't at all my type – but good, available and affordable plasterers were as rare as hens' teeth, so I accepted graciously, which proved to be a mistake.

Monday morning, promptly at 7.55 he arrived and held out his wiry little hand. I took it and found myself in a vice-like grip, being pulled into his chest and kissed vigorously while the icy tip of his nose tapped me on both cheeks. Tuesday morning I was standing ready to thrust a steaming cup of coffee into his hands, insisting he must drink it after his cold journey, and hoping it might distract him from the kissing ceremony. But no. He took the coffee, placed it on the table and launched himself at me. I wondered how long it was going to take him to finish his work on our walls.

I really felt quite sorry for him, as his wife had left him and he did seem to be a very sad fellow. His poor little face was covered with a network of broken red and purple veins, which extended into the whites of his eyes, and he lived a lonely life in his neat bungalow and beautifully tended garden. What he needed was some company and kindness and a sympathetic ear. Well, anyway, that's what I thought he needed, but he seemed to have a more comprehensive agenda and began inviting me to dances and dinners, all of which invitations I gently refused, pleading prior commitments or ill-health. The invitations were always delivered by telephone at around 10.30 p.m. and accompanied by little hiccups, or maybe sobs. They were never mentioned the following morning.

The walls began to look a great deal more suited for their task of supporting the house, and our relationship continued on an even keel, with the facial rituals each morning and evening being, I felt, a reasonable little bonus for his excellent work.

I suppose we were halfway through the project when François introduced a new and really quite intolerable ingredient to our greetings. As we shook hands preparatory to the kiss/nose thing, he unexpectedly jerked my hand in a quick downward movement into his expectant crotch. He was extremely strong for such a little man, and guided my fist effortlessly into the place he had designated for it. I had to resist an overpowering urge to raise my right knee hard and fast, because we did have to get the walls finished, but instead I pretended to trip, lurched forward into him, knocked him off balance, retrieved my hand, and handed him a cup of coffee with a big smile. Thereafter I started getting up earlier, leaving the coffee to waft invitingly on the table whilst I busied myself shovelling manure in the stables or the dogs' mess in their sleeping quarters to coincide with his arrival, calling out a cheery greeting whilst flourishing the shovel, which I found quite an effective repellent to his early-morning advances. I think it made some impression on him generally, because we reverted to a brief polite handshake and peck morning and evening.

I felt quite cruel for treating the poor lonely fellow so meanly, because it seemed that he had developed a passion for me, and I was loath to hurt his feelings. Then M. Meneteau mentioned obliquely one day that I should be careful, because 'le petit misère', as he was rather unkindly known, was not to be trusted and had a bad reputation as far as women were concerned. Shortly afterwards another Frenchman I knew came round to the house and saw François working there. He stared at the little fellow, who turned his back and continued working; very unusual behaviour, because no matter who turned up where, everybody normally greeted each other with a handshake and a few words.

The visitor warned that I should be careful not to get myself into a compromising situation, and confirmed what I'd already heard about François's behaviour with the ladies.

Knowing that I was not after all the sole target, but one of many, made it easier for me to deter his advances.

Terry arrived to stay for a week. He was aware of the unwelcome attention I was receiving and was mildly amused by it, recognizing that the poor fellow was rather lonely, and at his suggestion we invited François to come with us to visit the newly opened Monkey Valley just 6 kilometres from our home. It is a magical place where 25 species of monkeys live freely in the trees and bushes. There are no bars, and no cages; they are free to roam where they will, and will feed from your hand and sit on your shoulders. It's not a zoo, but a serious conservation project and an opportunity to see these creatures living as near a natural existence as possible outside the wild. On the central island there is a family of gorillas, a stern silverback male and his two wives, who had each produced a baby during the two years since they'd first arrived.

François was delighted at our invitation, and we collected him from his house after lunch, stylishly dressed in neatly pressed trousers, polished shoes and a smart jacket, and emanating a strong aroma of beer. He conversed energetically with Terry for the ten minutes it took to reach our destination, a one-sided exchange as Terry's French was minimal and François's English non-existent, but he was very happy to chatter on.

The first colony of monkeys we saw inside the Valley were the tiny, fragile squirrel monkeys, with their shrill, bird-like calls. Touching is something that monkeys can interpret as a sign of aggression, and it is a strict rule at Monkey Valley that while the monkeys may touch humans, the latter must not reciprocate. But that didn't stop François. He was entranced by the capers of the little simians, and he was also, as we suddenly realized with dismay, horribly drunk. He started making loud,

169

monkey-like noises, chittering and chattering and lunging at the monkeys running around our feet. People were staring at us. Terry shepherded him firmly on to the next colony, the Barbary apes, and then on to the lemurs, who enjoy sitting on human shoulders while they eat their hourly snacks. François told the one on his shoulder, rather emotionally, that he loved it, and that he had once had a cat that looked very similar to it. We progressed to the gorillas, who sat across the narrow river, mirroring the crowd's disapproving stares at our guest's loud shouts and uncertain steps.

Next to the gorillas were the pygmy marmosets, the smallest monkeys in the world. They are hardly bigger than sparrows, with the tiniest little faces imaginable, and they move slowly, like chameleons. On our visit, however, they were also very publicly and enthusiastically mating, a fact that even in his inebriated and wobbly state François noticed and commented on, turning to call the passing crowd to watch, encouraging the little creatures excitedly, and jabbing me rhymically in the ribs with his drunken elbow. He laughed and clapped and stamped his feet, getting ever redder in the face as I willed the ground to part and allow me to slip beneath it.

We dragged him onwards, past groups of astonished monkeys who broke off what they were doing to watch him perform a variety of drunken imitations, scratching his armpits and rear end, rolling his eyes and swinging his arms wildly around while making clicking, growling and whooping sounds.

It was a memorable afternoon.

Chapter Ten

It was summertime, our second here in France. During the spring I'd laboriously gouged out a pond that was attracting scores of amphibians, butterflies and birds; clouds of goldfinches came there to drink, fluorescent dragonflies zinged just above the surface, and big zebra-striped butterflies danced in the lavender round the edges. I watched a large frog ambushing, quite successfully, the butterflies, and cramming them into its mouth with its podgy fingers. At night I fell asleep to the sound of the birds singing and frogs croaking to each other; and when I woke, they were still going. In the fields the flamboyant sunflowers were at their radiant best, poor things, little knowing how fleeting was their life. In a couple of months they would be hanging their black and withered heads in shame, then a dragon would come and munch them all up.

Terry phoned late one night, an hour off the ferry on his way here, to say that he'd picked up two young birds. I dug out the cats' travelling box and lined it with a folded towel, and settled down to wait.

It was 2.30 a.m. when he arrived, walking softly. In the bedroom he opened his fleece, and two enquiring little black faces peered out from where they were snuggled between his neck and his shoulder. They were young

171

house martins. One stepped without hesitation onto my outstretched hand, and I popped it into the warmth of the cat box. The other decided to fly round the room, splash a nasty mess onto the pillow, and attach itself to a beam, from where we caught it without much difficulty and fed it into the box with its companion. While they settled down comfortably on the towel, Terry described how at mid-point across the cold, windy Channel he noticed a flock of birds swooping round the deck, so went outside to watch them. As he leant on the rails, one of the birds suddenly flew onto his wrist, and a few moments later a second bird joined it. They huddled together, and Terry put a hand over them to shelter them from the drizzle. Daylight was fading. He stood on the deck through the rest of the journey, keeping the little birds as warm as he could, and wondering what next to do with them. When the ferry docked they showed no inclination to fly away, but climbed a little further up his arm into the comfort of the sleeve of his fleece. He planned to let them go once he reached woodlands, but even here his little passengers would not disembark, clinging like feathery limpets to his clothing. And so he drove 400 kilometres with the small birds cosily and happily nestling on his shoulder.

In the morning they were perfectly composed inside the cat box, and looking at us with perky interest. I phoned the Ligue pour la Protection des Oiseaux to ask for advice.

The lady there didn't seen at all surprised to learn that our small visitors had travelled such a distance sitting on my husband.

'You can just let them go,' she said. 'They'll sort themselves out straight away.'

So we opened the box and scooped them out. Like arrows from a bow, they soared up and out of sight in seconds.

I knew about the LPO because, a little while before, somebody had noticed an owl in difficulty in the barn opposite Bill's place.

The poor bird was caught by the tip of its wing in a knot of wire about five metres up, and there was no way we could reach it. I went to see if M. Meneteau had a sufficiently long ladder. He didn't, but came down to see what was happening. The owl swung round and round by its wingtip, until it broke free and crashed to the ground. It scuttled awkwardly into a corner behind a pile of timber, from where I dug it out.

I put it in a box of straw, under an infra-red lamp, and made some phone calls to vets and a wildlife park who told me to get in touch with the LPO, who rescued wild birds. They were very helpful.

'Leave it until dark, and then take it out of the box and see if it can walk properly. Then you can take it outside and see if it flies. If not, you could bring it to us tomorrow.'

'What about feeding? I normally give birds tinned cat food. Is that OK?'

'Give it some raw liver, if you can.'

'What about a mouse?'

'Of course that's what it would most enjoy, but there isn't much chance of you catching one!'

On the contrary, one of the cats had brought one in this morning and left it dead on the doormat. I'd put it in the waste bin. It was still there, but rather dusty.

'Just brush the dust off, and put it in the box with the owl,' advised the LPO man.

I did so, and an hour later opened the box to find a pellet that was the neatly processed remains of the rodent. The owl gazed up hopefully and trustingly, so I gave it a few spoonfuls of liver. It ate with relish, and seemed quite relaxed in the box beneath the lamp.

In the evening I took it out of the box, but although it

could walk both wings were dragging, so it spent the rest of the night back in the box, and the next morning I drove it to Poitiers to the LPO.

'Ah yes, a female barn owl. I hope you wore strong gloves when you were handling her? She could tear your hands very badly with her beak and claws.' Hm.

They entered her into a log, and invited me to telephone at some time in the future if I wanted to know how she was doing. When I phoned a couple of months later, they said she had two broken wings, which had been mended at the veterinary centre. She would remain in captivity until she had grown new feathers, when they would release her back into the wild.

Terry had asked me to dig a trench in the garden for the pipe that would lead from the incoming water supply down to the tap that watered the horses.

With the crowbar I hacked along about five metres of heavy, sticky clay and arrived at an area of nice black friable earth. About two metres of that, and then I hit something grey, rounded, obstinate and very big – a hippo pretending to be a large grey rock. It couldn't fool me, though – I knew rocks simply didn't get that big. It was definitely a hippo. I tickled it with the crowbar and it did not move, so I tickled it a bit harder, and harder still. I wiggled the crowbar down its side and started heaving, and finally the hippo moved. It was a juvenile, but almost fully grown, and made no effort to get out of the way. I had to be very forceful. It was only one of many: I'd struck upon a whole colony of them, living in precisely the spot where the trench had to go.

Oh, they were placid enough, no signs of aggression, but all displaying that infuriating obduracy which is their trademark. Clapping my hands did not work, nor did whistling at them. I tried stamping my feet, and the guinea fowl pecked them, but move they would not.

They had to understand that they lay right in the course of my water pipe, and, loath as I was to disturb them, they did have to go. I used the tip of the crowbar to find their sensitive spots, and, with a wiggle here and there, eventually I made them move. My continued tickling caused them reluctantly, and so very slowly, to surrender the trench to me, and then I had a great pile of them, 160 in all, lying on the grass waiting to be rehabilitated.

My triumph was short-lived, however, because then the snake started playing up. Looking for all the world like a heavy-duty black and blue hosepipe, it gave its true self away by refusing to uncoil. Every time I straightened it and pushed it into my trench, it jumped out and tried to rewind itself. Both my energy and my patience were now very thin, and I resorted to banging the snake with some of the hippos to make it stay flat in the trench. When it was in place I started to bury it, but, because the trench had been previously occupied by more hippos than earth, and because it was far too shallow, there was insufficient soil to inter the snake. I would have to somehow find earth from somewhere else, but some other time. It had taken seven hours under a sizzling sun to get this far.

I was exhausted, with little to show for my labour apart from the upheaved hippos and one half-submerged snake. Just before he'd left the previous day, Terry had installed the bathroom fittings and a water heater, although the bathroom itself had no ceiling and no door because there was no wall to put the door into. A sheet of polythene draped over the beams afforded little privacy if anybody wandered into the barn. During the following winter months it gave no protection at all from the north wind that swept in, and even if I ran a bathful of scalding water, by the time I got in the ambient temperature had already cooled it to tepid.

I had dreamed of lying in a deep bath of hot water in

our own home for many long months, and after the day's efforts with the hippos decided that no reward could be more satisfying than to take an inaugural bath.

I assembled all the smellies, a book, a glass (well, a bottle) of wine, some clean clothes and a pile of fluffy towels, and, humming a contented little tune, folded the plastic sheet neatly to make the room as airtight as possible before reaching to turn on the taps. Sadly, they had locked themselves solid and even with a plumber's wrench I couldn't budge them a fraction or squeeze a single drop of water from them. The bath would have to wait for Terry's next visit in a month's time. Such is life, sometimes.

So I staggered to the bed and lay there comatose until darkness fell and I had to feed and water the livestock, after which I sat weakly with a glass of vodka and composed 'Ode to a Crowbar'.

> Crowbar, crowbar, I love you.
> When nowt else works, you always do
> When the pickaxe won't pick
> And the shovel won't shove
> You keep on crowbing,
> Crowbar, my love.

Then I wondered if I might be going slightly barmy.

To some people 'renovating a French farmhouse' means paying builders to do the work. It didn't to us, because we (or rather more accurately Terry, because my skills were very limited) were doing most of it ourselves as best we could, learning as we went along. The major part of our thin resources went on paying veterinary bills that we had never anticipated, so even buying a pot of paint was often a heavy drain on the budget. But we had scraped together enough to pay a builder to knock a doorway through from the small room into the main barn where the kitchen was, thereby reducing the trip from living room to kitchen by about fifty metres. It was no job for amateurs, because the wall was nothing more than flints, rocks and dust, a metre thick. Once the opening was made, it left a pile of rubble of approximately four cubic metres that I had to somehow lose. I spent many months filling holes in the field and sifting out stones to use as borders for flower beds.

Like most of the skills I didn't have, carpentry didn't seem to be one of my hidden strong points. One chilly night, as I lay unsuccessfully trying to convince myself I was warm and cosy in the damp little room on the uncomfortable sofa bed, there was a distant horrible crash. I mean, a really loud crash, then silence. My initial reaction was to stay where I was and hope the crash belonged to somebody else. But the more I hoped, the more I thought about it, and the more I thought about it – and the less enthusiastic I was about getting up – the more I accepted that unless I found out the cause of the crash, I was not going to get back to sleep that night.

Out of bed, on with boots, hat and gloves. Found torch and sploshed down muddy garden, flashing torch around. Nothing untoward visible. Went into barn; saw two horses' bottoms. Most of front parts of horses had disappeared through a great hole in the back wall of the barn. Splintered wood indicated that a horse had applied considerable strength to kicking the hole. Shone torch through hole. Torchlight picked up the neat rows of M. Meneteau's cabbages, rapidly shrinking before the assault of two sets of ancient but still eminently serviceable equine teeth.

With little further effort Leila and Cindy would be able to climb through the hole and eat his entire garden.

Feeling very cross, waded back to house. Found hammer and nails. Torch, as usual, fading rapidly. Back

177

to barn, elbowed horses away from hole. Tried unsuccessfully holding torch in mouth, then clutched it between knees, recovered several planks of wood from other side of hole, and started nailing them neatly back into place. Wondered if neighbours were lying comfortably in their warm beds, speculating what *l'anglaise* was doing hammering wood at midnight. Horses now eating the piles of hay left in the barn for that purpose. Quite proud of my handiwork, I retired to bed.

In the morning I examined my midnight carpentry project, and was crushed to see that it was all higgledy-piggledy, gaps where there shouldn't be, planks all over the place. It had looked fine in the dim light of the torch. I went and found my trusty crowbar, undid the previous night's effort and renailed planks. The nails didn't seem quite long enough, or sharp enough, and the planks were a bit splitty, but it was the best I could do.

Gardening was a challenge. Despite the fertility of the soil, it only extended to a depth of about two centimetres before becoming rock. No matter where I tried to jab the fork into the ground, it bounced back and jarred my shoulders. The only effective way, the only way at all, in fact, to dig a hole was to take my treasured crowbar and start tickling with it until something moved. Once the first stone had been extracted it was simply a question of pulling out all its neighbours, and in no time at all there would be a nice clean hole ready to receive a new tenant. However, I was left with two problems. A big pile of unwanted stones, and no soil to refill the holes with. Here I depended quite a lot on the colony of moles who allowed us to share their homeland, and went around collecting the piles of fine tilth they created to fill the plant holes with. How they managed, with their tiny velvet bodies and small claws, to find any earth at all to mine was a real mystery. With crowbar, fork and

178

shovel I was lucky to find a couple of cups of decent soil. Overnight they could produce four or five bucketsful, and never a stone to be seen. What did they do with them? Were there nightly cave-ins in their subterranean world? Did they wear small helmets to protect themselves from the rocks that must have rolled down their tunnels?

Mme Meneteau was watching me digging one day. A great pile of stones that bore no relation at all to the relatively small hole I had dug attracted her attention.

'There are a lot of stones in your garden!'

'Yes. It's absolutely full of them. I don't understand where they all come from. There isn't a square centimetre where there isn't rock.'

'I know! It was us, we did it!'

'But why?'

'Well, when we were small, and it was a working farm, the carts used to sink into the mud when it rained. So our parents sent us out into the fields with baskets, and we collected the stones and packed them all over the land. We collected *so* many stones!'

'Yes, I believe you! How would you like to come and take them all out?'

She laughed, and handed a bowl of strawberries over the hedge.

I tried to create flower beds against the walls of the house, and there too the rocks flourished. It was a question of personal honour not to be defeated by a piece of inert matter, no matter how big, and sometimes it could take several days to extract a particularly huge specimen. Many of them went right up to and in some cases a little under the walls of the house, and as I tugged out the umpteenth boulder I had a sudden vision of that corner of the house gently subsiding into the void left behind, followed by the rest of the building caving in behind it. Only one stone defeated me: I'd hit it within a couple of

179

centimetres of the surface, just below the grass, and poked around with the crowbar to find its outer limit, which it didn't seem to have. After scraping away the topsoil over an area of two-thirds of a square metre, I conceded victory and covered it back again. It could just have been holding the house up.

Where we'd bought Tinkerbelle there was a beautiful wistaria twining its way all over her owners' house, and they had kindly given us a cutting that I'd carefully planted; it had survived being eaten to the ground by sheep, chewed to the ground by dogs on its attempt to regrow, masticated to a pulp by the geese on its third try, and once again chewed down by dogs. With very little hope after the fourth assault, I put a protective net around it, and lo and behold off it went again, and within a year was already over two metres tall. Some survivor. You had to be resilient to last around there, believe me.

As a spasmodically enthusiastic gardner I was delighted to find that I had acquired really green fingers, or, as the French say, a green thumb. What we had in mind was a stunning garden where plants would grow to their correct height and spread, without requiring too much watering, weeding, feeding, spraying, pruning or any other tiresome attention. Whatever seeds I planted, whatever twigs I stuck in the ground, they all grew, and I congratulated myself on my newfound talent. But after a relatively short time I discovered that everything flourished in the fertile soil despite the stony substratum, and the neat garden I had created transformed itself rapidly into an impenetrable wilderness as twigs exploded into towering bushes and smaller plants gave up the hopeless struggle for light. In almost no time at all we were living in a jungle, and the more I chopped and hacked at the rampant greenery the faster it grew.

Apart from drought and flood, moles, slugs, snails,

greenfly, blackfly, red spider mite, leatherjackets and dozens of other pests and diseases, the other great enemies of the French gardener are the *Saints de Glace* – the ice saints. Every day of the year is dedicated to a particular saint (some have to share a day because there are so many of them). The saints Mamert, Pancrace and Servais belong to 11, 12 and 13 May, dates which, in 1897, saw serious overnight freezing. St Urbain, on 25 May, is regarded as the last ice saint, after which the night-time temperature is unlikely to drop below freezing, although Jean-Luc told me that in 1966 it snowed on 15 July. If you joined in a gardening discussion and said you'd planted a particular plant, or taken some geraniums outside, it was an invitation to the warning: 'Ah! Beware! Don't forget the *Saints de Glace*!'

Hoping to live off nature's bounty as far as possible I harvested walnuts, blackberries, blackcurrants, nasty little worm-ridden apples, rock-hard pears, and mushrooms. Mme Meneteau mostly knew which mushrooms were safe to eat and I would take them to her for advice. One day I found a large patch of voluptuous fluted yellow fungi that I hoped might be chanterelles. Were they edible? I asked hopefully.

'They might be,' she said, 'but I'm not sure. Why don't you try just eating a little bit?'

'Because I don't want to die in agony,' I replied, laughing.

So she suggested taking them to the local pharmacy, as all French pharmacists are trained to distinguish those mushrooms that could kill you from those that will not. Our mushrooms, it seemed, fell into the former category. Although we had several books which were meant to help in distinguishing edible fungi from toxic ones, when you held a specimen in your hand and tried to identify it among a whole load that looked quite similar, when a shade of pink or a length of stalk could make all the difference, eating it was like playing gastronomic Russian roulette.

The dotty old people returned from Spain and decided, after all, not to sell their house. As an apology for my rude response when they tried to appoint me as their estate agent, I invited them up for tea, and we sat out in the garden eating strawberries and cream. I'd bought French gingerbread for the first, and very likely the last, time. It had the weirdest texture, very dry, but at the same time bendy. You could fold a slice in half and it wouldn't break. I found that a little sinister. The old boy gallantly demolished three slices, professing it to be 'absolutely delicious'. I didn't believe him. She was slightly frenzied, as she always was if things didn't go entirely her way. Apparently somebody in the village hadn't said hello to her, so she was going to sell everything after all, and move away. He just smiled vaguely and I nodded sympathetically.

They had brought with them a large plastic shopping bag filled with plants – mostly irises and marguerites. Now I realized that this was well-meant, but what it entailed for me was several hours of hacking away at compacted dust to reveal rocks that had to be levered out of the way to make room for the plants, and the further problem of finding something to fill the gaps left around them by the evacuated rocks. And it wasn't any use discreetly depositing the plants in a far-flung corner, because I knew she would require regular updates as to their progress, and would more than likely spring a surprise visit just to check up.

Occasionally they needed a small favour, mostly in the form of transport somewhere, and they were insistent on rewarding me for these little excursions, both by replacing the fuel used and in other ways too. Sometimes it was an invitation to tea, or the much more welcome suggestion that I should enjoy the luxury of using their shower, something we still lacked. I'd had two showers there when I overheard the old lady telling one of her visitors that I was 'an absolute pauper', and 'always asking to use their shower', so I stopped. Pride won over self-indulgence.

During the summer, the horses stayed out in the field at night, and in the morning, as soon as the sun and the flies came out, they put themselves in the shade of their barn. Even there the insects pestered them, and I could hear them stamping and snorting irritably throughout the day, so I made them some cotton fringes for their eyes out of thick white woolly mops, and stitched a couple of old flowery-patterned duvet covers into light-weight fly-sheets for them. They looked a little strange, rather like medieval destriers but without the armoured riders.

A French lady arrived at the gate one afternoon, and asked whether we'd lost two horses.

'No,' I replied. 'I don't think so. Our horses are out in that barn.' I pointed to the barn where they sheltered during the day, and where they had been when I went to check on their water about an hour previously.

'Oh, well, the people in the village were certain that they belonged to you.'

'Where were these horses when you saw them?' I asked.

'Trotting around in Saint-Thomas.' She looked at me a little curiously. 'They were wearing fancy dress.'

'Oh, merde,' I cursed under my breath. 'Thank you so much, madame. They do sound like my horses. I'll go and catch them.'

I found a couple of ropes and set off in pursuit, and met my little war horses on their way back home, clacking down the road at a spanking trot, heads and tails high, ears pricked, and duvet covers billowing around them like giant wings.

They had a technique for getting past the electric fencing, which they did about twice a month. Leila, the more dominant of the two, herded and pushed poor Cindy into the wire, where she would receive a shock; with the jolt ahead of her, and her bullying companion shoving her from behind, Cindy would lunge at the wire and drag it down, so that Leila could step over comfortably and they were free to wander where they pleased. Quite often they simply took themselves off to another nearby field and grazed quietly. Occasionally they took to the road and headed to the village. And every once in a while they vanished into the hundreds of acres of sunflowers and maize that surrounded us, when all I could do was wait for them to return, either under their own steam, or more often than not attached to kindly strangers who had been directed to me. Most people within a radius of several kilometres knew of '*l'anglaise*' with all the renegade animals.

We were making a little gentle progress here and there as funds and circumstances allowed, and had managed to afford some floor tiles for the small room, where the old boards had given up all attempts to support themselves and had disintegrated onto the dirt below. We'd found an odd-job man to lay a concrete base, and once it was set I started laying the tiles on an impossibly hot afternoon, mixing the cement in heavy bucket loads, spreading it on the floor and positioning the tiles, not as simple as it sounds because no walls were parallel, no corners formed proper right angles and a decision had to be taken as to which formation would look the least odd. Sweat was running down my face and neck, and I took a few minutes to lie in the cool of the shuttered living room. The phone rang.

It was Jean-Luc's girlfriend.

184

'Susie, your horses are on the road.'

I didn't know why they should be on the road – they'd been standing comfortably and coolly in the barn last time I saw them.

Because of the dirty task I was involved in, I was wearing a very old pair of leggings with ladders all over, and in which the elastic waist had gone, and a baggy T-shirt smeared with blobs of paint and encrusted with dried cement. My footwear was a pair of plastic sandals. I dared not stop to change, but grabbed the only rope I could find and sped off down the lane in time to see two fat rumps jogging up the hill across the road. Jean-Luc's girlfriend came by in her car and I jumped in. We chased the horses for about a kilometre as they charged along a dusty ploughed field, and then they veered away from the road and I had to abandon the car to keep them in sight. Young vines were somehow maintaining their green crispness in the stifling heat and every so often the horses stopped to nibble at them. I could get within a metre of them before they tossed their heads and trotted off another kilometre. Chasing horses over a roughly ploughed field in flimsy sandals is the sort of activity that cannot adequately be described: you have to experience it at first hand to know just how uncomfortable it is, as fistfuls of tiny pieces of grit work themselves inside the straps, under your soles, between your toes, and between your heels and the backs of the sandals. It was agony, compounded by impossible heat, rising panic, increasing exhaustion and the necessity of holding up the ragged leggings in order to prevent them from slithering down my hips.

Reaching a fence, the runaways changed direction, found a gap and shot through it. I struggled along behind, desperate to keep them in sight, and found myself scampering between orderly rows of tomatoes. A man and child were hoeing round the vegetables.

'*Bonjour, madame*,' they called politely, as if dishevelled women and fat horses habitually ran through their garden.

Very soon I was going to have to give up the chase; my heart was pounding, and I was soaked through with perspiration and starting to see double. The horses were showing signs of flagging, too, tired by negotiating the deeply rutted fields. They nibbled at a hedge and with a lunge I managed to grab a handful of mane and get a rope onto a halter. With one secured the other was content to follow behind as we trudged around trying to find a pathway, and then to discover where on earth we were.

A bent old gentleman was leaning over his garden gate, and he raised his cap as I hobbled past.

'*Bonjour, madame*. Isn't it rather hot to be taking your horses for a walk?' The subjects in question were lathered into a soapy foam of sweat and their heads were hanging almost to the ground.

'Please, can you tell me where we are?'

He mentioned a name I'd never heard of.

'I'm trying to get back to Painville.'

'Oh, that's easy. It's over there,' he pointed, 'no more than three kilometres.'

Really no distance at all. It only took an hour for the three of us to stagger back.

In the meantime the tile cement had set hard in the bucket and had to be thrown away, but that suited me just fine because the last thing I wanted to do, apart from scuttling about in a ploughed field again, was lay any more tiles.

Chapter Eleven

As time went by Terry fitted a makeshift electricity supply – a dangling wire with some plastic boxes full of sockets – into the kitchen that was simply a collection of rather nasty units leaning against the old stone walls, and a few pieces of wood balanced on breeze blocks to form shelves. He also introduced some elementary plumbing in the form of a sink that filled from taps, and pipes that removed the water to the outside. The washing machine that had started off in the garden had worked its way into the house, progressing into the primitive kitchen and linking up with the electricity supply. This should have been a benefit, as it meant I could do the washing in all weathers, but it became a major operation. When Terry had installed the plumbing to the bathroom and kitchen, he had told me to dig a soakaway pit for the household water to discharge into. I had done my meagre best with the crowbar and excavated a pit measuring about one cubic metre, which doesn't sound much but had proved to be quite a large project, although I will freely admit my heart wasn't in it and I hadn't made it nearly large enough. The result was that every time the washing machine was used, the outgoing water soon filled the little pit and, having nowhere else to go, started backing up the pipes into the kitchen, bumping into the water that was trying to get out, and erupting from the provisional pipe into which the washing machine outlet was hooked, flooding the floor of the barn with gallons of grey soapy water to a depth of several centimetres. To stop this distressing occurrence, I had to drain the used water from the washing machine directly into a bucket, quickly switch off the machine before the bucket overflowed, empty the bucket outside, replace the bucket, switch the machine back on, etc. etc. I seem to remember that a complete washing cycle produced forty bucketsful of water. It was ideally a two-person job, one to watch the rising level in the buckets, the other to operate the on/off switch on the machine. Sometimes I wished the machine was still out in the garden. Life and laundry had been simpler then.

One day, to my great delight, the despicable cooker blew itself up. However, it was a well-established pattern that if one vital piece of equipment broke down, another always came out in sympathy at the same time, so it was not a surprise that the washing machine chose that moment, when we were at our most financially fragile, to strike too, putting itself into a wild spin that drove it across the floor totally out of control, until with an earth-shattering thunk it shivered to a standstill and gave up the ghost.

Tinkerbelle, bless her, was also having trouble keeping up. Every so often she'd give a rattling shudder and a tinkling sound as something fell out of her. Her ignition key had jammed in the lock outside the supermarket one day, and had had to be drilled out, and a switch fitted in its place to the steering column with some insulating tape. Only her left indicator worked, and the windscreen wipers didn't unless the indicator was on at the same time.

Gloria mentioned that Fred was trying to sell a car that

he'd picked up for next to nothing. It was a really ugly thing, but reliable and with a full set of new tyres, said Gloria, who knew where he'd bought it and how much he'd paid. He'd tried selling it to her and Bill, but they already had more cars than they knew what to do with.

'But it's so ugly,' I said.

'Listen, beggars can't be choosers. He wants to get rid of it, he's only asking two hundred pounds and it's got a good engine and sound bodywork,' said Gloria.

I'd no idea where we could get two hundred pounds, but thought that Fred would probably take instalments. But I knew that if he thought I was interested, the price would shoot up, so I kept quiet and let him bring up the subject.

He arrived with an ear-to-ear smile one day, and shouted, 'Don't worry, I don't want anything – I've come to do you a big favour!'

That sounded encouraging, but rather unlikely. I gave him a cup of tea and asked what shape the favour was coming in.

'Look,' he said, 'that car of yours is falling to pieces and you need a new one. I've got just the thing for you. You can pay me over several months if you like.'

I tried not to look like a starving piranha sighting a floundering swimmer heading in its direction.

'Can't afford it, thanks. We really don't have the money for another car – we've just had to replace the cooker and the washing machine. Tinkerbelle has to keep going for a while.'

'I've told you, you needn't pay me in one go. Just a bit now, and the rest when you can. I'm almost *giving* it away.'

Hiding my glee, I nibbled at the bait.

'What are you asking for it?'

'I won't lie to you. I picked it up cheap, but I've got to make a few pounds on it. You understand, don't you?'

189

I nodded. I supposed he was going to suggest two hundred and fifty.

'Well, then, dearie, it's yours!' He clapped his hands and stamped his feet with delight.

'So what do I owe you?' I asked happily.

He opened his mouth to speak, thought better of it, closed it and swallowed, then said: 'Six hundred and fifty pounds.'

I stared at him. 'No thanks, Fred. I'll leave it.'

He blustered a bit, and said maybe he could knock a bit off if I'd let him have Tinkerbelle for spare parts.

'No, I'd rather leave it, thanks.' I hadn't even liked the thing anyway.

Fred stomped off, shouting that I was a fool to miss out on such a bargain, and that if I changed my mind I'd better let him know quickly, because he'd be putting the price up the next day.

'By the way,' he yelled, picking up a cracked plastic watering can, 'do you want this, or can I have it?'

'It's buggered,' I said. 'It leaks.'

'But can I have it?'

'Yes, help yourself.'

He waved it triumphantly and climbed into the ugly car and drove away.

I'd no idea what he did with all the junk he gathered, but he collected stuff like a jackdaw. Anything he saw, he had to have. One day an old plastic handbag that was lying in the drive; another day an empty coffee tin; a small piece of rope, a rusty screw or a broken lamp. If he saw it, and could have it for nothing, he wanted it. And the funny thing was, he seemed to have loads of money, and frequently said that he did. I'd been in his house when he'd disappeared into a room and come back with a thousand pounds in notes.

Funny old boy, really.

* * *

That summer the weather was particularly humid. The living room floor, which I had painstakingly sanded back to clean wood, and oiled, was covered in green mildew. I had to drag all the furniture out into the garden so I could scrub the mould from the floorboards. The boards were collapsing round the edges, and a builder told us the joists too would be quite rotten and the whole floor would need replacing. When I spoke to the neighbours, they told me that their wooden floors were also covered in mildew, something they had never known before. It was attributed to the unusual humidity we were experiencing. Since we'd arrived, we'd experienced the coldest winter for twenty-five years, the highest winds, the driest spring and then the most humid summer. I wondered what extreme to expect next.

One Sunday morning I decided to drive into town, 10 kilometres away, to buy a loaf of bread. I could have bought one at our local bakery, which had gradually improved its products to the point where they were edible, but I thought I'd take a new acquisition, Virgil, a seven-month-old German shorthaired pointer, for a drive as he was still a little uncertain about cars, and it would also be a fine excuse not to have to mow the lawn. So off we set, parked the car, queued with half a dozen cheerful and friendly people buying *fougasse, pain, croissants, couronnes, tarte à l'abricot, éclairs* and *brioche*. I bought a small *baguette* that I didn't really need.

Now, the lane in which the bakery was located was very narrow. Two cars could just squeeze past each other if they rubbed wing-mirrors. The lane led to a T-junction, where you had to turn left. On the left corner of the junction a new building was going up; there was a vast crane, scaffolding, giant concrete pipes and a sturdy metal fence around the whole. All this made the left turn very, very tight indeed. Even a cyclist had to concentrate.

As I approached the junction, I noticed a young pigeon strutting backwards and forwards distractedly, watching its reflection in a shop window ahead of me, and there was something indefinably wrong with it. So I got out of the car, crossed the road and picked up the bewildered bird, which pecked me. In the few seconds this had taken, a line of traffic had appeared from the right, wanting to turn into the lane I was about to turn out of. Because of all the construction equipment on the corner, nobody could go anywhere until I had navigated the tight corner, and already people were starting to hoot. I got into the car with the pigeon, which Virgil immediately wanted to sniff. The pigeon didn't want to be sniffed, and struggled. More cars hooted. With my left elbow in Virgil's throat and the bird in my left fist, it took several backward and foward shunts to get the car round the corner one-handed without damaging it, whilst the hooting grew more passionate and arms started waving out of car windows. After two or three embarrassing and humiliating minutes I got round the bend, and could see male drivers pointing at me in the rear view mirror. Never mind, the road ahead was clear and there was a small copse behind the treasury offices, so I stopped the car, pushed Virgil off the pigeon, and put it in the grass, where it wandered around rather forlornly and tried to fly without success. I investigated and found that something had pulled all its tail feathers out, so it was quite helpless. It was very young, with straggly wisps of hair poking out between its feathers. Driving 10 kilometres fighting Virgil off was going to be really quite dangerous, so I stuffed the pigeon up inside my T-shirt and set off again. It didn't nestle quietly against me, but used its scythe-like claws to haul itself up my torso so it could get its head out through the neck of the T-shirt, while Virgil clawed at my shoulder in excitement. This wasn't going to work. My skin was lacerated and bleeding into the T-shirt and I couldn't take any more pain. So I stopped the car, put the pigeon into a convenient cardboard box in the boot and set off yet again. Although now relieved of the agony of the raking claws, I felt that something was still scratching me. I was certain I could feel my skin moving. I scratched at an arm, and left tiny spots of blood. My neck itched, so I scratched that and more tiny ruby pinpricks appeared. My hair was itching, both arms, my stomach, my nose. I looked in the mirror and noticed dozens of tiny, blood-coloured dots waltzing around on my face: yes, they were definitely moving.

Back at the ranch, I handed my new treasure to Mme Roly-Poly, warning her that it had things on it.

'Oh yes, that's normal – bird fleas. Poor little thing, it's just a baby. You're hungry, aren't you?' she crooned at the bird, which was pecking at her thumb.

I stripped off, showered in scalding water for a very long time, put all my clothes in the washing machine, soaked my trainers, burned the cardboard box, fumigated and hoovered the car. The *baguette*, which was the cause of the entire episode, ended up in the bin, because I was sure the pigeon had distributed the microscopic fleas into it, and I didn't fancy eating them, even if they had helped themselves to quite a bit of me.

My new friend and employer Red asked me very tactfully one day whether I was interested in having some new clothes that could be picked up for next to nothing. I did have a fine wardrobe full of smart suits, neat skirts and high-heeled shoes from my previous life, but everything that was of any practical use was stained or torn. So Red introduced me to a fantastic clothes shop. Well, it wasn't actually a shop, but a hangar behind the cement works. The clothes lay in piles several feet high all over the floor, arranged into sections. Men's shirts; denims;

sportswear; dresses; coats; nightwear; children's clothes; underwear; men's jackets; jumpers; shoes; and several miscellaneous heaps. As shopping expeditions go it was not for the faint-hearted, for you had to climb onto the piles to delve into those you were interested in, and there was an unpleasant smell all over the place from the stuff they used to fumigate the garments. It was a charity, receiving donations from all over France; certain items went straight away to needy areas worldwide, and those that were not suitable were sold, by weight, for a modest 25 francs per kilo. There were rags here, and riches. Unworn designer clothes and shoes; stained night-dresses and clothes with cigarette burns, zips removed, or gaping holes. Let the buyer truly beware. But for the discerning shopper willing to invest some time and energy there were some tremendous bargains, and there was really no need to lack for a comprehensive wardrobe. It was a great meeting place, too, the clientele ranging from the really poor through travelling folk to the wealthy, everybody together searching for a bargain. Shoes were piled in a heap, but seldom was a pair found together. Somebody found a shoe they liked, waved it aloft, and all the other hunters dug through the pile to find its partner. Someone discovered a gigantic pair of bloomers, and, laughing, waved them in the air; fat ladies, encouraged by their friends, tried determinedly to squeeze into thin dresses; the two resident dogs bounded around asking people to throw rubber toys for them; children climbed up the clothing piles and tumbled down; somebody took off their jacket to try another, and in no time another customer had picked up the discarded garment. 'Ah! No!' cried the owner, snatching it back. Everybody laughed. Nobody seemed to know the name of the place, so the English called it affectionately the Rag and Louse, and the French, a little more delicately Chez Dior. It quickly became a regular haunt, where I went with friends to spend a couple of hours laughing and replenishing my wardrobe.

My perfect mother-in-law Sophie came to stay. She was in her mid-eighties and still fit and full of fun. Before her arrival, her first visit to France, she hadn't any idea what to expect of the country. 'Do they have fridges?' she enquired. Once she was here, the lovely summer weather, the peacefulness of the life and the tidiness of the countryside seduced her. She took in her stride the lack of flooring, doors and walls all over the house, the bumping around in Tinkerbelle, and was happy sleeping on the divan in the living room, the only reasonably civilized place. The weather was perfect for outdoors, and she sat in the garden watching the chickens and playing with the cats, or watching the geese in the pond.

'Yes, it's lovely here,' she reported on the phone, 'the weather's wonderful, and they've got swans on their lake.'

Valérie, the estate agent's secretary, who had since become a friend, invited us for dinner. Her own house was being renovated, and we ate out in a cobblestoned barn, but before that she took us to visit her neighbour's farm, where we saw first the cows, and then the goats, being milked. In deference to my vegetarianism she served an excellent cheese fondue. As this was Sophie's first experience of the dish, Valérie's father initiated her into the dip-and-twiddle technique, and she enjoyed spearing the garlicky cubes of bread and dipping them in the melted cheese, and the mirth directed at anyone who lost their cube in the mixture. Her lack of knowledge of a single French word was mirrored by Valérie's father's ignorance of English, but that didn't do anything to prevent them from carrying out a cheerful conversation throughout the evening.

Sophie stayed for six weeks, and every moment in her company was a joy. As the end of her visit hove into sight, I wanted to take her out for a good meal. The dotty old English trout in the village always made it her business, twice a year, to phone all the English people she knew and remind them to change their clocks as we went in and out of summer time. She'd phoned the day before and instructed me to ensure that all the clocks and watches in the house were adjusted accordingly, which I did, exactly as she said. The following day Sophie and I were on our way to a pretty riverside restaurant in the town of Confolens, where I'd been treated to an excellent lunch a few months before and the service had been faultless. Knowing they were likely to fill up early, and not having booked, I made sure we were there in good time, just after midday. The staff were less welcoming than before, looking at us quite strangely, and the restaurant was deserted. It was very disappointing after I'd told Sophie what a special place I was taking her to. However, the food was as good as ever, although it took ages to materialize. The place only started to fill up as we were on our way out, and it was only later in the evening, when all the television programmes seemed quite out of sync, that it dawned on me that instead of putting the clocks forward, as the old lady had said, they should have gone back. Then we would not have unwittingly arrived for lunch at a little after 10.00 a.m.

Autumn started settling in; the roar of the chainsaw replaced the growl of the lawnmower, smoke curled from chimneys, the swallows left, and the bronze, gold and russet colours of the trees, and the misty mornings, were breathtaking. The days were generally still warm and sunny, and the damp evenings brought a lush greenness to the countryside, a relief after the dry, dusty summer.

The chestnuts were falling, and lay on the roadsides like herds of little green hedgehogs.

A brisk wind stripped every remaining leaf from the trees overnight, and the skyline was suddenly very stark. The hunting season got into full swing. Some evenings they started hunting towards nightfall, and the sound of yelping dogs, shouting men, and gunfire in every direction lasted until midnight, panicking the horses into galloping crazily around in the dark, leaving them sweating profusely and blowing hard. The hullabaloo had to be heard to be believed. The French hunting horn sounds like one of those children's party squeakers with a feather on the end. The whole thing was prolonged because some of the dogs got lost or stuck down holes, and instead of seeking them out their owners just squeaked on the horns. The horses didn't like that, either.

With the money that I'd earned working for Red, I went and bought the large wood-burning stove that Terry and I had promised ourselves, because I very much did not want to be cold all the time as I had been the previous winter.

During one of Bill's long absences, something belonging to him had disappeared, and he had aroused the enormous indignation of the neighbours by having me go and ask whether they knew anything about it. A little while afterwards he and I had unfortunately fallen out. What had begun as a simple misunderstanding developed into a minor war; we both felt we were in the right, and stopped speaking to each other. As a protest at what he believed was the theft of his property, before returning to Spain he had erected an edifice of scaffolding poles, rolls of barbed wire and heavy wooden planks across the entrance to his land. I'd bought a stack of firewood from M. Guillot, the son of the old lady who had died, and it was at the back of their cottage, next to Bill's establishment. The only way I could access it was by lying on my stomach in the freezing mud and writhing beneath the barricade, frequently tearing my clothes on the barbed wire. The neighbours watched anxiously, and said that I should report the situation to the local mayor or to the police, as it was an offence to prevent somebody from getting their firewood. But I never did get round to it, and spent the next few weeks becoming increasingly agile and progressively shredding my clothes.

So I ordered more firewood from a wood merchant, three cords, which should be sufficient, friends told me, to see us through the winter. The wood merchant phoned to say he would deliver the logs cut into half-metre lengths the following day. The idea of having a healthy and neatly stacked woodpile like all my French neighbours was quite exciting.

The logs arrived, on a trailer hauled by a tractor driven by a very nice man. I didn't know he had arrived until he knocked at the door to say the delivery had been made. He had kindly tumbled the logs, all 9 cubic metres of them, onto the drive in front of the car, where they formed a medium sized mountain, and apparently it was not he who stacked them into the neat piles, but me. Numb with disbelief, I wrote him out a cheque and watched him trundle off with a cheery wave, and then I stood and stared tearfully at the logs, and my car immobilized behind them. The forecast overnight was for heavy rain, and it was already drizzling softly, so I started assembling the logs into some sort of form that could be covered to keep them dry. It took me five hours, and until well after dark, to get them all moved the twenty or so metres to their designated storage area and piled up, and the end result in no way resembled the neat arrangements of everybody else, but at least I could get to the car, and cover the pile with a tarpaulin. Offhand I couldn't remember ever being quite so physically exhausted as I was then. I was drenched in perspiration and the last thing I wanted to do was sit by a fire.

Rain came that night, in torrents, and twenty-four dogs' paws transformed the living room into a sea of mud. Then the electricity failed in the kitchen, leaving me in the pitch dark with no means of cooking or heating water. I had to go out through the downpour into the garage and find the small spare cooker, which weighed about sixty pounds, and flounder with it through the mud to the living room where the power was still on. I really did feel quite disgruntled on this exasperating day, and when I thought that nothing could happen to make it any worse I had a worrying phone call from England, from a friend of mine to say she had seen Terry and he didn't look at all well. His face was very grey, she said, and his hands were shaking badly. When I called him he said he was just fine; he thought maybe he was just drinking too much coffee. Over the following weeks he complained of severe headaches. When he first told me that his doctor had diagnosed a blocked sinus, I remember thinking, 'That's what the little turkey had.' As the weeks went past, he didn't get any better; the prescribed painkillers weren't working and during his visits I was shocked to see that he had started stumbling a lot, talking rather incoherently and seeming unable to do simple tasks. It seemed strange that a blocked sinus should have such a dramatic effect, but his frequent visits to the doctor always produced the same diagnosis: it was just a simple case of a blocked sinus that would sort itself out in time.

He came for a 3-week stay over Christmas and the New Year, our second in France, and when he arrived after his 14-hour journey he staggered from the car, holding his head. The next morning his headache was gone, but he seemed vague and uncoordinated. I asked myself whether it could be a psychosomatic reaction to

199

the demands of this wonderful farmhouse that required never-ending supplies of money to hold it up, the animals who seemed to be for ever in need of veterinary treatment, the car that was falling to pieces, and the computer that caught fire or shed its peripherals with gay abandon. As well as the new gearbox, Tinkerbelle had needed a complete set of new tyres and brakes as well as a host of smaller components, and in the past year I'd gone through two modems, one hard disk, one monitor that had gone up in flames, and a motherboard.

I felt Terry's behaviour was extreme if all that was wrong with him was a blocked sinus. I was starting to get very worried. He'd been ill now for several months, but somehow he kept producing the income we couldn't survive without.

I had my job with Red, but the salary was more a token than anything else – a month's pay would possibly sustain the animals and myself for ten days, but no more. The trouble was that even somebody as mathematically challenged as I could see that her business was failing. She had been given some very poor advice by an unsavoury character who was trying to impress her. Unfortunately, she had followed it and transformed her modestly successful one-woman business into a French company with all the financial obligations that that entailed, and in no time at all it was sinking under the insatiable demands of the French exchequer. I watched as Red slid towards certain ruin, and could do nothing to help. The best proposal I could think of was to sell the boys, Joseph and Christopher, to a family of machochists, but Red thought her little sons were absolutely wonderful. I called them the Kray twins, and her Vi, and she just laughed.

The bailiff was a regular and not unsympathetic visitor to her office; less understanding were the representatives of the various governmental bodies to whom money was due. A strange car pulling up outside the office was the signal for Red to disappear out through the back door, leaving Carole to use her awesome streetwise talent to keep the unwelcome visitors at bay. I wasn't any good at that, my only tactic being to hide.

I felt like a tennis ball between the distress of Red's situation, and the increasing worry about Terry's condition. His behaviour was becoming more and more peculiar. Nevertheless he kept on making the long, tiring journey here, and becoming progressively frailer. I knew he was suffering from something far more serious than a blocked sinus, and that either he wasn't telling me, or his doctor wasn't telling him. I was certain that either he was in the early stages of Alzheimer's disease, or he had a brain tumour, and all through each day this was the only thought in my mind. My stomach was in a permanent state of liquidity; I shook constantly both within and without, frantic for a solution to this terrifying dilemma. We had nothing to fall back on, nothing put aside for a rainy day. Our only asset was a house that was crumbling faster than we could fix it up. My job was plainly not going to last for more than another couple of months. I was a prisoner of the animals: we had the six dogs, two cats, two parrots and two horses, and somebody had to look after them. But there was absolutely nobody able or prepared to do so for an extended period so that I could go to England to look after Terry. I could probably farm the horses out somewhere; likewise the parrots, and maybe a neighbour would feed the cats. But six dogs constituted an insurmountable obstacle, and I couldn't see any solution but to have them put to sleep. In one of Terry's more lucid moments, I told him I was going to do that and come back to England with him. He simply wouldn't hear of it, insisting that he was feeling a great deal better and that if I did put the dogs to sleep he would never forgive me. He made me swear not to do so and left the following day. In his befuddled state he continued to drive the car although it was indicating that it was overheating, until the engine blew up. He was 300 kilometres from here, on the side of a road, with no food, money or transport. A lady phoned me from a garage he had managed to walk to. For two days he slept in the car, living on a large crate of walnuts that we had collected in the garden and he was taking back to England, and cups of coffee kindly supplied by the garage. I had no money, and Tinkerbelle was out of action, so there was no way I could get to him, but each time he called he assured me that everything was fine; he was feeling quite well and making arrangements to get back home. He managed to find someone to give him a lift to the ferry; once it landed at Portsmouth another kind soul gave him a lift to London, and from there an off-duty taxi driver drove him, free of charge, right to the door of his flat. He then located a new engine, brought it back to France and had it fitted.

Eight months after he had first started complaining of the headaches, I received a phone call from England from people who had previously been our neighbours. Terry was with them, and was in a very bad way. He had fallen over, and they were very worried about him. Another neighbour's daughter was studying alternative healing, and had been invited round to lay her hands on him. I exploded.

'For God's sake, call the bloody doctor! He doesn't need hands laid on him; he needs a doctor quickly!'

'But it's Sunday. We can't call the doctor out on Sunday afternoon.'

'Bugger that. Ring the doctor now!' I slammed the phone down, and dialled Terry's sister, who lived 100 miles away. She agreed to take control and ensure that somebody started taking Terry's condition seriously.

An hour later, Julie, our daughter, phoned.

'Mum. The doctor's seen Dad, and he's not allowed to drive, or be left alone. He has to be at the hospital at nine a.m. tomorrow morning. I'm staying with him at his flat, and will take him to the hospital tomorrow. Don't worry too much. He's in good hands.'

'What do they think the problem is?'

'The doctor wouldn't say. We'll know tomorrow. I'll phone you as soon as there's any news.'

'I'll be at work. Phone me there, darling.'

I put the phone down feeling ill, the most frightened I had ever been; terribly frightened for my husband, and terribly frightened of the future. All through the night I lay awake, shivering and trembling, my mind racing and churning until it was dawn and I could busy myself with feeding the animals and getting ready to go to work, where I sat hunched up and shaking with fear and misery as I tried ineffectively to do the job I was being paid for.

Julie rang.

'It's OK, Mum. He's had a brain scan, and he's being transferred to a neurological hospital. I still don't know what it is, but Dad's quite cheerful and there doesn't seem to be any panic. He'll be transferred by ambulance this afternoon. Rob's here with me, and we'll stay with Dad and keep you up to date.'

I quivered through the interminable day, willing the phone to ring with good news. But it didn't.

When I got home I started phoning everybody I could think of who might have some news, but was unable to get any answer. I knew Julie was with her father, but rang her home just because I needed to keep dialling numbers.

Her husband Steve answered.

'Hello, Susie. How are you?' He has a most soothing Welsh voice, and it was exactly what I most needed to hear. You could not imagine this man ever panicking.

'Is there any news?'

'Yes. Julie's just phoned. It's serious, but not too serious. You don't have to be worried. He has a large quantity of blood inside his skull – it's called a subdural haematoma – and they're going to operate tomorrow to drain it. Are you going to come over?'

Of course I would go over. I made half a dozen phone calls and enlisted a brigade of helpers who would some-how hold the fort for me and mind the animals while I was away. I scribbled lists of feeding and medication requirements, threw an armful of clothes into a small overnight bag and, unable to get a ferry crossing for three days, was forced into taking the Shuttle under the Channel. To a serious claustrophobic this is all your worst nightmares rolled into one, but I absolutely had no choice.

In the midst of this indescribable panic, Michelle phoned. In her strange croaky voice, she said she needed some blankets to wrap her mother's furniture in, and could I let her have some.

'Not now,' I said. 'My husband is terribly ill in hospital and I'm leaving for England tomorrow morning.' It was 10.30 p.m.

'But can't you just bring me some blankets for my mother's furniture before you go?'

'Look,' I said, 'I'm packing to leave and trying to organize care for my animals. I've had no sleep for two days, will have none tonight, and I can't worry about your mother's furniture now. When I come back, I'll see what I can find. I'm sorry I can't help you now, but this is an emergency.' I put the phone down.

Half an hour later, she arrived at the door.

'Can I take some blankets now?' she asked. I felt my mouth drop open. She hadn't asked about Terry, or offered to help in any way, and in any case I had no idea why it was my responsibility to supply blankets to wrap her mother's furniture in, but it was quicker and simpler

204

to hand her a pile of dog blankets than to argue with her. She still has them.

Red was in England. She phoned at 11.30 p.m., and I told her what was happening. 'Have you got any money?' she asked.

'No.'

'Go to the office and take two hundred pounds,' she said. She couldn't afford it, but insisted I must have it. 'You're going to need it when you get there.'

The office was 25 kilometres away, and the key with Paul 15 kilometres in the opposite direction. I collected the key, just before midnight, and picked up the money on my way to the railway station the following morning.

I don't even want to think about the journey on the train through the Chunnel.

A few hours later I arrived at Frenchay hospital, to find that Terry had been successfully operated on and, astonishingly, was fully recovered and restored to his former self.

The doctor explained how blood had seeped from a small vessel into his skull, forming a mass that had pushed his brain to one side, and put it under tremendous pressure. Immediately that pressure was removed, he was back to normal again. The relief at seeing him recovered outweighed my anger that he had suffered unnecessarily for so long because he had not been diagnosed correctly. He was released from hospital two days later, and after a check-up four days afterwards was given his doctor's consent to come back to France to convalesce. We travelled back slowly and arrived on a Friday evening to find that the menagerie had survived without us and was still intact.

It was now late spring, and with Terry stretched out in the garden soaking up the early sunshine, we mutually breathed a sigh of relief at having survived this dramatic episode.

But it wasn't over.

On the Sunday afternoon Terry complained of a headache, but wouldn't hear of my calling the doctor. He said he was simply hungry, so off we set to a local restaurant. We'd ordered and were waiting for our meal to arrive, while Terry was clutching at his head and looking very grey, but insisting that as soon as he'd eaten something he'd feel better. Two minutes later he was on the floor of the restaurant, slumped against a radiator with his jacket over his head. I asked the restaurant owner to call a doctor very urgently, explaining that Terry had had a major operation only a week before.

The local doctor arrived within minutes, a funereal-looking person all in black, very thin and very mournful. I recited Terry's recent medical history, and he flicked a light into his eyes before pulling his jacket back over his head.

'Madame, your husband is dangerously ill. He must be taken to hospital without delay. I am going to phone an ambulance. Could you please give me the details of your medical insurance while we are waiting.' Nothing like being practical.

The paramedics came quickly, and they wheeled Terry from the restaurant to the obvious interest of the other diners, and the relief of the owner. I paid the full bill for the single prawn Terry had eaten and the meal that I had left untouched, and started to follow the ambulance as directed, not knowing quite what was going to happen next.

This was our first experience of the French health system when it leapt into action. When the doctor summoned the local ambulance he'd also alerted the hospital in Poitiers, who had despatched an emergency medical team which was even now whizzing down the motorway towards us. The two ambulances kept in radio contact and met up at a junction, where Terry was transferred to the specialist care of the three doctors in the vehicle from Poitiers. It parked up on the roadside whilst they carried out emergency treatment, took blood samples and blood pressure, and radioed the information directly to the hospital. The first ambulance then returned to its base, having extracted my medical insurance details and a solemn promise to see them the following day to settle their account.

In any other circumstances being in the ambulance with three of the most wickedly handsome men I have ever seen would have been a pleasure, but once again I was shaking with fear, my teeth were chattering and I was frozen. The three doctors were relaxed and cheerful as they flourished needles, connected drips and machines, twiddled knobs.

'Has he eaten this evening?'

'Just one prawn and a little . . .' I couldn't remember the French word for 'piece', 'a little part of a slice of bread.'

'*Ah! Un petit morceau! C'est "un morceau", le mot que vous cherchez!*'

In the middle of this frightful drama, he was giving me a French lesson.

'*OK! On y va!*' cried one of the handsome ones, slapping merrily on the window behind the driver. 'You follow, madame, and don't be afraid, French doctors are very good!'

The ambulance started speeding to the hospital 25 kilometres away, with Tinkerbelle and me stuck like glue to its bumper for fear of losing it, as I had no idea where the hospital was.

With the benefit of continuous radio contact, the emergency team at the hospital knew exactly what to expect when Terry arrived, and he was whisked away whilst I was led to a comfortable waiting room and told not to worry. I was actually quite worried not only about

Terry, but also by the fact that all the way there the petrol gauge on the car had been indicating that it was virtually empty and I hadn't any idea where or if I would find an open petrol station. Back at home all the animals were unfed and heaven knows what revenge they would be wreaking.

A large kindly-faced surgeon in a powder blue gown appeared about an hour later, smiling as he shook hands, and speaking perfect English.

'Your husband has another haematoma, but there is abolutely nothing to worry about. I'll operate in the morning, and he will be just fine. You can go and see him, and then you must go home and sleep. But first of all, I'll show you the X-rays. Come.'

The X-rays of Terry's brain were pinned up to backlights.

'Here, you see, the two halves of the brain, and down the middle, the line between them. It should be a straight line, but because of this,' he pointed to a large dark mass to one side, 'which is the blood, his brain is pushed to one side.'

Instead of a neatly bisected oval, Terry's brain looked more like the yin-yang symbol.

He was tucked up in bed in a quiet room, and on the verge of sleep. I squeezed his hand, said I'd be back in the morning, and told him that the doctor had assured me everything was under control and there was nothing for us to worry about. He nodded wearily and closed his eyes.

When I finally reached home at just after 2.00 a.m. the animals had put themselves to bed, and, bless them, stayed curled up and didn't ask for anything, so I was able to climb gratefully into the loft and spasmodically doze through what was left of the night.

Terry was operated on the following morning, and after having a litre of blood drained from his head (under local anaesthetic) spent a week enjoying the excellent hospital facilities in Poitiers before being released once more to convalesce. Each day during his stay in the hospital the surgeon called to sit on his bed and chat about aeroplanes and boats and other little boy things.

It had been a very, very long eight months.

Chapter Twelve

I'd realized fairly soon after my trip to the market with Bill that I had made a serious mistake in buying a cockerel. The dreamy prospect of having lots of fluffy little chickens happily scratching and pecking all over the place was one that I had looked forward to, and it hadn't crossed my mind that amongst the company, inevitably, would be a certain number of cockerels. A fact you might like to consider, if you ever plan on keeping chickens and share my vegetarian lifestyle, is that 88 per cent of all the chicks hatched were little boys, and as they grew, they fought. At one count there were twenty-two cockerels fighting energetically throughout the daylight hours and seven hens watching with mild interest. It was a disastrous situation that could only get worse, so I had to start making gifts of the little cockerels to the neighbours. For days afterwards I couldn't look at my treacherous face in the mirror.

As a poultry keeper I was a novice; our only previous experience had been the purchase of some battery hens who, having spent the few short months of their desolate lives in boxes the size of an A4 sheet of paper, laying themselves into exhaustion, were destined for the cat food factory. We had bought six of these pitful creatures and put them in our garden shed, with access to an outside run. For the first week they would not come out of the shed. Not only would they not come out, they wouldn't step over the line between shadow and sunlight, because never having seen it before they didn't know what it was or what to do about it. They didn't even know how to walk, never having previously done so. We had to lift them over the sunshine line and put them on the grass, and when we sprinkled some grain in front of them they soon learned to walk; within another week they were carefree and confident and generously supplying us and our friends with healthy eggs, and absolutely no trouble at all. When we left England we gave them to Sandra, the kind lady who was looking after the horses.

If you ever decide to keep chickens and don't know much about them, here's a tip: catching them is quite a lot more difficult than you might suppose. They are fleet of foot and you can look and feel extremely foolish lunging around and being outwitted by a bird of charm but minimal brain. Wait until dark, when they become completely tractable; I don't know whether they're worn out, night blind, or whatever, but you can pick them up without resistance. The hens are also manageable when they're broody, because they appear to be in a permanent state of trance, and if you lift them up they stay in a sitting position without moving a muscle.

Shortly after I'd started working for Red, she'd found a stray dog, a sad-eyed beagle-type bitch spotted limping along a road many miles from the nearest village. She wasn't much of a dog to look at: long-bodied, long-tailed, long-eared, short-legged. Black and tan coat that looked wiry, but felt soft. White muzzle indicating advanced age. Left eyelid turned almost inside out. I had never seen a dog who knew such fear. Red's ghastly children could do what they wanted with her, and her tail, which was almost as long as her body, would wave tall behind her.

211

But if anybody laughed or shouted, or moved quickly, she was reduced to a shivering wreck. Anybody picking up something even as inoffensive as a tea cloth had her cringing flat to the ground, flinching and trembling. And yet she was enormously affectionate, and would sit with her grizzly head resting on any lap available to her, gazing up at the lap's owner with the gentlest, deepest brown eyes imaginable. She was ready to risk a kick in the hope of a caress. Her life was divided into three elements, love, fear and greed. She never stopped hunting for food.

I'd tried unsuccessfully to find her owner. She wasn't tattooed (it was before tattooing with a unique identity number became obligatory for all dogs in France), and phone calls to every *mairie, gendarmerie* and vet within a radius of 15 kilometres drew blanks. I concluded that she had been deliberately abandoned. There was no possibility of finding anybody who would want her. She was old, and her damaged eyelid was rather gruesome. There is a French equivalent to the RSPCA, called the SPA which I think stands for Société pour la Protection des Animaux, but from talking to local people I knew that dogs taken into the shelter were only kept for a short time unless they could be rehomed, and her chances of being adopted were less than none.

If there was anything we didn't need, it was another dog to feed, but each time I saw Amy, as Red's boys had christened her, my heart ached. I knew Red wouldn't keep her indefinitely – she already had one dog, and her circumstances were worsening by the day. Soon she'd have to move, and a second animal would add to her problems. One day I just put Amy in the car and brought her home. She didn't look the sort of dog to be any trouble, and she probably wouldn't eat much and thus add any unwelcome burden to our delicate pecuniary equilibrium, so she moved in with us, bringing our canine headcount to six.

Our other dogs, sociable to an extreme, welcomed the new family addition, but as if she knew that she came from humbler origins and didn't share their aristocratic lineage, Amy kept herself slightly apart. Despite living now in an environment where she was loved and secure, she still clamped her tail to her belly and flattened herself to the ground if I picked up a magazine, or if somebody walked past her carrying something. Her fear was too deep-rooted to be overcome, but she was relaxed and happy with her five new friends. We had her neutered and tattooed, and her damaged eyelid eye operated on.

She settled in with us in no time at all, and demonstrated her gratitude by killing as many of our chickens as she could catch, which was quite a lot, twelve I think at the final count. Amy certainly solved our surplus chicken dilemma. Within a month of her arrival, we didn't have a single one left.

There was a message on the answering machine from Agnes, the nicest English lady you could possibly meet, and who lived about twenty kilometres away.

'I need your help, but only if you're not afraid of snakes.'

How could anybody resist? I called her back as soon as I heard the message.

'It's a grass snake, trapped in the raspberry netting. I can't think of anybody mad enough to help me, except maybe you.'

As Tinkerbelle was, as so often, non-functional, Agnes drove over and collected me.

The snake was as thoroughly enmeshed as it could possibly be in masses of square metres of netting lying in a tangled nylon heap, threaded through with long grass and raspberry canes which pinned it to the ground. Next to the badly decomposed body of another snake, the beautiful black and green reptile lay motionless beneath a broiling sun. It looked as if our mission of mercy might have come too late, but I touched its tail, and it responded by moving slightly. Armed with a gigantic pair of scissors, all that Agnes could find, we considered our strategy. It had gone in head first through one of the small loops of the netting, and then through another, and another, and another in its efforts to get free. About two dozen green plastic circles were digging into its body, giving it the appearance of a loaf in the process of being sliced. Where the netting had cut most deeply, layers of skin were peeling away. I suppose the diameter of the netting was at most three centimetres, whereas in places the snake's body must have been getting on for six. Starting at the tail end, crouching in the grass and raspberry canes, we began cutting it free, one holding it while the other manoeuvred the scissor blade between the netting and the skin. It was a laborious and lengthy task, our backs and legs aching as we worked, but greatly encouraged by the increasing movement of our patient we progressed up the body, snipping and pulling away the nylon from where it was embedded in the snake's silky skin. It was by now alert enough to be taking an interest, its head turned to watch us, the forked tongue flickering, but its attitude was relaxed as if understanding that we were trying to help. As we got closer to the head end and the snake became livelier, Agnes said: 'You know what? It's beginning to look like an adder to me.'

'No, it's far too big. Adders are much smaller, and they always have Vs on their heads and down their bodies. Adders have slit pupils, whereas this snake has big round pupils. It's just a grass snake.'

'I hope you're right, because I don't want to have to phone your husband and tell him you've been bitten by an adder.'

'Trust me, this isn't an adder.'

The final circle of netting was tight just behind the snake's head, and meant getting very close to the open mouth, but with Agnes holding the several feet of freed body I was just able to snip the last of the nylon and pull it away. As if it had never been there, the reptile vanished. It moved so fast we quite literally didn't see it go, and had it not been for the residual aches and pains in our strained muscles, and the overpowering stench of the decomposing body, we might have thought we'd imagined the whole thing.

If Agnes had asked a French neighbour to help her with the snake, the response would probably have been to shoot it, or, even worse: 'Leave it there. It will soon die.' They just don't like snakes, even useful and harmless ones like grass snakes that do such an excellent job of rodent control, and a sighting in our hamlet is a signal for M. Royer to fetch his shotgun.

I'd seen one of these snakes before at close quarters, when I went to Jean-Luc's field across the road to move the electric fencing to give the horses a new area to munch at. In the long dried grass just beside a copse, as I bent to yank one of the poles out of the ground, I saw what looked like a hosepipe neatly coiled up. I bent to get hold of it. In one movement the coil formed itself into a straight line measuring the best part of two metres and took off at high speed, whipping the grass into waves as it went. I stood rooted to the ground in disbelief. I hadn't imagined there were snakes that size in France.

Reptiles and Amphibians of Europe identified it as a western whip snake, which can indeed grow up to two metres in length, and although non-venomous is active and aggressive and will bite if disturbed, so it's a fairly good idea not to go up and touch these snakes if you see them, although they're more likely to rush away than to let you get close enough to do so. For all the long hours I wandered around our meadow and the vast fields behind the hamlet, it was the only snake I ever saw, although the large green lizards were fairly common.

It was time to bid *adieu* to Tinkerbelle. Dearly as I loved her, for all her crankiness, there were limits. The fact that I had to wear plastic bags on my legs to protect my feet from the rain that gushed in from the corroded bottom of the windscreen was not a sufficient reason to pension her off, even coupled with all the little unscheduled stops we made in strange and inconvenient places, or the loud and embarrassing grinding noise she emitted from time to time. However, she had developed a new habit of spewing out her spark plugs periodically and unpredictably, sending them crashing into the underside of the bonnet. Nobody seemed able to find out why she did this and it was a cause for some alarm, because I didn't want a high-velocity spark plug to plough through the bonnet, the windscreen and my head, as the mechanic assured me it certainly might. She had served us well for over four years, like some bent and creaky-boned crone still faithfully caring for her employer, but she had earned her retirement as soon as we could scrape up sufficient funds to replace her.

As if she knew that our days together were numbered, she played ever more little tricks, gurgling, squealing, sometimes sending up small jets of steam from under the bonnet. I stroked her steering wheel and encouraged her along. 'Just a couple more kilometres, Tinkerbelle, just let's get back home, please. Please don't collapse here, in this deserted lane, in the middle of rural nowhere, at midnight.'

Terry rang to say that he had found a replacement car and it would be arriving within a couple of weeks and I passed the news to Tinkerbelle, who seemed to take on a new lease of life, behaving faultlessly, rolling smoothly and quietly, starting when asked and not making horrid smells with her brakes. It seemed that she was making one last desperate effort to convince me that she was still a good reliable car.

She did have one final trick up her automotive sleeve. In our small local town there were some traffic lights at the top of a rather steep hill, and on the day in question we arrived at the lights as they turned red, always a bit of a blow as Tinkerbelle's handbrake had stopped working some while back, and she had to be held at the lights with one foot revving the accelerator to stop her stalling, and the other foot on the brake but ready at a moment's notice to switch to the clutch. It was at this slightly nerve-racking moment that her seat collapsed. The seat of the 2CV is a primitive thing, a metal frame stretching the width of the car, covered with a thick plastic material held taut by some little metal clips, over some criss-crossed webbing straps which provide the support for the driver's weight. When they cease to do this, the driver suddenly finds him/herself sitting in a hole on a piece of sagging plastic, with the top of his/her head approximately level with the middle of the steering wheel. This is not a satisfactory driving position at all. You cannot see out of the windscreen for a start, generally a bad sign. Because there is nothing to support your weight, you have to do so yourself with your legs, while operating the pedals at the same time. So you are standing in a racing skiing position, and juggling three pedals with two feet.

Somehow we managed to get away from the lights and pull into a slip road where I dug out a length of rope from the boot and wove it around the metal seat frame, then padded it with a couple of dog blankets from the back seat. I drove home in more comfort than style, parking Tinkerbelle to one side for the last time, to leave room for her replacement.

For a couple of weeks she'd been displaying a rather optimistic '*A vendre*' sign in her rear window, and a Frenchman phoned and said he was interested in buying her.

'She's very old, and both her bodywork and her engine need a lot of work,' I told him. 'I don't want you to come all this way and be disappointed.'

He assured me he quite understood but that he was a 2CV enthusiast and Tinkerbelle's condition was immaterial. He loved her already without seeing her. It was a brief love affair, because as soon as he arrived he started making most offensive remarks about her, kicked her tyres, mocked her red roof, rocked her from side to side and spat next to her. He offered me a ridiculously small amount, and badly as I needed the money, she wasn't going to somebody who wasn't prepared to love her for better or for worse, and I suspected this man was going to chop her up for spare parts. I withdrew her from sale and he became quite unpleasant.

'I came a long way to look at this car. I'm offering you far more than it's worth. You are very foolish not to accept.'

'She's not for sale any more. I've changed my mind. I'm sorry. Goodbye.'

He stomped away with a muttered '*sale anglaise*', and Tinkerbelle rested on her tired axles until my friend Red came to visit one day. She asked what I was going to do with her.

'Sell her, if I can find somebody who'll love her. Otherwise she can just stay here as a large ornament.'

'I'll buy her,' Red said. 'The boys can learn to drive in her. They'll love her.'

And monstrous as they were, I thought they probably would, so Tinkerbelle travelled to her new home in style, driven away on the back of a transporter. As I watched Red winching her aboard, I felt rather weepy and had an urge to touch her and tell her that I still loved her. She had a lot of character, that little car.

Not long afterwards, Red's business collapsed, the bank took away her house, and she and her family moved away.

One day Amy went missing. We didn't know how she had escaped from the garden, and searched in vain.

Two days later the local hunters' president arrived at the gate.

'Have you lost a dog, madame?' he asked. He pointed to a smug face looking out of the window of his car.

'She joined in our hunt on Sunday, and it was only at the end of the day we discovered that she didn't belong to any of us. She's been staying with me, and I've just heard from your neighbours that you've lost a dog similar to her.'

She was none the worse for her adventure, and after that, whenever the hunters were in the village, we kept the gate carefully closed.

If she had one fault, it was gluttony. If there was food around, no matter what, she'd go after it. Horse food, chicken food, wild birdseed, she wasn't fussy.

One summer day we took the six dogs out for their usual walk and noticed that Amy was lagging behind slightly, which was unusual for her. Normally she galloped around with the rest of them. When she abruptly sat down and wouldn't move, there was no choice but for Terry to carry her, heavy lump that she was, all the way back home, where she flopped into her bed and didn't stir.

The following day she still seemed completely drained of energy, so I took her off to the vet, who examined her with increasing furrows on his brow, scanned her and said: 'She is very ill. She has diabetes. You will have to decide what to do.'

219

'What are the choices?'

'She will need insulin daily, for the rest of her life.'

'Can she have that in tablet form?'

'No, only by injection.'

I felt poorly. 'Is it very expensive?'

'Yes, quite expensive.'

'I couldn't do that myself, stick a needle in her. Is there no other solution?'

'Yes, of course there is. We will put her to sleep now.'

'No. We can't do that. I don't want her put to sleep.'

'OK then.' He reached for a syringe, speared a needle on it, loaded it from a small bottle and handed it to me.

'Give this to her now.'

'I don't know how to. I've never injected a dog before.'

'Just put it in her neck.'

'But how far? How deep does it go?'

'Just put it in her neck and push. Please hurry up.'

I put it in her neck and pushed. Amy didn't move.

'There you are. I told you, it's very simple. It's a very small needle.'

So here was something new to look forward to: injecting a dog every day with a small needle.

The first time I did it unsupervised, the needle went in one side of a fold of skin, straight through and out the other side. But within a week I'd got the hang of it, and Amy was recovering her bounciness.

It was a few months later that I went out for a while, and returned to find that Amy had vanished. I hunted around until I found her in a muddy outbuilding.

Crouched behind a pile of timber, in a pool of mud, Amy cringed and shook. I hauled her out and carried her to the house, where she started turning round and round in circles, alternately yelping and barking.

I phoned the vet, who was at lunch, while Amy continued her spinning singing show.

'Give her sugar, as much as you can get her to eat. It's a diabetic crisis. And bring her to the surgery at two o'clock.'

But the sugar only mixed with the strings of saliva she was producing, and her whole body became stiff. I jumped into the car with her, and she insisted on sitting on my lap with her head hooked around my neck. Her fat body made it all but impossible for me to operate the steering wheel or see where I was going, and she shouted and yelled increasingly loudly. By the time we reached the vet, I was soaked in perspiration and copious floods of Amy's urine, and we were both as rigid as scaffold poles. I carted her into the surgery, where she was quickly hooked up to a transfusion while the vet examined her.

'In fact, this isn't a sugar problem. It's something a bit more serious. She's having a stroke.'

Oh, heavens. Whatever was going to happen next?

'We'll keep her here tonight, and we will ring you tomorrow morning.'

Off she disappeared into a back room, and I thought we probably wouldn't see her again.

The vet rang the next morning.

'Your dog is fine: you may come and collect her when you like.'

She was proving to be a great survivor, although not quite the low-cost minimum maintenance pet we had envisaged.

Only a few months after he'd had his haematomas, Terry had a horrible accident and burned himself severely. Our daughter Julie and her gorgeous little daughter Catherine had come to visit for a week, and we were having a barbecue, something we never really have got the hang of properly. I'd put great bunches of rosemary and thyme over the coals hoping to impart their fragrance to the fish we were trying to cook. There didn't seem to be much heat getting through, so I asked Terry if he could relight it. He found a bottle of barbecue lighter fluid and sprinkled some into the coals. There was a very loud bang; the plastic bottle exploded in his hands and erupted into a ball of fire. It happened unimaginably quickly. He was engulfed in flames from his head to his shoes, reeling around and shouting and burning. Julie screamed at him: 'Dad, lie down and roll! Lie down and roll on the ground.'

He fell to the gravel and rolled around, but still he was on fire. Little Catherine, six years old, was transfixed with horror. I turned the hosepipe on him and drenched him until the flames were out and ran to fill the bath with cold water. His shorts had stuck to his legs, his shirt was burned away, his hair was burned and he had awful wounds on his shins. We led him into the icy bath, but the heat of the burns quickly heated the water, and we had to keep running fresh cold. His pain was obviously unbearable, and he kept screaming for help. Somebody had told me, a short while before, that in France you cannot just summon an ambulance, but must first call a doctor who will call the service if he feels it necessary. I calculated the time it would take to contact the doctor and for him to get to the house, and decided to drive Terry directly to the hospital in Poitiers, over thirty kilometres away. As soon as he got out of the cold bath he was screaming with pain again. We sat him in the front passenger seat of the car, Julie and Catherine, white-faced, in the back, and I drove like the wind, screeching round corners, while Terry urged me to go faster. He put his legs out of the window so that the wind could give some relief, and every time we were stopped by traffic lights he screamed at me to take no notice of the lights, just keep going. Finally we reached the hospital and rushed him into the emergency unit. A

222

nurse took a large bottle and poured it over his shins, where the burns were worst.

'It's new, this stuff,' she explained, gesturing at the colourless gel. 'It gives instant relief.'

Which it did, to all of us.

The nurse admonished me for not calling an ambulance.

· 'They would have been able to help your husband far sooner. In future when there is an accident, call them straight away.'

Terry was admitted to the burns unit of the hospital, and as he was wheeled down the corridors the hospital staff, remembering him from his previous stay, welcomed him back cheerily. The surgeon who had operated on him came to visit him and to check that he hadn't sustained any damage to his head when he'd fallen. He spent two days in the hospital, undergoing an immensely painful treatment that involved having the burned flesh vigorously scrubbed with a hard linen cloth, which promotes clean and quick healing, and which resulted in the wounds leaving almost no scarring at all. Because both he and Julie had to return to England two days later, when he was discharged from the hospital they sent him away with sufficient medication to cope with a national emergency, including lotions, creams, bandages, tablets and *tulle grasse*, a large gauze pad smothered in a thick layer of some kind of grease like petroleum jelly; it can be applied directly to wounds to give protection without risk of sticking.

It wasn't very long afterwards that M. Meneteau arrived at the gate one day, limping badly. I asked him what had happened, and he said that when he was washing out the great wooden barrels in which he made his wine, he had been tipping a bucket of scalding water and caustic soda into the barrel and had slipped and tipped it into his wellington boot. He raised his trouser leg and showed me the most terrible burns and sores all down his shin and ankle. What did I think he ought to do?

I still had some of the dressings that Terry hadn't used. I gave them to M. Meneteau and suggested he took them home and asked his wife to disinfect the wounds and cover them with the *tulle grasse*, and then get himself to the doctor as soon as possible.

Later that afternoon I went to ask how he was.

'Oh, he's fine.' Mme Meneteau smiled. 'The doctor said that the *tulle grasse* was exactly the right thing to do.'

Possibly as a result of watching too many French farces in which the doctor is mad or incompetent and always prescribes suppositories no matter what the ailment, I'd been quite worried about finding a good doctor, and in particular one who wouldn't prescribe suppositories for everything from tuberculosis to a hangnail. Red had recommended a surgery about eight kilometres away, where there were two doctors to choose from, and a little timetable to learn. Each doctor was available by appointment only on certain days, alternating mornings and afternoons, not at all on Thursdays, and on a first-come, first-served basis on other days, but you had to be prepared to wait quite a long time then because those were the times when the medical reps visited with their large black cases, which was rather irritating when you were quite ill and they went in ahead of you.

An English friend living some way away used another surgery, where there was always a vase of red plastic roses on the table in the waiting room. People would come in and some would take a rose. My friend's daughter thought she'd have one, and helped herself. When the doctor came out she was quite angry and told the girl to put it back straight away – the roses were to distinguish reps from patients.

One of our local doctors spoke perfect English, and

had a thriving list because of the growing English community. A big man, with thinning sandy hair, blue eyes and a manner that was mostly avuncular but held just a hint of rakishness, he dressed casually and smoked heavily, although not in front of his patients. On the day I went into his office and didn't smell smoke, I asked, 'Have you given up smoking at last?'

'Yes,' he sighed. 'I've given up. If I didn't, I would die. Like a rat.'

The other doctor was smaller, dapper with a neat moustache and sports jacket and didn't speak any English at all. They always came out personally into the waiting room to usher in their next patients, shaking hands and enquiring after family and neighbours. They were both charming and highly competent. I had a visitor from the United States who'd been treated there for diverticulitis for two years. While she was staying with me she was in great pain and visited our doctor, who examined her for three minutes, said she didn't have diverticulitis, sent her for X-rays which proved he was right, and had her admitted to hospital the following day for an emergency operation. What she actually was suffering from were two large kidney stones, which had they not been removed when they were would have left her with permanent kidney damage, and almost certainly the loss of one kidney. We felt ourselves very fortunate indeed to have such excellent medical expertise on our doorstep.

There is nothing I am more afraid of than a visit to the dentist. Each morning I wake up terrified that I might have a cavity, or a broken tooth, and sometimes I do. Sure enough, one morning as I brushed my teeth a large filling fell out. Although the French vets and doctors had proved themselves, it was difficult to imagine that a rural dentist would have either the temperament or the skills necessary to deal with an Englishwoman who was frightened out of her wits. Through a friend I was recommended to a dental surgery in a very small village about six kilometres away, and having made an appointment I set off in tears. Twenty minutes later I lay on a padded leather couch watching the downhill ski racing on a television mounted in the ceiling, hardly aware of the fingers and hardware filling my mouth, and still waiting for the moment of agony when something would hit a nerve. The dentist was young, startlingly handsome – what an American friend calls 'eye-candy' – and clucked disapprovingly: 'English dentists.' Deep brown eyes welling with sympathy for my plight, and a gentle, seductive voice saying that I needed two fillings, and was it all right if he did them straight away? I nodded feebly and braced myself for the worst. He sprayed something on my gums, waited a minute, injected a local anaesthetic. So far, I'd felt absolutely nothing at all. Was I comfortable, he asked? I nodded, but knew it couldn't last. The pain would come. He reached for the drill 'just to clean out the cavity' he explained, and I clutched at the arms of the couch, sweat pouring down my hands and running to my elbows. There was a distant purring noise, and I focused on those gorgeous brown eyes. Every two or three minutes my man kept asking whether I was comfortable, whether he could carry on, and I gazed back adoringly as he pouted a small sad smile.

'*Et voilà, c'est fait!*' he murmured.

And so it was. And really I hadn't felt a thing.

He liked a little joke sometimes. Knowing that each visit was still an ordeal for me, he might show me Polaroid photographs of the bloody gums of a previous patient who had just had all her teeth extracted, and wait to see if I'd fall to the floor. But I could drive to my appointments without crying any more.

Chapter Thirteen

Our dogs and cats succumbed to every complaint in the veterinary text books, and them some more. Having so many animals, many of advanced age, made it inevitable that veterinary treatment would feature in our lives from time to time, but our poor animals really did have bad luck. M. Audoux's wife, a friendly and enviably slim lady who epitomized French chic and sometimes acted as his receptionist, was sympathetic.

'You don't have any luck at all with your animals,' she said one day. 'I feel so sorry for you every time you come here.'

They got mysterious diseases, sunstroke, and fearful injuries. Two of the cats contracted cat flu, and one was in intensive care for nearly three weeks. I had no hope at all that Beau would survive, as he was weeping tears of blood and hadn't eaten for days. Several times each day he was placed in an incubator and given a steam treatment to clear his airways. He was being fed through tubes, and had a permanent drip into his leg. One of the other vets, an adorable Belgian lady named Catherine who spoke perfect English, tried every type of food to tempt Beau's appetite. She bought jars of baby food, cooked sardines, and minced liver, and still the cat wouldn't eat. I used to visit him daily, and one Friday held his thin body to my shoulder. As plainly as if he had spoken, I felt him say: 'Take me home. I need to be at home.'

I asked Catherine if I could take him with me for the weekend, and we agreed that if his condition worsened I'd bring him straight back. Once at home, he ran straight to rub himself against all the dogs, while I cooked his favourite meal. If this didn't work, nothing would. I put the dish down and called him over. He didn't even bother to sniff it, but started gulping great mouthfuls of the food he loved more than anything else – spaghetti. Over the weekend he ate ravenously and the improvement in his condition was immediate. He didn't look back.

A year or so after she became diabetic, we noticed that Amy had started bumping into furniture, and then running into walls. Her brown, limpid eyes were clouded over. The vet confirmed that she was totally blind. And strangely enough, this made her life easier. From the time we adopted her, she was terribly afraid if anybody held anything in their hands. She cringed flat to the ground if I picked up a broom, a saucepan, a book, even a teacup. She was the most abjectly terrified dog I'd ever seen, and even after three years she hadn't lost her fear, nor her expectation that sooner or later somebody was going to hurt her. Once she lost her sight, however, she also lost the fear, and became more confident, and could soon find her way around the house and garden. Her tail no longer stayed between her legs. She had found peace. She started to enjoy long walks across the fields, galloping blindly along and returning frequently to our sides to reassure herself that she wasn't lost, her beautiful gentle blind eyes seeing nothing, but her ears listening for our voices, her nose following familiar scents, her feet keeping her to the paths she knew, and her extraordinarily long tail wagging high behind her. Despite her

228

earlier massacre of the chickens, and the unwelcome expense of daily medication, she was a joy and an inspiration as we followed her madly waving tail through the lanes and paths, where she stopped from time to time to dig holes, pounce on mice or stand with her head cocked to one side to listen to things she could hear but couldn't see.

Ever since our arrival in the hamlet, a very large, long-coated evil-looking tabby cat had been skulking around in the hedges and fields. When we met, it crouched with back arched, ears flattened, green eyes glaring, and lips drawn back to show fangs. Its obvious dislike of us did not discourage it from coming into the house at night and raiding the kitchen, spilling dishes and tearing open any packages it could get at. Our two cats loathed it and terrible fights broke out in the small hours, to the tune of dreadful wailing and the sound of furniture being over-turned. In the morning piles of detached cat hair testified as to who had been involved in the scrap, and if I took into account the quantities of different hair I could work out who had been the victor.

Then one hot day I found the tabby casually curled up asleep on the couch in the living room. That first time it took off like a missile, but it kept coming back and even started approaching me cautiously and asking to have its head rubbed. It was during one of these getting to know each other events that Louis, our black cat, crept up behind it and prepared to pounce. To avoid a fight I grabbed the tabby and swept it into the air, thus saving it from a potential pasting. It showed its gratitude by sinking four fangs that a sabre-toothed tiger would be proud of deeply into my arm, and causing four separate ruby-coloured springs to surface and race each other down to my fingers.

But gradually it insinuated itself into our domestic

non-routine. It monopolized my lap and chased the dogs, and the two other cats hated it, but it didn't care.

Its arrival made life rather difficult for Amy, who had by then adjusted to her sightless world and made her way confidently around the house and garden, wagging her tail a little ruefully when she bumped into a piece of furniture or a plant that had been moved from its usual position. Once it had installed itself the tabby cat made friends with the dogs and demanded frequent attention from them in the form of bottom and ear-sniffing, planting itself in front of them to attract their notice. When it stood in front of Amy, she, having no idea it was there, blundered straight into it. The cat responded by soundly boxing her ears. Amy lived in a permanent state of puzzlement for some months, wondering what it was that kept attacking her, and why, until the cat seemed to understand that the collisions were caused by circumstances beyond Amy's control, and either got out of her way or simply accepted their intermittent impacts.

During the summer the parrots stayed outside during the day, in their cages in the garden, sheltered from the sun. Twice I had found Rafiki, our grey parrot, exploring the garden, having somehow managed to open her cage, and each time she was delighted to climb on my hand and return to her cage. But one day a gust of wind toppled the cage, and as I picked her up she panicked and flew into the hedge. I called to her, but she flew a little further away, into a plum tree. No matter what I did, she just kept flying a few metres further from the house, exploring the tree bark and leaves, whistling and chattering to herself as she went further and further. I scrambled frantically over hedges and wire fences, sometimes no more than three metres from her, but she just kept on going and then I lost sight of her completely as she found her wings and flapped away behind a barn.

For three days I hunted, called, shook tins of food. Bill kept saying he'd seen her, she was in a tree, or on the roof. But each time it was a false alarm – a pigeon, or a crow – and I was devastated and resigned to having lost her for good.

On the fourth day, the phone rang, and it was dear old Mme Grimaud. 'Madame, your parrot is in my garden!'

'Are you *sure* it's my parrot, madame?'

'Yes. Absolutely. I heard it talking a little while ago, and all the neighbours are here listening to it. It's speaking English, so it must be yours!'

There, in her garden, sitting comfortably on a walnut tree branch, surrounded by amused French people and waiting for somebody to bring her something to eat and drink, was Rafiki.

'Hello!' she chirped when she saw Terry, and sidled down the branch and onto his arm.

She was none the worse for wear, but very hungry and slightly dehydrated, and after four days at almost the limits of her survival capability.

At the time, Terry was engaged in some building work, and wheeling a barrow backwards and forwards. The wheel had developed an irritating squeal, so he'd lubricated it. The squealing stopped. The next day he was working at the front of the house, where the parrot cages were. From the window I watched him examining the barrow, wheeling it again, lubricating it again, frowning, examining it again, taking the wheel off, putting it back on, and then staring at the barrow in exasperation.

'What's wrong?' I asked him.

'I can't understand it. I can't seem to stop that blasted noise. Watch.'

He pushed the barrow a few steps and sure enough it squealed, but when he turned the corner of the house it stopped. It only squealed at the front of the house, where Rafiki sat in her cage, perfectly imitating the wretched noise, and quietly chuckling to herself. That bird knew exactly what she was doing.

Her companion, an Amazon parrot called Cervantes, was usually no trouble, content to sit in his cage watching the world go by, or playing with his toys. Given the opportunity, he'd bite you to the bone. Unlike Rafiki, who was English-bred and hand-reared, he was a bird who'd been captured in the wild, and had never forgotten or forgiven man's hatefulness. We'd bought him as a companion for Rafiki, but unfortunately she despised him; he was very sociable with other birds, but if he tried to befriend Rafiki she attacked him. One day, I promised him, we'd buy him a companion.

I sometimes wondered whether the animals tried consciously to make life as difficult as possible, or whether it could possibly be accidental.

At night the parrots came out of their cages to explore the barn. After a period of not being able to sleep at all, I took two strong sleeping tablets one evening. Unfortunately I'd been unable to get Cervantes back into his cage before I went to bed, and around midnight was dragged from deep, drugged sleep by mad squawking and the sound of things crashing about. For some reason he was flying around in the dark, and had managed to knock over all sort of ornaments. When I got to him he was on top of the computer with one claw trapped in the casing. It took me fifteen groggy minutes to release him, holding his attacking beak at bay with a wooden spoon with one hand and working his claw free with the other. He flew away growling, and I went back to bed. At 5.30 a.m. there were more crashings and bangings, squawkings and yelpings. He was sitting on one of the dog's heads, and it was difficult to decide which of them looked the more startled. This time it took a broom and towel and an hour-long struggle to get him back into his cage.

*   *   *

Apart from wondering what I did with myself to keep from being bored, the other thing most people wanted to know was how I found the French. It was easy – I just stepped outside the house and walked 50 metres down the lane, and there they were.

The local people were gentle, slow, dignified and friendly without being intrusive. They were always courteous; even strangers always nodded, smiled and said '*Bonjour, madame*' when our paths crossed. We learned that when going into public buildings like the post office, bank, bakery, or local shops, it was customary to acknowledge everybody else with '*Messieurs/dames, bonjour*', and that going into a restaurant you should wish everybody whose table you passed '*bon appetit*'. Soon we could always tell if somebody was English, because they were the people who walked in without greeting other customers. The French people found this incredibly rude, and were shocked to know that in England this was normal behaviour, and not discourteous.

Our neighbours enjoyed a little harmless gossip; they were always interested to know what the various English people who were moving into the area were up to, and they enjoyed sharing such small scandals as occasionally broke the surface of village life. They were quietly sociable, and not effusive. I admired Mme Grimaud's epiphyllum, and next day she handed me some cuttings. Mme Meneteau often passed bowls of figs or strawberries over the hedge, or bundles of leeks or a crispy lettuce, and asked whether I'd like cuttings of this or seeds of that. They were all country folk, and could identify any bird by its call. One night a ghastly, blood-chilling noise split the darkness. It sounded like somebody or something *in extremis*, almost as bad as the cockatoo, and went on for several minutes while I tried to summon up the courage to go and investigate, and failed. The following day I asked M. Meneteau if he had heard it and whether he knew what it was.

'Yes, it was the barn owl. When they scream like that, something terrible is going to happen.'

'What sort of terrible thing?'

'Pff. I don't know. It's just what people say. I don't believe it myself.'

I waited hopefully for two or three days for some terrible disaster to occur, but nothing did, so I didn't believe it either.

I mentioned to M. Meneteau that blackbirds were nesting in a hollow cherry tree in the little orchard next to our garden, and he shook his head.

'Not blackbirds. They don't nest in hollow trees, they nest in the hedges. They're probably starlings.'

I was a little surprised because they had certainly looked like blackbirds to me, but when I dug out the binoculars for a closer look I could see that he was absolutely right. They nested in the same place each year, and had a struggle to raise their young because of the magpies who lived in the big oak tree and tried to get at their nest. Every year I built a network of interlocked branches around the nest so that the starlings could get in, but the magpies were kept out.

Walking the dogs in the fields behind the hamlet, I often met Mme Meneteau carrying a sack, bending to pick something from the ground. Sometimes it was dandelions for her rabbits, and sometimes the beads of maize left after harvesting, which she collected for her poultry. Mme Grimaud hunted snails, popping them into a flowerpot, and showed me which were worth harvesting, and which were too small. I helped her once, but felt terribly guilty each time I plucked another plump snail from where it was cowering beneath a leaf, and found myself apologizing to them as I popped them into the flowerpot, knowing that it wouldn't be long before they were boiled alive and eaten with parsley, garlic and great enjoyment. I really don't like harming anything, but the quantities of slugs and snails that lived in our garden devastated just about everything I tried to grow, and as an alternative to poisoning them I hunted the snails by torchlight when they are easy prey, and delivered heavy bags of them the next morning to Mme Meneteau and Mme Grimaud. I subsequently learned that nocturnal snail hunting is illegal in France, as is hunting them out of season – i.e. before mid-summer – because they are a protected species.

When I grumbled about stinging nettles to a farmer, he told me how useful they were for growing tomatoes.

'Dig a trench, and fill it with nettles. Then plant your tomato seedlings into it, and the nettles will not only provide fertilizer, they'll prevent disease too.'

Mme Grimaud added that at one time they used to chop up nettles and feed them to poultry and pigs, who'd eat them chopped, but not whole.

I'm sure our French neighbours thought us very strange; we kept horses that we didn't ride, our dogs were gundogs but we didn't go hunting, and I had a gun that I used for target shooting only. With all the land we had, all I grew were flowers, instead of useful things to eat, because vegetable gardening is very labour-intensive, requiring hours of hoeing under the baking sun, and I didn't feel I'd the energy for that. My gardening efforts were limited to putting things into the rocky ground and leaving them to fend for themselves.

Sometimes the neighbours had a laugh at my expense.

In the days when I had thought it was actually possible to have a vegetable garden and five dogs, I'd bought a box of seed potatoes, hoed a bed for them and planted them in rows. My only source of gardening information was a small book entitled *Adam the Gardner*, a *Sunday Express* publication that had cost 45 pence when it was first published, which I think was in the early 1970s, or thereabouts. The potato-growing instructions were quite straightforward: you stuck them in the ground, and waited for the green bits to grow and produce flowers. Once the flowers had withered and died, you dug up your potatoes. Simple. The green bits on our potatoes flourished, but they didn't produce any flowers, even after the things had been in the ground for several months. Then one of the horses needed an injection. Thanks to Amy's daily insulin jabs I was by now quite confident with the needle, but I needed a strong person to hold on to the horse while I did it; so I asked M. Meneteau if he could please help. Afterwards, he pointed to our potato patch and asked when I was going to dig them up.

I explained that the flowers hadn't arrived yet, and he looked at me a little strangely. What flowers, he wanted to know? I told him about the little book and how Adam said you had to wait for the flowers to bloom and die. His shoulders shook a little, and his eyes filled with tears as he started to laugh and shake.

'They don't all have flowers!' he spluttered. 'If you don't dig them up soon, they'll be as big as footballs. I dug mine up six weeks ago!'

How stupid of Adam not to have explained properly. I got the fork out and poked around in the ground and was rewarded with a large crop of very fine potatoes that tasted delicious and were so big that one was suffcient for two people.

M. Royer kept a few sheep in the field next to ours, which they shared with Mme Grimaud's hens. One evening I noticed one of the sheep lying down, moaning, and the others standing at a distance watching it. It seemed very distressed, and was lying in the wet grass, and after I'd watched it for about five minutes I thought I'd better go and tell M. Royer. I knew that the neighbours thought I was soft in the head where animals were concerned, but anyway, I went and banged on his front door and interrupted his supper. I blurted out that one of his sheep didn't look well, and I thought there might be something wrong. He took off his slippers and pulled on his boots, and we walked down the field together. By the time we arrived the damned animal was standing up and munching grass and looking perfectly normal. I apologized for having disturbed his meal, and was feeling pretty stupid when he smiled (he was a very shy man, but when he smiled it was like watching the sun come out) and pointed: 'Look.'

In the grass beside the sheep a new-born lamb was struggling to its feet.

'It's a good thing you came for me – it's too cold for it to be out tonight. I'll get them into the barn. I didn't know she was having a lamb. Thank you for telling me.'

I blessed the sheep for not having made me look a fool, for giving me an opportunity to make a neighbourly gesture, and for enabling me to have the longest conversation I'd so far had with M. Royer.

When we went shopping, we recognized more and more people who waved and chatted, and after three years we started to feel we were beginning to belong, although the sheep whose domain ours had previously been still glared at the dogs and us through the fence with undisguised hostility as we walked where they once had, saying: *Go home, get off our land, stupid English people and dogs*.

When Jean-Luc came and said he and his girlfriend were going away for a long weekend, and asked if I'd mind feeding their dog, I was so pleased to be asked that I almost burst into tears.

Gloria moved from Spain with her three dogs to live next door permanently. What she enjoyed doing was reading, smoking, soaking up the sun with her dogs around her, and gardening in a haphazard way. That was all it took to keep her happy. When she mowed the lawn, she did it in the altogether, and in times of crisis she changed her hair colour or style. She was uncrushable, it seemed, always looking on the bright side of life, which in her case quite often must have taken some doing. Their house progressed slowly. Bags of cement formed an obstacle course and there were ladders and timbers and plasterboards and sanitary fittings as far as the eye could see. Electric wires poked out and dangled at face-height. She and Bill lived in one of the caravans at the back of the barn, and the dogs lived in another.

Their two Great Danes were ageing, and their health was visibly deteriorating by the day. One of the symptoms of their illness was terrible nosebleeds, and the vet had given Gloria some powder to staunch these haemorrhages before she went on a visit to England, leaving Bill in charge. The phone rang one night just after midnight, as it so often did. It was Bill (who had his own telephone by now).

'Lolly's having a nosebleed. Can you come?'

The room looked like the aftermath of the Texas chainsaw massacre, and the blood was still pumping fast.

'Where's the powder?'

'I can't find it.'

'But Gloria said she'd told you where she'd left it.'

'I know. But I can't remember where she said.'

We searched for a few minutes, in vain, and still the blood poured.

I couldn't find any cotton wool, so as a last resort I took a broom handle and started collecting spiders' webs from the corners until I had a small wad, which we pressed to the nose until the flow finally stopped.

One morning, after another post-midnight call that had hung up when I answered it, Bill said: 'I rang you

238

last night. But when I realized how late it was, I hung up.'

'Why did you phone me?'

'Well, I'd papered the hallway, and it looked right nice. But then all these little bumps and bubbles started coming up. I was going to ask you if you thought they'd go down if I stuck pins in them, but as it was so late I peeled the paper off and saved it. Now I'm going to put lining paper on first, and stick it all back on again.'

And he did. I've never met anybody who was so meticulous and prepared to put so much time into getting things right. He had the most amazing patience. If something of mine broke down, he would willingly drop whatever else he was doing and spend hours dismantling things and trying to get them to work. Mostly they didn't, but it certainly wasn't because Bill didn't try hard enough.

If only he would have tidied up his property. Everywhere you looked there was stuff: bags and sacks and boxes and cartons and vehicles and rolls of pipe and weeds and stone fountains and garden furniture and caravans covered in green algae. Sometimes Bill would say, with the familiar faraway look in his eyes, 'I must tidy this up, make it all look nice', but he never did.

Because the local people were generally so courteous and friendly, it was rather shocking to meet somebody who wasn't. Gloria went with me to the bank one day, and a newly arrived member of staff, a woman, pounced on us and started trying to sell me some life insurance, which I politely declined on the truthful grounds that I couldn't afford it. She was not easily discouraged, but we parted on what I thought were fairly friendly terms.

'She looked like an angry chicken, don't you think?' Gloria asked loudly, as we stood in the queue. 'With that hair sticking up on the middle of her head and those funny eyes.'

'Shh.' I jabbed her. 'She can hear, and I'm sure she can understand, too.'

The woman had flushed rather red.

The next time I put my card into a cashpoint machine it was swallowed up without any warning, leaving me stranded with no petrol, and causing me considerable embarrassment and inconvenience. I hied off to the bank to enquire what had happened to the card, and the man at the counter assured me that there was a problem with that particular machine and that my card would be returned within a couple of days. It was not. Further visits to the bank continued to produce the same information, until on one occasion I was invited to go into the office of the chicken-faced lady.

She was not at all friendly, and marched into an office and slammed herself down into a chair. She did not invite me to sit.

'I have taken away your card.'

'Why is that?'

'You were overdrawn.'

'I'm always overdrawn.'

The bank made most of their money from my overdraft fees. It was not coincidental that since I had been with them they had undergone tasteful and very expensive renovations.

'Well, that's *not* allowed. You card has been confiscated.'

'Could you not have warned me beforehand?'

'I did. I wrote to you and you didn't bother to reply.'

'I haven't had any letter from you. When did you write?'

'A long time ago.'

'Please may I see a copy of the letter?'

'Are you calling me a liar?' Her voice rose. Now she even sounded rather like a chicken that had just laid an egg.

'Of course not. I'm just asking to see a copy of the letter you sent me that I didn't receive.'

'Well, I didn't send you the letter, actually, because we don't have your address.'

I wondered if I'd heard correctly.

'But you must have my address. You send me monthly statements and cheque books. Of course you have the address.'

'So you *are* calling me a liar?'

'I am not calling you anything, but I'm very disappointed that after I have banked with you for several years you withdraw my card without any warning. I've introduced a lot of new customers to your bank, and I'm very shocked by your behaviour.'

She bounced up from the chair, and shouted: 'Now you're threatening me! I don't have to listen to this,' and ran out of the office.

I was quite distressed by this unpleasant encounter, and sat wondering what to do for a few minutes; then she came back in.

'Anyway, no card for you. Not now; not again. Ever.'

'Whose decision was that?'

'Mine.'

'And what is your position here with the bank?'

'I'm the manager.'

'I don't think you are. Who is the person in charge of the whole bank here?'

'The new manager's name is Monsieur Vampire.'

Couldn't get much more fitting than that.

'And Monsieur Vampire' – I started giggling – 'supports your decision, does he?'

'Yes.'

'Then I'll have to move my account elsewhere.'

I stood up.

'I hate this job!' she cried suddenly, in English. 'I hate the people here, and I hate the work! The only thing

I enjoy is being able to talk English to the English customers.'

'And withdraw their cards. You've got one less English person to talk to now. Goodbye.'

She burst into tears as I let myself out.

To my very great glee, only two days later the head office of the bank, as part of a country-wide survey, sent a questionnaire on customer satisfaction that I completed as fully and in as much detail as possible, emphasizing my opinion of M. Vampire and his chicken-woman.

A month later, they sent a refund for over seven hundred francs of charges that the chicken-faced lady had taken from my account for her services in confiscating the card. Then I closed the account.

The opening hours of the post office in Saint-Thomas-le-Petit were rather erratic, so I started going in the opposite direction, to la Petite-Eglise. The post mistress there, Agnès (not to be confused with the English Agnes, of the snake episode), was slim and very attractive, with dark wavy shoulder-length hair and a splatter of freckles. She spoke near-perfect English, as did her husband Danny. They were both Anglophiles, and had two young sons, who were very nice little boys of about eight and ten years old. Danny bought English taxis, double-decker buses and milk floats, and hired them out for publicity campaigns and weddings. They were his passion. Agnès collected teapots and had a great cabinet full of them. They also collected models of buses, and telephones, and their little house was jam-packed with all kinds of ornaments. Agnès was a talented painter, and all in all a very busy lady. From the first time we met over the counter at the post office, we became friends. From Danny and Agnès I learned some very picturesque and interesting French, delightful sayings such as, when referring to somebody who wasn't quite all there: 'there's a spider on the ceiling', or 'there's a little bicycle going round in his head'.

They were renovating a farmhouse a few kilometres away, and sent us an invitation to an 'evening of friendship' there, from 7.30 onwards.

Unfortunately Terry could not get out for that date, and on the evening of their get-together I wasn't feeling quite on top of the world. I would have liked to go to bed with a hot water bottle, but felt that as I liked these people so much, and they had been kind enough to invite me to their friendship evening. I would make an effort. I calculated that if I arrived at around 8.30 p.m., by 10.00 p.m. I could politely take my leave. I set off with only a very sketchy idea of where to go, and spent forty minutes driving around spidery lanes in the approaching dark, and thinking it would be a sensible idea to go back home. Finally I stopped at a small bar to ask for directions. The clientele were all in various stages of intoxication and it was quite difficult trying to explain what I wanted to know, as they shouted and laughed and beckoned me to join them. When I eventually got across the message that I was trying to find the hamlet where Agnès and Danny lived, three of them staggered up and pointed in three entirely different directions, bellowing and emitting alcoholic fumes. I focused on the one who was staggering the least, and repeated the name of the place I was looking for. He pointed twice in the same direction, so taking that as confirmation I set off and duly arrived at just before 9.00 p.m.

I was aghast to find a crowd of forty people in the courtyard, all French, none of whom I knew. Agnès waved me into their bosom, saying gaily: 'Good! Now Susie has arrived, so we will eat.' This was not the casual gathering I'd envisaged, but a formal sit-down dinner.

In a rustic barn beside their house, beautifully

decorated with flowers and paintings, three long tables were set for a banquet. Over the next three hours we ate through plate after plate of fragrant melon, stuffed eggs, marinated vegetables, followed by a main dish of succulent chicken which I had to decline, but there were accompaniments of assorted vegetables and a green salad. Crisp-crusted bread was piled in baskets on the table. Cheese came next, creamy cheeses and crumbly cheeses; cheeses that smelt of hay and cheeses that smelt of old socks; blue cheeses, white cheeses, golden cheeses. And the wine. Ah! Everything was perfection. Agnès had prepared all this herself, while still running the post office that morning. She explained that friends from the Gironde had brought up the melons. 'They're the best melons.' The cheeses had come from friends in Normandy. 'The best cheeses!'

Most of the vegetables were home-grown, including black potatoes that I'd never seen before. The bread had been collected from a bakery some kilometres away, where they baked the best bread. And the wine came from the vineyard of a close relative just next door to Saint-Emilion. The guests were mostly family and old friends and I felt greatly flattered to be there with them. Although the wine flowed as if from an eternal spring, and the barn was loud with animated talk and laughter, nobody misbehaved. One old boy whose face was startingly red stood up and sang, a bit off-key, to kindly applause. The children entertained themselves happily. More food arrived, chocolate profiteroles, plum tart, apricot tart, strawberry tart, and still we ate.

Just after midnight, Danny and Agnès's two sons, Kevin and David, came in and clapped their hands loudly, shouting, 'Silence.' They had our full attention.

'The firework show is about to begin. Everybody outside.'

Dutifully we trooped out into the courtyard, where a

group of young children were crouched around a small mountain of sand studded with fireworks.

'Everybody behind the stones. Nobody must step forward. This is dangerous.'

The elder son, Kevin, indicated two rocks connecting an invisible line over which we must not step, and we obediently assembled behind it.

A child struck a match, and nothing happened. The other children examined the firework that hadn't gone off, and applied another match to it. It went off this time. It was a colourful and noisy display and really well put together, and I could imagine what an outcry there would have been in England if children had been seen lighting it. The grand finale was one of those rockets that goes off and divides itself into several dozen howling, shrieking things that whirl in every direction. Either this had not been securely placed in the sand and it had moved, or else the young organizers of the event had wanted to have a laugh, because when it was lit it came directly towards the assembled spectators at knee-height and at about a hundred and fifty kilometres an hour. Despite our heavy payload of food and drink, we who were assembled securely behind the invisible line all managed to leap to safety, although with little dignity as we clung to and collided with each other before retiring for coffee and cognac. When I made my way home at half past midnight, everybody else was revving up for dancing till dawn.

Chapter Fourteen

The English colony grew; few weeks passed when new settlers didn't arrive. The region was still inexpensive in comparison with the better-known parts of *la belle France*, and was said to benefit from the 'micro-climate' off the Atlantic coast, and these factors attracted the new wave of immigrants. Also there were many who came to visit friends or family and succumbed to the peacefulness and simple charm of the area: the gentle rolling hills, wooded valleys, abundance of ancient buildings, and impression that the march of time had bypassed the place about fifty years previously.

As English estate agents grasped the opportunity and set up shop, property prices rocketed, and old houses started to become scarce. Young French couples found themselves being priced out of the market. There were ever more British-registered cars on the road, and more English-speaking voices in the shops and restaurants. Friends asked whether I thought the French felt any resentment towards the English who were, as one French gentleman said, invading the area. If they did, they were normally too courteous to show it: only occasionally did I overhear French people lamenting that there were now more foreigners in their village than French; and most of them I asked said that they were pleased to see

246

old houses being renovated that would otherwise have decayed into ruins. French people had little use for collapsing old farmhouses, and were amused and puzzled as to why the English had so much, and why they were prepared to spend huge amounts of money on these ruins, and further great sums on making them habitable, when for a great deal less they could have bought a nice, comfortable modern house. A very jovial man I was talking to one day confided that he much preferred English neighbours to Parisians, who seemed to be universally loathed.

Not everybody who moved here settled happily ever after.

Once the initial euphoria faded, some people found that the endless peace and quiet they had thought they wanted was *too* endlessly peaceful and quiet, and after a few months they were bored. Others had over-optimistic expectations of the weather, or the cost of living, or the ease of integrating into a foreign country, and, disappointed, returned to wherever they'd come from.

There were people who found that country life didn't suit them. They didn't like the gorgeous agricultural pongs that reeked off the fields, or the clods of tractor-borne dirt shed outside their houses. They didn't like the lowing of the cattle, or the bleating of the sheep, or the crowing of the cockerels, or the fact that their neighbours were all farmers and only talked about farming.

Some missed their families and friends back in England. Others missed being close to theatres and museums; and the odd person here and there found that they didn't like the French or couldn't cope with the sometimes tiresome bureaucracy. Most people made efforts of varying degrees to speak the language, but there was a strange band who didn't have any intention of doing so, on the basis that they 'couldn't get their tongues round it', or were 'too old to learn new tricks', although all of them peppered their conversations with 'boulangerie', 'gendarme' and 'baguette'. Everybody could manage those three words, and I felt that if they made a point of learning just one common, simple word each week, at the end of the year they'd know fifty-five words instead of only three.

One way and another, of the English who settled here quite a large proportion didn't stay long, but their spaces were soon filled by others.

Those of us who made it our permanent home integrated in different degrees: some surrounded themselves exclusively with other English; some were equally at home with French or English, and there were others who immersed themselves totally in French life, joining all the local activities and becoming involved in all aspects of their communities, even if they couldn't speak the language. They followed the fortunes of the local football team, played mysterious card games they didn't understand, and bought tickets to the various village entertainments; there were even people who steadfastly refused to have any contact at all with other English.

The availability of excellent wine at silly prices meant that tales of drunken English people disgracing themselves were common, seemingly regarded with amused tolerance by our French neighbours, less so by the sober English who felt that the drinkers were rather disgracing us as a nation.

A disturbing factor that started to become apparent was that not all the people who emigrated to France did so for love of the country. Some openly admitted that they were only there because they couldn't stand living in England any more, chiefly because there were too many immigrants there who couldn't even speak English. These were the ones who were continually critical of the French, and demanded that their local *maires* should learn to speak English. It was this attitude that sent cold shivers up the spines of those of us who loved the country and its people just as they were. We feared that if it continued the French might start to lose their tolerance towards us.

When we met our English friends we lamented the fact that more English were moving into the area. Having found our own little piece of France, we were jealous of it and didn't want to share. But often the new arrivals became new friends, and soon they too would be sighing and saying: 'The house next to ours has just been sold to Brits,' and we'd all commiserate. Oh, well.

It always astonished me when friends didn't fall head over heels in love with our wonderful home. They stared in blank-faced disbelief at the bare stone and dirt walls and floors, the holes where the doors should be, and the dozen or so electrical extension leads which served the house from the sole socket in the living room. They were shocked by the fact that we lived 10 kilometres from the nearest town, by the frightful mess of Bill's establishment, by the absence of locks on the surviving doors, and the lack of glass in some of the windows.

'My God, you can't live here! It's falling down! What on earth do you do for heating? You'll never get it finished – it'll cost a fortune.'

'Susie, you can't stay living like this. Can't you move to somewhere normal, or back to England?' asked one very dear friend.

'Seriously, you've got to think about getting away from here,' another advised.

The thought never crossed my mind. Regardless of weather, financial dilemmas, and problems with the animals, I'd never wanted to live anywhere other than that house since the moment I saw it. And not for one moment had I ever felt unsafe leaving our doors and windows open and unlocked by day or by night.

Where else would we have neighbours who were always kind, always considerate, always ready to help? Where else could we have toads coming into the house on warm summer evenings and spending the night sitting fatly in flowerpots, or watch the twinkling green lights of glow worms blinking in the grass? Who would have rescued the plump hedgehog trundling round the patio with its body wedged into an ancient horseshoe from which it couldn't free itself, whose irritable whiffling combined with a metallic scraping, clunking sound woke me up? Where else could we lie in bed and hear a symphony of owls performing through the night, or the nightingales who sang to each other from spring to summer, and watch the sun float up over the hill opposite the tiny bedroom window in the morning?

A friend sprang a surprise visit during October, and we went out for a meal in the evening. Many restaurants were closed, as they only opened at lunchtime out of the holiday season and we had to drive around for a while to find somewhere to eat.

'Susie, you can't possibly stay here,' he said earnestly. 'You'll be bored out of your brains. Look at it.' He pointed to the quiet square in town, deserted at 10.30 p.m. 'There's nothing happening.'

I tried to explain that it was the nothingness that I loved: the being able to park my car easily, without having to feed money into a machine; the polite, gentle people; driving home at 2.00 a.m. through deserted country lanes and not being afraid. Lying in the dark listening to the night noises, or standing outside, sometimes when the stars came down so low that they grazed the rooftops, and the moon lit up the whole countryside. I described how one night, coming home very late, I had seen the house shining in the dark, as if lit by lasers. I had driven up the lane and found that it was the Milky Way hanging directly overhead, beaming its light down so that the whole house was illuminated. These were the things I saw, while some people saw only cracked walls and a sagging roof.

As a matter of fact, there wasn't nearly as much nothingness as I would have liked. Forgetting for the moment the perpetual round of trying to mend things that were falling to pieces, like gates and fences, the pitiful efforts at home improvement and the garden I was trying to develop, I had two horses, six dogs, one of whom was a chronic invalid, three cats, two parrots and innumerable poultry, all of which needed regular feeding, continual medical attention, clearing up after, and frequent hunting down and retrieving from far-flung places.

And surprisingly, normal domestic life had its place too. If I didn't shop and cook, I didn't eat. I washed dishes and clothes, occasionally swept and polished in the house. Planted flowers, mowed the lawn twice a week, translated, took phone messages, and baby-sat animals for other people.

When I pointed this out to a friend, he said, 'It's funny, but somehow I imagined that living in France, all you would have to do was sit in the sun reading, and picking flowers and drinking too much wine.' Funnily enough, I had once had a similar vision. Living in France is not synonymous with being on holiday. It's like living in England, except it's foreign and much more fun. And the wine is cheaper.

It was a rare week when at least one of the animals didn't cause some disruption to my day, even the most undemanding of them, like our oldest bitch, Natalia. She was the most obedient and obliging dog imaginable, even in her dotage, and had never caused us a moment's anxiety. In her old age something affected her sense of direction, and once she got moving in a straight line she didn't seem to be able to stop or turn until she reached a fence or a wall. She moved at an easy trotting gait that was difficult to overtake. Being rather deaf meant that she was oblivious to yells and shouts, and unless she was forcibly arrested she'd just keep trotting on. One day somebody left a gate open, and by the time I realized she was missing she was nowhere in sight. I searched fields, rivers, woods and ditches in every direction; I phoned the local vets, the *gendarmes*, and the mayors, with no success. Somebody phoned to say she had been found meandering round the village and been taken to the dog pound, 12 kilometres away. But when I got there it wasn't her, but a sad brown spaniel. After four days we were resigned to not seeing her again when a local farmer drove up in his white van, and out from the back bounced Natalia, sprightly as ever, and making a beeline in the wrong direction.

He smiled. 'She was trotting down the road about three kilometres away, with traffic dodging round her. We took her home and looked after her, and then I heard at the *mairie* that you had lost a very old dog. Well, she's certainly very old, but she was running along the road like a pup and I had to run quite hard to catch her!'

Another day a passing visitor had luckily discovered her, in my absence, swimming aimlessly round the pond and fished her out.

One day there was a whole string of messages from Michelle on the answering machine, saying it was vital that I contact her as soon as possible. Against my better judgement, I called her.

'Do you go shopping?' she enquired.

Yes, I said, like most people.

She said: 'I need help. I am very ill, I cannot drive, and I need some shopping. Will you do it for me?'

'Of course I will. Do you have a list?'

'Which supermarket do you use?' There were two in town.

'I can go to either, whichever you prefer.'

'But which one do you usually go to?'

I told her.

'Oh no, I don't want you getting my things from there. You'll have to go to the other one.'

'Fine, that's no problem.'

There was quite a long list, about twenty items in all, and all with complicated instructions, such as taking apart multiple packs of tinned cat food and changing the flavours round, and she made me read the list back to ensure that I had fully understood just what she did and didn't want.

'When are you going?' was her next question.

I wasn't falling for that one. 'I'll go whenever it's best for you,' I said.

'Tomorrow afternoon.'

She had to choose the only time in the whole of the next week, or possibly the entire month, when I already had an appointment, but never mind.

'OK. I'll go at one o'clock,' – always the best time as all the French people are having lunch and the super-market is almost empty – 'and I'll bring your things at about two o'clock.'

'No! You can't come before four o'clock – I'm taking my mother out for lunch and we won't be back before then.'

At the time, I was so confused that the fact she was able to drive sufficiently well to take her mother out didn't register; I just wanted to get her off the phone.

'Fine. Then I'll go later' – when it's nice and crowded – 'and see you at four o'clock.'

The shopping expedition was worse than I could have imagined. The brand of ham that she had specified only came in a packet larger than she wanted, and with a rind that she didn't want. There were insufficient tins of the correct brand of cat food, and the cat biscuits only came in large boxes when she wanted a small one.

Some of the other things she wanted weren't there, so I had to decide whether to go back to her without them, or improvise. I improvised, queued up for a long time, stowed the shopping and drove to her house, arriving at precisely four o'clock. Her car was parked in the drive, and a horde of noisy little dogs was racing up and down barking, but there was no sign of her. The gate was chained up and padlocked, and too high to climb over. I roamed up and down calling, then sat in the car and hooted, and after fifteen minutes decided to give up. I placed the boxes of shopping in the shade of a bush, wrote a little note and attached the bill for the money she owed me, and started the car.

She flew out of the house like a bullet from a gun, waving her arms angrily.

'So you were just going to drive away and leave all my things in the sun?' she shouted.

'Look, I've been here for fifteen minutes. I arrived at exactly the agreed time, and have done all I could to attract your attention. I couldn't stay here all night.' I felt like driving away but she owed me quite a bit for the shopping and I didn't want to risk not getting paid.

'Well, bring it in,' she said, unlocking the gate. She didn't look at all ill.

I lugged the shopping into the house and handed her the bill and said I was in a hurry, which was quite true. She ignored the bill and started pulling things out of the boxes and slamming them down on the table.

'Wrong!' Slam! 'This is wrong!' Slam! 'This is wrong!' Slam! 'This is wrong!' Slam! 'You've got me all the wrong things, you stupid woman.'

Alarmed in case she used my inefficiency as an excuse not to repay the quite large sum I'd forked out on her behalf, I bit my tongue and said that if she wanted me to take some things back I would.

She handed me the money and said that if I got it wrong next time, I'd have to take it all back and change it. She forgot to thank me. I apologized for my poor effort and ignored all her phone calls for the next few months.

From time to time the telephone rang in the very early hours.

'Hello, Sue, it's Mrs Malucha,' boomed the familiar voice.

'Mrs Malucha, it's four o'clock in the morning!'

'I know, Sue, but I couldn't sleep, so I thought I'd ring and see how you are.'

'Well, that's kind of you, but couldn't you ring during the day instead, when I'm not asleep?'

'Oh no, it's too expensive during the day. By the way, Sue, have you found my brown shoes and my kettle yet?'

'Mrs Malucha, I told you two years ago, nobody knows where your brown shoes or your kettle are. I'm really sorry, but there's no point in keeping on asking me, because I'm never going to find them.'

She told me she had somehow got herself to England and had a nice flat somewhere or other. Later she wrote to say one of her suitors was taking her to live in Switzerland. They were buying a house together. She was an unquenchable old thing. I always wondered what happened to her.

Then there was the man I mentally called the Pope, because he was such a great pontificator. His hobbyhorse was 'the *Eng*lish', of which he was one. In his view his fellow citizens just didn't understand the French, or their way of life. He poured scorn on everyone he knew, despite the fact that after living here for more than a decade neither he nor his wife could speak more than three words of French.

I asked them once if they didn't feel they should learn the language. His wife looked nervously at him, seeking guidance, but he laughed and said: 'No – there's no need. The French can understand you well enough if they want to. And we can always find somebody to translate if we need to. Which reminds me, we've got this tax form here. I'll get our papers out and you can fill it in while you're here.'

I explained that understanding how to complete a French tax declaration was beyond most native French people and quite out of my league, but he wasn't to be deterred and dragged out a large filing box full of receipts and cheque books. He unfurled the triple-folded sheet crammed with boxes, lines, columns and rows all containing symbols and enigmatic strings of letters that meant absolutely nothing to me, which is the French tax declaration form. I said if he went to the tax office they were very obliging there and would certainly help him to complete his declaration.

'Yes,' he replied, 'but the problem is, Susie, they don't speak *Eng*lish.'

I saw a visit to the tax office looming on my horizon. 'But as you said, if they want to, they can. I'm sure you'll get it sorted out. Sorry, I must dash, late for something.'

The next time I saw him he needed me to speak to the insurance agent, then write a letter in French to him, then go back and translate the response. This led to a disagreement with the agent, which caused further correspondence, all of which needed translating backwards and forwards, as the agent, if he could understand *Eng*lish, certainly wasn't letting on.

On another occasion I was to investigate how he could get a new pair of glasses completely free from the French social system. The Pope had been to see the local social worker, a charming man whom I'd met several times.

'Stupid boss-eyed git couldn't understand a word I was trying to say. Can't you phone somebody up and make some enquiries?'

I held my breath for several seconds, and said, 'No. Sorry, got to rush, late for something else.'

'I've got a little project for you,' he announced happily one day. 'Give you something to do.'

Oh, good. Exactly what I was looking for, something else to do. I waited.

'Well, you know how many things there are to do around here.'

I nodded.

'There's so many places for tourists, and our guests' – they owned some *gîtes* – 'are always asking for suggestions. What I'd like you to do for me is this: go round all the tourist offices, find out everything there is within an hour's drive from here – say within a radius of about forty miles. Get hold of all the brochures and information, and start making it up into a book. Put things into categories: all the museums in one section; places of historical interest; boating areas; zoos; lakes and rivers; theme parks. You know what I mean. Find out the entrance fees – don't forget to check if they vary according to season – and find out the opening hours. Of course, you'll have to translate them all into *Eng*lish, but that's easy for you. So each place will have full details. Then get out a large map of the area, and work out the best routes. Draw a map showing how to get there, and mark all the road numbers. Do you see what I'm getting at?'

Yes, I felt I was getting the gist.

'So a guest can get out the book, find the section they're interested in, and see at a glance all they need to know.'

'It seems like a very sensible idea.'

'Well, there you are then. How long do you think it'll take?'

'Far too much time for me, I'm afraid. I'm busy enough with my own life.'

He sneered. 'You're always *busy*. I've never known a woman who's always as busy as you say you are. What do you actually *do* all day?'

I counted to ten. 'Well, you know the things your wife does – shopping, cooking, cleaning, washing, ironing?'

'Yes.'

'Well, I don't have a wife to do them for me, so I do them for myself. Then, you know how you look after your garden – mow the lawn, weed, water, prune, plant, keep it looking nice?'

'Yes.'

'Well, I do those things as well. And painting and decorating and trying to mend things. And helping *Eng*lish people with their various problems. And looking after twenty-eight assorted animals. And if I ever had any spare time to call my own, I'd probably enjoy sitting down and reading or watching a film.'

He sniggered. 'Goodness me, you do make it sound hard work!'

I breathed deeply. 'But,' I said, 'I do need to earn money. So I'll do your book for you, but you'll have to pay for my time. Let's say a hundred francs an hour, to take account of travelling to the tourist offices, translation, typing and so on.'

His mouth dropped open, then it closed and broke into a smile. 'You're pulling my leg,' he chortled.

I smiled back. 'I can assure you I'm not.'

His face reddened a little, but then he smiled again. 'I don't know. You women. You do come up with the oddest ideas.' He chuckled patronizingly at the female oddness.

'Yes, don't we just! Anyway, got to rush now. Lots to do.'

Although she was living there, it wasn't where Gloria's heart was. She wanted to move back to England; life was too quiet for her bubbly nature, and she missed her children and grandchildren.

'Once the boys have gone,' she said, referring to the dogs, 'I'll go back.'

Because of the dogs, she and Bill usually took it in turns to go to England, but this time they were going together, and Fred Bear and his little wife were to come and hold the fort for five days until Bill returned.

All the arrangements were in place, and they were just waiting for somebody to come and collect a vehicle they had hired out. When he turned up, Gloria came round and beckoned me.

'Come and have a look at this! Quite a tasty number, the chap who's hired our truck,' she said.

He was OK, better than we generally saw round here, but just a little too tanned, a little too white-toothed, a bit too smooth and a little bit too pleased with himself. As soon as he had driven away, Bill and Gloria left, she snapping and snarling at him in her normal half-serious, half-joking way, he murmuring under his breath and rolling his eyes.

Two days later Terry and I set off on a sunny afternoon for a drive up to town to do what the French call 'window licking' – window shopping. At the end of the lane, where it joined the road, a car was parked, and as we approached out stepped two men wearing armbands, who raised their hands in the air signalling us to stop.

'Uh oh! Cycle race going through,' I said. During the summer, when cycle races were a daily event, it was common for traffic to be held up or rerouted while the cyclists passed.

The armbands walked towards the car, one on each side, and one leaned in on my side.

'*Bonjour*,' I said politely.

'Your papers, please, madame.'

What a bloody cheek! Since how long had cycle marshals had the right to ask for motorists' papers?

'Is this normal?' I asked.

'Perfectly normal, madame. It's part of our job. Please step out of the car.'

This was ridiculous.

'What's happening?' asked Terry.

'They want our papers, and we've got to get out of the car.'

We climbed out and handed over the car documents. From our house 100 yards away our dogs could hear our voices and were barking madly.

'I'm just going to put our dogs away before the noise disturbs our neighbours,' I told one of the armbands.

'Do not move. Stay where you are.'

Really, this was becoming intolerable.

'Your passports, please.'

Terry handed over his, but mine was in the house.

'Where do you live?'

'Just there.' I pointed to our house.

They flicked through the passport.

'You are not Mr Smith, then?'

'No,' replied Terry.

The light was beginning to dawn, and I noticed belatedly that the armbands had '*Douane*' printed on them.

'Oh God, this has to be something to do with Bill,' I muttered to Terry.

One of the armbands took out a mobile phone and made a call.

'You are to come with us. Please follow in your car.'

'Where are we going?'

'Just to the village. Please follow.'

We set off behind them, but after a couple of hundred metres they pulled over to the side of the road as a police car coming in the opposite direction flashed its lights at them and came to a halt. We all turned round and followed the second car 2 kilometres in the opposite direction, until they turned off into a field. The second car disgorged three policemen with guns on their hips and handcuffs hanging from their belts. Two more cars arrived and more policemen spilled out into the field.

I was starting to feel frightened. All these guns, but worse, the handcuffs.

Yet another car arrived and its passenger walked over to us, holding out his hand.

'Good afternoon. I'm sorry you are being bothered. I am a judicial policeman, and I'm here to ensure that the police and customs officers carry out their duties in the correct manner.'

'Could you please tell us exactly what this is all about?'

'No, I'm sorry, but we are going to search Mr Smith's house. Is there anybody there?'

'Yes, some English people are looking after the house.'

'Do they speak French?'

'No.'

'Then in that case, madame, I have to ask you to act as interpreter. The law requires that these people can understand what we are saying. Please will you follow us.'

Back we went, now a convoy of six cars, sweeping into the hamlet and stopping outside Bill's barn, to the great interest of the other inhabitants.

Fred and his wife were standing in the space where there should have been a front door.

'What the hell's going on?' asked Fred.

'They're cops and customs officers, and they're going to search the house.'

261

Fred seemed to be simultaneously furious, excited, and positive that whatever Bill was suspected of having done, he was guilty.

'We don't know anything. Let's not jump to any conclusions yet,' I said.

A seventh car arrived bearing two more policemen and a German shepherd dog, and they set about exploring the barns and the skeleton of the house, pointing at the bare dangling wires, the dusty furniture, a pile of ancient records. The dog showed no interest in any of it.

'How long has the septic tank been here?' asked one of the officers, pointing to the open channel that carried effluent to the said tank.

'About two months,' I replied. Oh God, no, please don't say they're going to open it up.

The officers conferred for a few minutes and said: 'OK. We've finished here. Do you please have a table where we can fill out our report?'

While they had been searching, Terry had been heroically making tea and coffee for our new friends, numbering fourteen in all. It was quite a task as we only had six mugs, and the instant coffee offerings didn't seem to be very enthusiastically received. At the same time they were checking our passports on their computer.

Eight of them piled into our living room and installed themselves at a table and started putting together their report. We still weren't meant to know what was going on, but it was impossible not to pick up the frequent use of the words '*drogues*', 'cannabis', 'Dieppe' and 'Smith'.

While several of them made verbal contributions, one of them tapped away at his computer, and two others wandered casually around the downstairs of the house, glancing about.

It took them over two hours to complete the report to their mutual satisfaction, and then it had to be read aloud to ourselves and to Fred and his wife, while I translated. When we got to the nitty-gritty, we learned that the truck with the bit of all right driving it had been searched at Dieppe and found to have 475 kilos of cannabis aboard.

Fred seemed undecided as to whether to be angry or pleased at this dramatic revelation.

I said: 'Let's wait and see what happens before jumping to any conclusions. Gloria and Bill weren't even in the vehicle.'

As far as Fred was concerned, that was proof in itself.

The eleven officers in our living room with their handcuffs and guns watched this exchange with polite interest, then took their leave with much hand-shaking. Terry and I resumed our trip to town, while the news snaked through the local English community like a bush-fire out of control. By that evening it was the hot topic.

However, the next morning we all awoke to the news that Princess Diana had been killed, which over-shadowed all other events for the following week or so, during which time calls came and went between Bill and Gloria, still in England, and ourselves, and we learned that Bill's solicitor advised him not to return to France.

Fred had worked himself into a fit of rage. 'If they think we're staying in this hovel looking after their bloody dogs, they've got another think coming!'

He was afraid that he'd end up having to buy the dog food when it ran out.

'I'm not bloody buying it. When it runs out, that's it. They can bloody starve. They said they'd be gone for five days, and we're not staying a minute longer.'

Gloria returned the following weekend, looking worn and bewildered, and she took the dogs and went back to Spain. Although everybody forecast that as soon as he set foot in France Bill would be instantly arrested, much to my surprise he arrived one day and we discussed the raid. He said he had been cleared of any involvement with the drugs and was just getting on with life as before. He started coming and going freely, and nobody arrested him. Gloria returned and things became as normal as they ever did in their household. Bill worked on the house; he'd got a staircase in by now and was putting down some floorboards when he dropped a hammer on Gloria's head. They settled back into their own tumultuous concept of married life.

Chapter Fifteen

Gloria was like a champagne bottle shaken well before opening, and just bubbled over with fun. I think why we got on so well is that we both had an odd sense of humour, and we laughed nearly all the time we were together. Even a drive to the shops, when nothing much was happening, could turn into a giggling spree. We'd be going along in silence, and she'd suddenly wave her hand and snap: 'What's that man doing there, driving a blue car on a Tuesday?' It was absolutely nonsensical and utterly hilarious. She told me that her father had kept a pet shop, and they had a pet Capuchin monkey. One night it had let itself out of its cage and entirely destroyed the shop. She shook with laughter as she told the tale. I could imagine how entertaining it must have been to find a whole shop ruined by one small monkey.

We walked down to the village café one morning for a coffee, and as we approached a man emerged on all fours. He laboriously crawled across the pavement, down the kerb, and across the road to where his car was parked. He dragged himself upright and into it, while Gloria and I watched in astonishment.

'Blimey, it's only eleven o'clock. He's started early!' laughed Gloria.

At the bar, the postmistress/waitress asked what we'd like.

'I think I'll have whatever he's had,' I joked, indicating the crawling man.

'Pardon?' she said.

'Whatever got him in that condition, I'll have the same, please.'

'He had polio,' she said.

'Oops!' Gloria murmured.

She came to tell me I had to go to a party. I said I didn't like parties in general, and the host in particular, and I'd feel bad about accepting his hospitality.

'Oh, don't worry about that – you have to take your own food and a bottle, anyway.' Oh, it was one of those parties.

'No, Glo, I'll give it a miss, thanks.'

'You have to come. If you don't, then we won't, so you'll be spoiling our fun.'

Reluctantly, with my bowl of food and a bottle, I went with them.

Nobody introduced anybody to anybody else, apart from the single French couple there who went round politely introducing themselves and shaking hands; all the other people who knew each other formed into protective enclaves and turned away if you made any attempt to break in. The three of us stood huddled in our own mini-enclave in the kitchen near where our food was laid out, hoping that somebody else we knew would arrive and provide a little variety. I was earnestly hoping we could go home quite early, but Bill and Gloria were enjoying themselves just standing and watching the other guests, and after most of the other people had drifted away we were still lingering around somebody's bowl of fruit salad. Just as I thought we could decently leave, we were shepherded into the living room and scattered around with a handful of other lingerers, quite pleasant people with whom we passed an hour or so of vague conversation. There was that feeling hanging in the air that everybody was ready to stand up and leave, but nobody wanted to be the first. I did want to be the first, but reliant on Bill and Gloria for transport I could not escape until they were ready, and although I rolled my eyes and made as many meaningful faces as I could at them, Gloria just smiled and made faces back, and still we sat.

Our glasses were dry and the wine had run out. Conversations struggled to start and once one did get going we all did our best to keep it in the air. Our host and his partner talked about their three houses in England, and the new house they were planning to buy in Spain.

He suddenly stood up, walked to a cupboard and took out a bottle of cognac.

'What the hell,' he laughed, 'it's my birthday!'

Oh good, thought I, a nice cognac and then we'll all go home. We all sat more upright with anticipation.

He poured a good measure into a tumbler, watched by every hopeful eye in the room, and then he recorked the bottle, returned it to the cupboard and sat down with the full glass, beaming happily. His sipping and swallowing was the only sound in the place; you could have heard a feather drop as we all stared in wonder at this novel approach to hospitality.

'What did you think of the party, then?' Gloria asked later.

'Try not to drag me into anything like that again, will you?'

Sometimes, I managed to wreak my revenge in small but satisfying ways.

Finding hay and straw for the horses in small bales was really difficult. Most of the farms boasted great rolls of the stuff in their fields, but they needed a tractor and fork to lift them. We didn't have a tractor and fork, and just needed a couple of hundred manageable bales to keep us going through the winter. It took quite a while before I was introduced to a local farmer who could supply me, and in the midst of almost intolerable heat which was certainly the precursor to a thunderstorm our delivery of hay arrived, 2,000 kilos of the stuff lying in a tumbled heap of bales in the meadow, and needing to be got under cover before the predicted storm arrived and ruined it all. Gloria, who suffered badly from asthma and probably hadn't done anything more energetic than smoke a cigarette for the last five years, very nobly volunteered to help me, using her little trolley, and the man who'd delivered it kindly mucked in too. I could see him keeping an interested eye on Gloria, and making sure that as she was going through the narrow barn doorway he was coming out, so that they sort of rubbed together. Within a very long hot hour, we had the hay all safely stacked under cover. I went to organize some cold drinks, and through the window saw the hay man becoming quite amorous towards Gloria, feeling her back to see if she was wearing a bra, playing 'round and round the garden' on the palm of her hand, and at one point trying to slide his hand in through the sleeve of her T-shirt. She was both amused and rather alarmed, and I deliberately took my time with the drinks, watching her fielding his assaults.

'Blimey, you took your time with those drinks! I was starting to have a problem holding him off,' she laughed once he'd driven away.

'Did you really?' I asked innocently, trying not to laugh.

Most days we had a cup of tea together in the morning, and on one of these occasions Fred arrived, brandishing something small in his hand.

'It's me toenail – it's come off!' he exclaimed, as we both stared in dismay at the thing in his hand.

'Will you stick it back on for me?' he said in my direction. I have a very weak disposition and faint at the sight of wobbly teeth: detached toenails are right out of my league, so quick as a wink and disregarding her glare, I said: 'Gloria's the one for that. She's more of a nurse than I am.'

No point in trying to tell him that once the things have fallen off they can't be stuck back on. As he turned towards her with his offering, I beat a hasty retreat, and she called out, 'I'll see you later,' in a tone that was half laugh, half threat. I sprinted home laughing my head off.

An English couple moved into a hamlet about two kilometres away, and the poor man fell ill and died very soon after their arrival, leaving a petite fluttery widow who was always perfectly made up and carefully dressed, and a little out of place there in the backwoods. It was plain that she was going to have an uphill struggle adapting to life alone in a country she hardly knew. A week or so after the funeral, quite late one night, the phone rang. It was the dead man's son, to say his mother was distraught and had disappeared into the night, dressed in lightweight clothing and no coat. The neighbours had searched barns, stables, and frosty fields, but there was no sign, he was worried out of his mind, and could I suggest anything. I made a few phone calls in the hope that somebody more enterprising than myself could think of a way to find the lady before she froze to death, which was a real possibility on such a bitter night. The only thing everybody could do was to wait for a sighting, and immediately let everybody else know. I went back to bed feeling frustrated by my inability to do anything. The countryside around was just a whole lot of space dotted with little copses, hamlets, and farmyards: impossible to even know where to begin to look for a missing person.

From the depths of uneasy sleep I heard male voices calling my name, and somebody banging on the patio doors that Terry had fitted to replace the ineffective plastic sheeting, which did a much better job at keeping the wind out and didn't fall down every time there was a gale. As luck would have it I was dressed in standard winter nightwear: an odd assortment of long johns, mountaineering socks, a little woolly hat and several jumpers to counter the terrible cold. I climbed down the stairs and found, standing at the door, our youngest and most attractive neighbour Jean-Luc and his dazzlingly handsome friend, supporting between them a sobbing little figure that they had found tramping down the road to the hamlet. The panic was over, but I didn't feel I'd been seen at my best.

For someone who had lived her married life wrapped in conjugal cotton wool, as Joan had, the change in her circumstances was very hard. Living in the French countryside can be bliss, but it can be hell too: on icy winter days logs need cutting and splitting, lugging into the house, and jamming into the fire; every crack and crevice of old buildings sucks out whatever warmth you are able to generate and replaces it with icy draughts. Chimneys get blocked and instead of filling the house with warmth, fill it with smoke and dust, and layers of ash cover every surface. Torrential rain can turn gardens into an expanse of mud that gets trailed unavoidably into the house; marauding cats and dogs knock over dustbins and scatter their putrid contents over the driveway. When you most need it the car won't start, or breaks down on a bend on a narrow lane, or the boiler fails and there's no hot water. At times like those you could sometimes wonder if you wouldn't be happier in a sheltered housing unit.

She was plagued by a well-meaning, generous but overwhelming neighbour, a buxom lady from the south of France and her Parisian husband, who were openly disliked by the other French residents of the village, as far as I could understand for no other reason than that they weren't local. Mireille just exuded energy and fun, but Joan didn't want either. She mostly wanted to be left on her own, but Mireille was not easily discouraged. Each day she arrived at Joan's front door, always bearing a little gift: a bunch of radishes, a small bouquet, a magazine. While she stood tapping at the door and singing, Joan crouched behind a cupboard in the kitchen until she went away. One day, though, Mireille persuaded her to go and have dinner with them, and invited me along. I explained that I was a vegetarian and didn't want to be a nuisance, but that was no problem, cried Mireille. She loved cooking for vegetarians. And she produced a superb meal, which was wasted on Joan who sat tearfully looking at her watch the whole evening. I felt it my duty to try to scintillate to draw attention away from her, and spent three agonizing hours trying to converse in French, and at the same time politely disregard the huge lump of boiled bacon that had arrived in my bowl of *soupe au pistou*, that quintessentially Provençal dish. I dreaded to think what vegetarian ingredients the main course might include, but Mireille produced a *pissaladière* so perfect that it was almost criminal to eat it. The pastry was thin, transparent, golden, with its filling of caramelized onions, sprinkle of thyme and scattering of olives. The green salad was beyond perfection. Mireille dressed it at the table: a tiny amount of mustard in a little bowl, a splash of best olive oil, and a clove of garlic grated on the tines of a fork.

'Don't crush it; don't chop it, don't use a grater. You won't get the same result,' she explained. 'And no salt, no pepper, no lemon juice or vinegar. Just oil, garlic and mustard.' When she poured the dressing it glistened on the leaves of the salad, and was delicious beyond any description. She was a simply brilliant cook and an enormously affectionate lady, but just too much for a reclusive widow to cope with. She did things like hiding amongst the rhododendrons wearing a miniature yellow and blue umbrella on her head and leaping out waving her arms and yelling 'Aiieeee'.

Try though she did, life here just didn't work for Joan. One well-meaning woman, another expatriate, started on a crusade to prepare her for remarriage.

'You'll have to get that thing removed from your neck, and get something done about your eyelids. Then we'll be able to start circulating you in the right area,' she said encouragingly.

But Joan didn't want to circulate in the right area, or have things done to her neck or eyes, and she didn't want to get married again. She sold up and went back to England.

Chapter Sixteen

An elderly relative died, and left us what would to many people seem a small legacy: to us it was a small fortune. We could have used it to finish our own house, but instead we decided to invest it in restoring two of our decaying buildings: the one which served as the garage, and the small dirt-floored one-up, one-down that flooded to a depth of nearly two feet during heavy rain. Both had once, in the mists of time, been dwelling houses, with their original mantelpieces, inbuilt cupboards, and stone sinks still intact. Despite decades of neglect, both had managed to remain upright with shreds of dignity still clinging to them, though their roofs sagged and allowed unhindered access to the weather, spiders and other assorted insects, and birds. If they weren't renovated very soon they would fall down, leaving us with tons of rubble.

To bring the buildings up to a habitable standard, our small fortune was going to have to be managed with surgical precision, and so we began searching for a builder who could undertake the work without gobbling up all the pennies. We were introduced to an Englishman who was renovating his own house, quite artistically and apparently competently, although it was swallowing up a great deal of money he didn't have. We felt rather sorry

273

for him because he seemed to be a bit of an oddball without any real friends; he was delighted to be asked to undertake our roofing, the first step in renovating the buildings, and within a few days was enthusiastically removing and replacing damaged timbers. The sun shone; I cooked lunch for him daily, three-course meals, with wine; and the roofs started taking shape in a very agreeable fashion. For a few weeks he had a lad assisting him, and we were all happy.

As the roofing project was approaching its end, he asked what we planned to do about the remaining work, and whether we would let him carry it out. As he'd done quite a nice job on the roofs, we agreed that he would continue with the next phase of the work the following year. In the meantime he had his own house to work on and other jobs to keep him going.

The one cloud hovering on the horizon was the state of Bill's property, and the effect it would have on holiday-makers. Bill hadn't been around for several months, and we were going to have to take a very firm hand, and if necessary even enlist the help of the local authorities to get the mess cleared up. But within the next few months fate was thoughtfully going to step in and set up a chain of events that would eventually solve that particular problem.

Gloria went to England that Christmas, leaving Bill dog-sitting. He appeared at our house one morning, grey-faced and almost in tears.

'She's had a heart attack. Gloria's in hospital.' He looked utterly heartbroken.

A few days later we were able to telephone her at her bedside, where she was her habitual perky self. 'Don't worry about me,' she chuckled, 'I'm not ready to pop my clogs just yet,' and after several weeks of convalescence she returned to France.

During her absence Bill had worked frantically to make their house habitable so that she wouldn't have to sleep in the damp caravan, which aggravated her asthma, and by the time she returned she had a cosy bedroom, a warm though rather dishevelled kitchen, and the beginning of a living room.

'He hasn't done too badly,' she said, which coming from her was high praise indeed.

January came round again, cold, wet and miserable. The log burner we'd bought kept the living room reasonably warm, but consumed wood at a frightening rate, so I only lit it in the evenings, and the rest of the house was arctic. Rather than sitting indoors all day shivering, swathed in clothes and flailing my arms around to keep the blood flowing, I started going for long brisk walks, and found I rather enjoyed it. Every day I walked for about two hours, and one day, like a light bulb clicking on, the idea put itself into my mind that I would have an adventure. I'd go for a really long walk.

Back in the freezing house I dug out a map of France and made up my mind to walk from la Rochelle, on the Atlantic west coast, across the country to Lake Geneva in Switzerland, and to write a book about the venture.

My motives were a little hazy, but one thing that appealed quite strongly was the prospect of being out of reach, for a few weeks, of mad French women who wanted me to kidnap animals, and demanding English people who expected me to act as a communal unpaid secretary for them.

I started to prepare for this escape/expedition, with the help of Bill and Gloria who took me on forays to locate tents, boots and the other equipment that was necessary for the enterprise. They were very supportive and encouraging, and Gloria joined me on my daily hikes. She'd been told by her doctor that she must give up smoking, and showed what a very strong character she was by stopping immediately and never mentioning cigarettes again, although she had been a heavy smoker up to then. At first she was not overly enthusiastic when I suggested some exercise might be good for her, but soon she was waiting at her gate each day, with a tiny backpack containing her mobile phone and wearing a pair of high-heeled lace-up boots, and we tramped round the neighbourhood together. It was quite fun, especially once the weather improved. We ambled along – she was not up to my speed, or to any great distance – and after about half an hour we sat on the ground for a while and put the world to rights.

To get used to the weight I would be carrying, I wore a backpack loaded with encyclopedias. The neighbours frequently nodded and waved as I trundled past, and if they thought it strange that I disappeared each day for several hours with a loaded pack which was still with me when I returned, they were too polite to ask why. I wore a pedometer to measure the distance I covered. On the first day that I walked 20 miles, it told me that that had involved 43,680 footsteps. If the journey to Geneva covered 600 miles, as it well might, that would mean a total of 1,310,400 steps. The thing about the pedometer was that in order for it to record each step accurately, it needed a little jerk, a harder jerk than my normal walking style produced. And so I had to put my right foot down with a slight stamp, and I doubted that I could keep that up over half a million times.

In mid-March Gloria returned to England again for a medical check-up, and while she was away, one Sunday morning, Bill called out: 'Could you come and help? There's a couple of people here, but they're French and I can't understand what they're saying.'

They were a relaxed couple in their mid-thirties.

I introduced myself and asked how I could help them.

'Well, we're looking for a house to buy in the country,

and we understand this one is for sale.' They indicated the cottage betwen Bill and myself, where old Mme Guillot had sat outside on her bench enjoying the late afternoon sun until her death.

'Yes, that's right. I can give you the phone number of the owner, if you like.'

'We'd really like to have a look round the outside, if that's possible?'

I knew that M. Guillot was keen to sell. The cottage had been with an estate agent for over two years, but the eyesore of Bill's place was enough to put off any prospective buyers, and I often saw people drive up, take one look and drive away again without even getting out of their car.

'Yes, I'll be happy to show you round,' I said, and proceeded to lead them over every inch of land, burbling about each tree, bush, bird and boundary, until they finally excused themselves and said they would ring the owner. They were pleasant and very sociable, and asked how long I'd been living here. Something they said made me realize that they thought I was Bill's wife.

'No,' I laughed, 'he's not my husband – we're just neighbours.'

'Ah! And did you know each other before you moved here?'

No, I explained, it was just by coincidence that we came to be living next to each other.

They asked whether I went back to England often, and whether Bill did, and whether I worked, and whether I enjoyed living here, and I thought what very charming people they were.

When they'd gone, M. Meneteau called over the hedge. 'What did those people want?'

'They're interested in Madame Guillot's house. They're from Poitiers and want a weekend cottage.'

He wagged a finger. 'Be careful. They were parked

here yesterday. Don't trust them; they aren't what you think they are.'

'How do you mean?'

'Just don't trust them,' he warned.

I assumed he meant that they were potential burglars, but from their clothing, car and general manner I knew there was no chance that was the case, and thought he was just being rather melodramatic.

Bill and I went to town next morning and rummaged through second-hand shops and junk yards. I found a wood-burning cooker which was far too heavy to fit in the car.

'Don't worry,' Bill said. 'I'll go back and collect it for you this afternoon in the pick-up.'

We got back home, and I'd just finished lunch when the phone rang. It was Gloria.

'What's going on with Bill?' she snapped.

Well, for heaven's sake, I thought. What on earth is she talking about?

'Sorry, Glo, what do you mean?'

'I've just phoned him. He picked up the phone and said "The police have got me", and then the phone was slammed down. I want to know what's going on.'

'OK. I'll go round and see if I can find out what's happening. Don't worry. I'll ring you back in a few minutes.'

I snatched up a cup and ambled round the corner humming nonchalantly. Outside Bill's front door stood two men in plain clothes.

'*Bonjour*,' I called cheerily and tried to glide past them.

'Stop, madame! You cannot go in there.'

'Of course I can. I need a cup of sugar.' (I know it wasn't very original.) I waved the cup at them and kept walking towards the door. They moved into the doorway, blocking it.

'You cannot go in there.'

'Why not?'

The door opened and over the shoulders of a couple of uniformed policemen I could see Bill's anxious face.

'Are you OK, Bill?'

'Do not talk to this man. Go back to your own house,' said one of the men in the doorway rudely.

'No, please wait a minute,' called one of the policemen. 'Are you the English lady who lives round the corner?'

'I am.'

'Well, we would like you to look after this gentleman's dogs for a couple of days.'

'Why? Where's he going?'

'It's nothing to worry about. We're just taking him to answer some questions. Will you look after the dogs?'

'Yes, of course I will, but I don't know where the food is kept, or what they have. Please can I just ask Mr Smith?'

'No, you cannot. You must find the food and decide for yourself how much to give them.'

They led Bill into one of the cars and sped off.

I phoned Gloria to tell her the news.

'That's great, isn't it! Here's me just recovering from a heart attack, and he goes and gets himself arrested! Stupid bastard. I'll get the first train back.'

It was seven months since Bill's truck had been found with the cannabis aboard, and we had all assumed that nothing more was going to be heard of that affair. And we were all quite wrong. Many months later, Bill told me that when he was taken to the police station, the young couple of 'house-hunters' were there. They were plain-clothes detectives.

Word of Bill's arrest spread rapidly, and locally the debate about whether or not he was guilty, and what would happen to him, was the focus of conversation.

Most people, it seemed from listening to them, wanted him to be guilty, because that would be far more exciting than if he wasn't. With hindsight, nearly everybody could remember something suspicious he had said or done, or might have said or done. The concensus was that he was getting what he justly deserved. Most people simply enjoyed the scandal; one or two people defended him whole-heartedly; Fred seemed to be ecstatic and said he hoped Gloria would be arrested too.

Untidy and infuriatingly unreliable as he could be, Bill had a lot of nice qualities and I was quite fond of him when he wasn't irritating me. I didn't want to think of him mouldering away for the rest of his life in an *oubliette* if he was innocent.

The two days passed. Bill was charged with drug trafficking and remanded in prison.

Gloria arrived back and started a daily routine of phoning solicitors in England, and the French solicitor appointed by the court to represent Bill. As the solicitor didn't speak English, nor Gloria French, I interpreted these calls. Things weren't looking good for Bill.

Their situation was dire. She had no money; she was recovering from a heart attack; Bill was being held in prison and there was no indication how long he was going to be there. Somehow she had to find enough to keep herself – and, more important to her, her dogs – fed. She sold off bits and pieces; the buyers, knowing her situation, tried to beat her down. People who owed her money avoided her. People who didn't owe her money avoided her.

I started getting phone calls from people I knew.

'You want to watch yourself. You're getting a bad reputation,' one person told me.

'What do you mean?'

'Well, running around with that drug dealer's wife. You can imagine what people are saying about you.'

'No. I can't. What are they saying, exactly?'

'It's obvious, isn't it? You're in it with them.'

'In *what*?' I was so angry I nearly grew feathers.

'Well, I'm just giving you a friendly warning. Watch out before you find yourself in prison.'

A 'friend' rang.

'Oh, Susie, I'm so worried about you. You're going around with that woman. I'm terribly afraid you'll be arrested.'

'How can I be arrested for going shopping with somebody, or having coffee with her?'

'Well, he's in prison for drug dealing. You'll be branded with them.'

'Can we just put this straight: he's been charged. He has not been tried, or found guilty. Gloria hasn't even been questioned. She isn't under suspicion. And just at the moment she can use all the friends she can get. What's happened to you recently?'

The phone went dead.

I felt I learned a bit about human nature during this episode, but none of it seemed to crush Gloria. She was her normal spirited, cheerful self. She had a computer, slightly elderly, which frequently gave her additional problems.

'One day,' she said, 'I'm going to get one of those Pantechnicon Two computers.'

'A what?'

'You know – the Pantechnicon.'

'Do you mean a Pentium?'

'Yes, that's right. That's what I said.'

It was bad enough when the computers went wrong; trying to explain the problems to a French engineer was virtually impossible, and through enquiries we found an English one.

'Bring it over, and I'll have a look at it for you,' he said.

So off we drove and met a gorgeous cuddly man named Keith, with a very nice wife called Beryl with bright blue laughing eyes. Over the years Keith patched up and repaired my computers more times than I could count.

'I don't know what you do to them, Susie,' he used to say as I turned up for the umpteenth time.

'I don't *do* anything to the damned things. *They* just keep doing weird things.'

'Never mind, let's have a look.' If it hadn't been for Keith, I'd never have been able to write.

'Are you going to put me in your book?' he asked.

'You bet.' There you are, Keith. And thanks for everything.

Despite her bleak situation, Gloria wasn't going to let an opportunity to have a bit of fun pass her by, and she spotted a poster for a Country and Western evening in a nearby village hall.

'Shall we go?'

I mentally groaned. It wasn't how I'd have chosen to spend an evening, but it seeemed a bit mean to deprive her of an opportunity to get out, so I agreed.

'What are you wearing?' she phoned to ask on the afternoon.

'Oh, usual, jeans and a sweater.'

'No, you can't! I thought we were going to get all dressed up nicely.'

'But people don't round here. Jeans and a sweater *is* dressed up.'

'Come on, let's give them something to look at. I'm getting myself dolled up. You put on something nice. Be a sport.'

How could I refuse?

Reluctantly I climbed into a mid-calf skirt with a short slit up the back, and a demure top. I dabbed some

282

make-up on and put on a pair of high heels.

Gloria was a sight to stop the traffic.

The long crimson skirt she was wearing was like a big tassel: almost down to her ankles, it was slit to the hip in about eight places. She wore black fishnet stockings and black patent stiletto heels. Her freckled golden bosom pouted over the low-cut black top she wore beneath a black leather fringed jacket. She sported huge gold hoop earrings, a gold necklace, several chunky gold bracelets and about a dozen rings. Her hair was piled high in a bouffant blonde crown; false eyelashes, startling turquoise eye shadow, scarlet lipstick. She was showing them all.

When we sashayed into the village hall, silence fell, jaws fell, and eyes blinked as we strolled casually over to a table. It was quite fun seeing the reaction of the other merrymakers. Two unsavoury characters grabbed four beers each and headed over to our table.

'May we?' asked one as he plopped into a chair.

'Sure. Nice to have some company,' Gloria chirped, just as I opened my mouth to say no.

The second chap, who looked like a cushion with a string tied round it, sat down next to me. I ignored him.

Gloria chattered away brightly, sometimes kicking me under the table and indicating I should smile, but I didn't.

'So you've got a *van!*' Violent kick. 'We've got a cooker to be collected from town. And you two want to be shown round the second-hand shops. Well, we'll show you round if you bring the cooker back. Won't we?' She kicked me again.

I smiled weakly and said I'd be glad to take them sightseeing. We arranged to meet the next day.

'May we invite you two ladies out for lunch on Sunday?' enquired one of our new friends.

'No thank you.'

'Yes, we'd love to!' Another kick.

I scowled at Gloria, but she babbled on.

'We'll go to the . . .' She named a local restaurant.

'It's Easter Sunday. Their menu is priced at two hundred and twenty francs,' I told them.

Cushion-body paled a bit, but his friend said, 'No problem. Two lovely ladies deserve the best.'

They went to restock with beers, another four bottles apiece, and I snapped at Gloria: 'Why on earth have you got us lumbered with this pair?'

'Look, dearie,' she had started calling me 'dearie', like Fred, because she knew I hated it, 'you need to collect that cooker, don't you? How else are you going to get it back? You've got to be practical.'

She was right – I'd paid for the thing and Bill had inconsiderately got himself arrested before collecting it.

The next morning we called for our chauffeurs and found them still asleep. They were not at all enthuiastic about the cooker project, but Gloria trilled and smiled and flashed her eyes, made them each a cup of tea while they got themselves ready, and finally succeeded in forcing them into the van, completely ignoring their obvious reluctance. We kept to our part of the bargain by taking them on a guided tour of the second-hand shops, and got the cooker back; after they had struggled to manoeuvre it into our house, we never saw them again. Easter Sunday came and went.

'Shame, really,' said Gloria ruefully. 'I'd have liked a good meal out.'

And for ever after, when we reminisced about that evening, she would say, 'Hey, remember when we went out dressed like a couple of tarts?'

Because Terry couldn't stay here and look after the animals whilst I went walking across France, and I couldn't possibly expect Gloria to do so, I had put out a message on the Internet and found a quite extraordinary lady called Jennifer Shields, from San Antonio, Texas, who was coming to hold the fort during my absence. Her ticket was booked, and it was far too late to cancel the project, but I did rather feel I shouldn't be going away with Gloria in such a sorry state and poor old Bill banged up in the pokey. Up until the last minute I dithered with the idea of calling the whole thing off, but very happily Jennifer and Gloria hit it off immediately, so abandoning them, my animals, and anybody who wanted anything at all, I set off for seven weeks of glorious solitude, phoning home daily to keep up to date with events.

With Bill under lock and key, Gloria had somehow to keep their removals business running, because it was her only possible source of income. The occasional job came in, she still had one truck left, and she managed to find drivers when they were needed. But while I was ambling over the *massif central*, I learned that a new driver, crossing the border from Spain into France, had chosen to make the crossing at a very remote and unlikely point, where he was stopped, searched and found in possession of cannabis. Gloria had to get herself there to try to sort out this new dilemma, risking arrest herself because drugs had been found in her vehicle. When she arrived the driver had been allowed to go, and had disappeared with the truck's keys. The truck was thoroughly searched by police, customs and a sniffer dog flown in by helicopter. And when I say thoroughly searched, I mean that they ripped open soft furnishings, drilled through garden statuary and took apart everything that could be dismantled. Finding nothing, they departed, leaving Gloria to put the mess together and find another driver and a new set of keys for the vehicle so that it could continue on its journey.

The truck contained two loads of furniture. When it arrived in England at the first point of unloading, the person whose furniture had been slashed and drilled was understandably distressed and sequestered the vehicle, which still had the second person's belongings in it. The first person wouldn't pay the bill, the second person couldn't get their goods so wouldn't pay either and was threatening police action, and the truck was immobilized and out of service. And the driver wanted his money.

'How on earth is Gloria coping with all this?' I asked Jennifer during one of our daily telephone conversations. Remember, only five months previously Gloria had suffered a heart attack.

'Oh, she's just fine,' Jennifer assured me. 'Don't worry about her, she's doing great.'

The day I reached Geneva, I learned that Bill had been released from the prison where he had been held on remand.

Chapter Seventeen

Once I was back home from my travels I started writing an account of my journey across France, based on the reams of notes I had written along the way. With a nice stack of clean paper and a blank screen, I settled down to get on with it.

It had taken me fifty-two days, hobbling and slithering for over five hundred and fifty miles, alone, with an overweight backpack, from la Rochelle to the shores of Lake Geneva. Despite the months of training I'd done beforehand, I was unfit when I set off, and just as unfit when I finished. Most of the time I was lost, and I was always at the limit of my stamina; but the trail had led to many fascinating places, from the tiny villages hidden away from the beaten track to lovely towns like Paray-le-Monial and Digoin; and from the lowlands of the Charente Maritime across the endless bumps of the *massif central* to the exquisite uplands of the Jura.

Travelling alone had been a challenge, as had coping with a terribly inadequate tent that leaked and manufactured its own abundant condensation, and a sleeping bag that was no thicker than a tea cloth. Daytime temperatures soared into the 80s, and at night the mercury frequently fell below zero. My feet were blistered from the day I started until two days before I finished;

sometimes I'd felt like giving up, but the people I met along the way – who were almost invariably helpful and friendly, apart from an occasional lunatic – the beauty of each region I crossed, and the sense of personal achievement I felt each night when I reached a new stopping point, inspired me to keep going. Having a sense of humour had helped, too, being able to laugh at myself, a fifty-something Englishwoman struggling for hundreds of miles across terrain she knew nothing about, laden, exhausted, and lost, for no other reason than that it had seemed like a good idea at the time.

Anyway, now I was back home and the scars had healed, I was thoroughly looking forward to reliving the adventure and getting it down on paper.

It turned out to be much more difficult than I'd anticipated, in fact more difficult than the journey itself, because all sorts of people regularly descended unannounced to demand my services. At first I tried explaining, gently, that I needed some time to myself, without unnecessary interruptions, and would be delighted to see them some other time, but not just at the moment. Their reactions were unanimous: it was a total and silly waste of my time, writing a book that nobody would want to read, when I'd be far more usefully employed sorting out their various problems.

Polite hints, blunt words, nothing deterred these people, so I put a little notice at the gate, which read: 'Hi! Sorry, but I'm busy at present, and would be grateful not to be disturbed, but if you leave a message using the pen and paper in the letter box, I'll give you a call later on.'

People read the message, and came to the front door tutting with sympathy.

'Oh, you *poor* thing! People really are *so* inconsiderate not to leave you in peace. Come on, let's have a cup of coffee. By the way, I've just had this letter from the tax office; you'll have to translate it for me. Then you can write your book later.'

I padlocked the gate with a heavy chain and stuck a mirror on a broom handle. When the dogs barked, from the office I could see who was at the gate without being seen myself. If it was somebody I wanted to see, I could let them in; the rest I could ignore. Most people gave up after five minutes, although more determined parties tried to find a way in through the field and up the garden, but the geese usually got them.

Unable to attract my attention physically, they started a telephonic offensive. Sometimes I just had to laugh. People arriving here unable to speak the language bestowed upon me a moral obligation to solve their problems. The telephone answering machine allowed me to hear who it was and what they wanted.

'Really, this is the fourth message we've left this week, and we've been round three times. We've got a problem with our electricity/gas/neighbours/car/cooker, and we can never get hold of you. Kindly phone back as soon as you get this message.'

Why me? There were plenty of other English people locally, none of whom seemed to be so continually in demand. Eventually the penny dropped. When Terry was here, I was left alone, but as soon as he'd gone my customers returned. I overheard somebody saying to one of their friends, 'Ask Susie to do it. She's got all her time to herself; she's probably bored out of her brains and will be delighted to have something to do.' I think they really believed it.

With the dogs barking as people rattled the gate several times a day, the telephone ringing half a dozen times, and people screaming as they fled from the geese, I admitted defeat and confined my writing to the hours between 10 p.m. and 2.00 a.m.

For all the phone calls I made, and letters I posted,

often for complete strangers, it was a very rare fish who offered to pay for the calls or stamps. A friend said she found the same thing, and somebody else overheard our conversation and said they too never got reimbursed for such items. One of them said, 'I think it's because people who come out from England think that because we live in France we must be rich and won't mind buying their stamps and things for them. Nobody ever offers.'

I looked at the state of our house, the bare stone walls with bits missing, the empty window frames covered in plastic sheeting, and supposed such people merely thought I was a wealthy eccentric.

Fred was still a regular visitor, and seemed to be fervently hoping that Bill would be arrested again. I'd never known anybody act in what seemed to me such a malicious way.

Round the corner Bill and Gloria's situation was worsening. Although he was out of prison, he would have to stand trial, and in the meantime he wasn't allowed to leave the country; he also wasn't allowed to work in France, as he didn't hold a residence permit, so he was unable to earn a living. Every Tuesday he had to drive to the local *gendarmerie* and sign a register. Failing to turn up on time could lead to his rearrest and return to prison. Whatever money they had previously had been swallowed up by lawyers, both in England and France. The original truck containing the drugs had been confiscated by customs; their truck in England had been appropriated by customer number one with customer number two's furniture still on board; the lawyers still wanted paying in order to continue representing Bill until a trial had taken place, and there was no indication at all of when this might be – it could be years hence. It was a nightmare.

They started selling off bits and pieces, of which Bill

had accumulated a multitude, but it wasn't much more than a small drop in a very large ocean. Gloria returned to England to try to sort out the problem with the truck that was still immobilized in one customer's garden with the other customer's furniture.

While she was away, Bill came across one afternoon, looking more worried than usual.

'I haven't seen Horace since this morning,' he said. Horace was one of the Great Danes. 'He's not been looking at all well. Would you come and help me find him?'

I knew what we were going to find, and so I think did Bill.

We went to the old caravan where the dogs had their beds, and found Horace there, curled up peacefully, in a ray of sunshine, just as if he was asleep. He'd popped his clogs. This seemed to hit Gloria harder than anything else that had happened to them.

Bill kept working away at their house and finally got it to a habitable state. Outside it was still a jungle, but he'd tiled the floors, papered the walls and put in a staircase and a bathroom, and he was very proud of his work. Gloria dug out furniture from the Pandora's boxes in the barn; she hung curtains and dotted pot plants and plastic flowers and orrnaments around, and if you could close your eyes to the desolation outside it was quite homely.

Gloria was delighted. 'Now we can sell it!' she declared.

It was their only option. Nobody could give any indication at all of when Bill would be free to leave the country and start earning again. But he was angry and heartbroken that he was going to lose the home he loved and had worked so hard to build.

Gloria contacted an estate agent and put the property up for sale.

As our house was still looking very much the worse for wear, I felt I ought to do something about decorating, so

I dug out a few pots of paint and a brush. I didn't tell Terry, as I wanted it to be a surprise. Then he did one of those impenetrably thoughtless things that husbands sometimes do. He phoned and said: 'Guess what? You're having a visitor!'

'How lovely,' I responded, trying to sound enthusiastic, as if I wasn't sick to death of uninvited visitors. 'Who is it?'

He named an old friend of his, Ken, whom I'd met a couple of times, the last time at least ten years previously.

'Oh, yes, I like him. It'll be nice to see him. When's he coming?'

'Tomorrow.'

'Right, I'd better organize something for lunch. How long will he be here for?'

'Six months.'

'What? Where's he going to stay?'

'I said he could stay with you.' The ensuing silence must have conveyed more than words ever could. 'It'll be nice for you to have some company.' Why could nobody understand that I didn't *want* company?

'Where's he going to sleep? We only have one bedroom, or had you forgotten?' I was steaming.

'Well, surely you can sort out something for him. What about the living room?'

'I'm painting the living room,' (ruining the surprise). 'It's full of ladders, paint pots, brushes, splashes and cloths.'

'You'll sort something out,' chortled my spouse confidently, and dumped the whole problem squarely on me.

I stared round at the devastation that was the living room, the makeshift kitchen, the half-finished bathroom and the sleeping space that didn't exist, and I cursed and stamped my feet and shouted at the heavens, then picked up the phone and booked a room for my portending visitor at a local guesthouse.

* * *

One day, Gloria dropped a bombshell.

'How much would it cost to have the house put in our name?' she asked.

'What house?'

'This one.' She waved her arm at their place.

'I'm sorry, I don't understand what you mean. Surely it's in your name already?'

'No, apparently it isn't, because when Bill bought it he paid cash to the lady, and got a receipt, but he never went to the *notaire* to do the official paperwork, so it's still in the previous owner's name.'

I stared at her while I digested this information. 'Then legally the property still belongs to the previous owner. Why on earth didn't Bill go to the *notaire*?'

'That's Bill, isn't it? He paid, he got a receipt, it's his. That's how his mind works. But it doesn't really matter, does it?'

I had until then thought that the biggest obstacle to the sale of the property was its condition; this latest news bleached that into insignificance. In the almost unimaginable event that somebody wanted to buy the place, the chances that they would be prepared to do so if it was not in the name of the person selling it were practically non-existent.

'Does the estate agent know about this?' I asked.

'Oh yes, but he says it doesn't matter.'

Of course he would. Estate agents say things like that. The last thing I wanted to do was give Gloria any more worries, but I knew that the paperwork to register the house in their name would cost at least a couple of thousand pounds, which I also knew they didn't have. So I just said, 'Oh, well, that's OK then. Let's just see what happens.'

The estate agent called them from time to time promising he was bringing 'an almost certain buyer', but nobody bought.

Months went by. Their situation was hopeless, despite support from the French state and regional authorities who were not unsympathetic and did what they could to help financially within the framework of their system. With Bill grounded and unable to earn a living, there was nothing for it except for Gloria to return to England and find work, which she did with her usual cheerfulness, as a companion to elderly people. We joked about her 'going into service', and christened her 'Little Effie'.

Some people came to visit Fred, and expressed an interest in buying Bill's house. Actually it was Fred who was pushing them to do so, as he needed a lot of storage space, which his own house didn't have. He confided to me that if he could get his friends to buy Bill's place, he'd get the use of the space for nothing.

The prospective purchasers made an offer; Bill was half pleased, half sad. He knew he had to sell, but he really didn't want to. He called Gloria in England, and told her of the offer.

'Take it,' she said. So he accepted.

The next day, the deal was off – the purchasers had thought it over and changed their minds. Bill was half pleased, half sad once more, and decided to double the asking price.

Ken, who had moved into our living room as soon as I finished painting it, was spending more and more time with Bill. 'You know, I rather like that house,' he murmured one day.

'Are you going to buy it?'

'I might just do that.'

It seemed ideal. Bill and Gloria would sell the house, and Ken would have a house he liked, next to us, his friends. He would tidy it up and we could stop worrying about the effect the place would have on our holiday guests. I explained the hitch about the ownership of the house to Ken, introduced him to the legal owner, and said that I knew the sale could and would go through and that neither Ken nor Bill need have any fears regarding payment and title. So off went Ken, and made an offer. And in doing so, he made one very small but important error.

He told Bill he was a cash buyer.

Most of us understand that as meaning you've got all the necessary money, and don't need to get a mortgage. Bill understood that Ken would pay him in crisp notes, and in return Bill would give Ken the keys and a receipt. Again Bill was half sad, half happy. Gloria, when Bill phoned her, was ecstatic. They were getting rid of the house she didn't want, and an end to their immediate financial worries was at last in sight.

Ken asked me to make arrangements for the *notaire* to start getting the necessary paperwork together. I went to tell Bill that I was making the appointment for Ken and the actual owner to do the signing of the preliminary agreement to purchase. They were all happy for Bill to be present, although in legal terms it did not concern him.

'I'm not selling through the *notaire*. Ken said he was paying cash.'

Through long hours, I tried to explain that a cash buyer didn't hand over large amounts of cash without the legal paperwork being in order, but Bill wouldn't listen.

'I bought this place cash. I paid cash, and I've a receipt to prove it. It's my house, and I can sell it any way I like.'

My short temper, which had stretched such a long way that I was proud of it, finally snapped. I said: 'It isn't your house. It doesn't matter how many receipts you have, whether they are carved in stone or written on tablets of gold, it isn't your house until you have a legal document saying so. And as you haven't, you're very lucky indeed to have found a buyer.'

Later, Gloria rang from England.

'You just go ahead,' she said. 'It's a waste of time trying to reason with him. You sort out the meeting with the *notaire* for Ken and the owner.'

Bill didn't want to be involved in the meeting, so Gloria came back to France and together we met the owner at the *notaire*'s office, where I was the 'official translator' and Ken paid the agreed deposit for the house. Gloria was pleased that the wheels were in motion, but Bill was unsatisfied and becoming more difficult by the day.

'You'd no business involving a *notaire*. This was meant to be a cash deal.'

There are times when you have to accept that you are never going to succeed in getting a point across to a particular person; this was one of them. When Bill made up his mind about something, there wasn't much you could do to change it.

There was some land involved, which by law had to be advertised and offered to the local farmers before it could change hands, and it would be almost three months before the sale was finalized.

Ken went off to England, and now Bill really did start getting difficult.

Every day he came to ask when Ken was returning. I couldn't tell him, because Ken wasn't answering my messages, but I said I was certain he'd be back before too long.

'I've seen no money from him yet.'

'Well, I keep telling you, you won't. The deposit has been paid to the *notaire*, and the balance will be paid to him when the final papers are signed. He has to pay any outstanding taxes due, then he'll send a cheque to the registered owners, and they'll pay you. That's the way it works.'

'I'm not accepting that. I want cash. He said he'd pay cash, and now he's trying to cheat me.'

We encircled the 'cash buyer' scenario yet again. I just wasn't making any headway.

'Anyway,' said Bill, 'I'm putting the price up. Doubling it.'

'OK, fine.'

'Or I might take it off the market completely.'

'OK, fine.'

The poor man was stressed to breaking point. I understood, I sympathized, but I was seriously beginning to feel I'd had enough of this drama on our doorstep. I started creeping down through our field and out of the back gate to go for long walks without having to pass Bill's house and risk being ambushed. Some days I went off in the car with a book and drove to a field somewhere and sat and read quietly.

The days passed infinitely slowly. Two days before the signing of the final papers was due to take place, the *notaire*'s secretary phoned to say that he had decided to go on holiday, and the meeting was put back a fortnight. Now everybody was furious and suspicious of everybody else. So frustrated did I become that I would have wished the place would explode, except that I knew it wasn't insured.

Then something else happened.

In between Bill and M. Meneteau stood the tiny vine-strangled tumbledown house and large barn that belonged to the Guillot family, who also owned the empty cottage the other side of Bill's place. Bill had often talked in the past of buying the small house once 'his' house was sold, and both M. Meneteau and myself were very curious as to whether or not he was going to do so. Bill had been playing his cards very close to his chest on this one. We both liked him as a person, but the constant eyesore his property represented had been a thorn in our flesh for years. The prospect of the mess's simply migrating twenty metres and being with us for ever was not a happy one.

One day M. Meneteau came round and said that Bill definitely wasn't buying the place because Gloria wouldn't let him, although how he knew that I'd no idea. But it put both our minds at rest, anyway, until I got a phone call about four days before the final transaction with Ken was due to take place. It was Gloria, highly excited because Bill had had a row with somebody who was trying to buy the little house from under his nose. 'He's fit to be tied!' she said. 'He's going to buy all the spare land in the village and turn it into a pig farm!'

That sounded like one of Bill's schemes. But her call had confirmed my worst fears – the junk yard wasn't going away, it was just planning to relocate.

I picked up the phone and rang M. Guillot, and asked if he really was selling to Bill.

'If he has the money, yes. I'll sell to the first person who pays a deposit. Bill is bringing me the money as soon as he has sold his house.'

'If I can find another buyer for you before then, will you sell it to them?'

'Yes, of course. We'd like to sell to somebody who'll make the place look nice. We don't really want to sell to Bill, but if he has the money . . .'

I called Terry immediately. 'We've got a problem.' I relayed the latest news to him. 'If Bill stays here, we can say goodbye to our *gîte* project – our guests will be demanding their money back if they arrive and see the state of the place. Do we know anybody who might want to buy the house?'

Terry phoned back half an hour later. Somebody he knew would buy it. I phoned M. Guillot, arranged to see him the following day, and put down a deposit on the house. We shook hands, and the deal was struck.

The day before Ken's final signing, Bill came round in high spirits. 'I've got a surprise for you!' he announced gleefully.

'What is it?'

'You'll have to wait and see tomorrow. Maybe you'll be having a new neighbour that you didn't expect!'

He was beaming with delight, and the last time I'd felt so terribly mean and treacherous was when I gave the cockerels to the neighbours to eat.

The signing day came and the air was as taut as a violin string. For some reason Bill had blocked the lane so I couldn't get my car out. He didn't want me to go to the signing.

'Bill, I have to be there. Somebody has to translate, and they don't have anybody but me.'

'How do I know I'm not going to be cheated?'

'Well, Gloria's going to be there. She'll see what's happening and I'll explain what's being said. Please don't worry. Nobody is going to cheat you.'

'This should never have happened. He said he was paying cash.'

'Please, Bill, move your truck.'

He eventually let me out.

We all arrived at the *notaire*'s office and sat facing him across his antique desk. He read out the *Acte de Vente*, I translated it for Ken and Gloria's benefit. We came to the part when the money is handed over, and Ken explained, via myself, that he was going to pay the whole amount in cash to the lady who had sold the property to Bill but was still, legally, the owner. This is what he'd agreed with Bill. I'd told them that it wouldn't be acceptable to the *notaire*, but nobody ever took any notice of anything I said, and this was no exception.

'Ah no.' The *notaire* shook his head. 'I'm sorry, but the payment has to be made to me, by cheque or international money order. I have to pay any taxes due, and will then pay the rest by cheque to madame.' He indicated the owner of the property. Ken had to return to England later that day, and so was allowed to sign the documents. The owner would sign once the money was received.

Gloria was utterly crestfallen, and her mobile phone started ringing.

Outside, she explained to Bill why the sale hadn't gone ahead, and confirmed his worst fears. He started yelling at her, she yelled at him, and I wanted to get drunk.

Ken returned to England to sort out the money transfer to the *notaire*, and to arrange shipment of his furniture.

Bill and Gloria had already moved out, under much protest from Bill, into rented accommodation nearby, which was just as well because the new owner of the tiny vine-covered house arrived the next day to inspect his purchase. We crept around the property at dawn, anxious that Bill should not see us, as he had no idea the house was sold.

When it seemed the drama would never end, the *notaire* telephoned to say Ken's money had arrived, the owner had signed and the house now belonged to Ken. Now everybody should be happy. Little Effie was once more back in England working, and the previous owner telephoned Bill to tell him that they'd pay him as soon as they'd received the cheque from the *notaire*.

Ken returned with a truck full of furniture, and telephoned Bill to ask him to bring the keys to the property. Bill said he'd be there in a few minutes. When an hour later there was no sign of him or the keys, we phoned again. Bill was feeding his dogs, he said. He'd come when he was ready.

About five hours later, he materialized, and I can't recall ever seeing anybody in quite such a rage. He was absolutely glowing with fury. He'd just learned that the little house had been sold to somebody else, although he didn't yet know who.

'You stupid bastard,' he yelled at Ken, 'I've lost a damned good property because of you. It was meant to be a cash deal!' He raised his fists, which was both brave and very foolhardy as Ken was at least a foot taller and 50 pounds heavier than him.

I stood in the kitchen, watching these two men squaring up to each other and shouting, and thought back to our arrival and my dreams of a peaceful pastoral existence. How had I ended up standing here with a fist fight just about to break out? Why was all this happening in our house?

The men were shouting at each other and waving their fists, and my little rubber band snapped once more.

'You, out!' I shrieked at Bill. 'Get this nonsense out of our house! I've had enough. ENOUGH!'

The men broke off their engagement to stare at me in shared astonishment, and lowered their arms. Bill stamped away, muttering dire threats, and that was the last I saw of him.

I wanted to run after him and shake him and say, 'Bill, I understand. I know what you've been through, and I know you're hurting. I'm not proud of what I've done, snatching that house from under your nose. But fond as I am of you, we just couldn't live with your mess on our doorstep any more.'

But I knew it would be a total waste of time.

Ken started moving in, and we wandered round the property, hacking at the brambles and nettles and pulling things out of the undergrowth. Amongst an extraordinary collection of diverse objects we found 3 engines and 2 exhaust systems; an ice-cream trolley; a box containing somebody's family photographs; 2 King Edward cigars (smokeable) and a bundle of soft pornographic magazines; the cow-catcher from a Range Rover; a single flipper; a mechanical fertilizer distributor; a damaged but complete sports car and an enormous lawn roller, the sort that a tractor pulls.

That evening I just stood and looked at Bill's house for a while. It was going to take years of work to make it and the garden look respectable, but it was a relief to know that the days of mess were over. And yet I couldn't help feeling quite sad, because it was the end of Bill's dream, and however irritating he could be, however messy and disorganized I found him, and although we had fallen out from time to time, he was well meaning, and he had loved his house very much. He'd worked enormously hard, and it wasn't a bad effort by just one man. In many ways I'd miss him.

The only time I'd ever seen Gloria weep was when one of her dogs had one of its monumental nose bleeds, when she had sat with her head on her lap and her shoulders heaving. We were so different from each other: she was a bright bubbly extrovert, I was more of a hermit; she craved a bustling life in a busy place, I loved being far away from all that; the only things we really had in common were a rather weird sense of humour and the fact that we both loved animals. I had very great admiration for her strength under extreme pressure; we'd been through quite a lot together, and I knew that I'd miss her flashing smile and our ridiculous expeditions.

The last time I saw her, I said: 'You'll come and say goodbye before you leave for good, won't you?'

She'd looked away for a moment and said: 'I don't like

302

saying goodbyes, but I'll be in touch one of these days.'
And she drove off.

Bill was still awaiting the trial for which no date had
been set. He did what most of us would have done, and
slipped back to England.

In his absence, he was tried, and found not guilty.

Chapter Eighteen

Our building project was under way again, and there
were signs of discord. Terry was only here for a few days
at a time about once a month, so during his absence it
was my job to explain what we wanted doing. I don't
think our builder, for want of a better word, particularly
liked feeling that he was taking orders from a woman,
and in no time at all every little thing I wanted became
the focus of a minor skirmish. What layout did I have in
mind? I drew a floor plan showing how I wanted the
house to be. He frowned, and said he thought I should
have three bedrooms upstairs, and the bathroom and
toilet downstairs at the back of the lounge. I said that this
wasn't what I wanted. I wanted two bedrooms and the
bathroom and toilet upstairs. Well, he said sternly, he'd
have to talk to Terry about that. So he phoned Terry in
England and explained, man to man, my eccentric ideas.
Diplomatically, Terry agreed with him, but said that, as it
was my project, they should go along with my cranky
plan. Shaking his head and saying mysteriously, 'Be it on
your own head,' the builder started knocking down a
wall.

Slowly, at first, things got worse. Where I wanted a
window, he said there should be a door. Whatever I
suggested, he advised something different. It became a

continual battle to get anything done how I planned it. He started muttering darkly, glowering and talking of hypertension. He complained about the materials we bought: bloody crap, he spat, kicking at the floorboards I'd ordered. Junk, in the direction of the windows. An additional strain was added to our daily encounters because he loathed animals. He'd tolerated them without complaint during the roofing period, but now that he felt he was indispensable, he became more and more aggressive towards them. That couldn't possibly help our relationship. We don't like people being unpleasant to our animals in our home, and particularly not when we're paying them.

'I can't drink this cheap wine,' he complained one lunch time. 'It's too acid. It's giving me heartburn.'

I apologized and started buying château-bottled wine.

Although he was a sun-worshipper, he couldn't work outside for very long, because he became dehydrated and needed to stand indoors drinking long cold drinks for fifteen minutes to revitalize himself. If he was hammering he had to wear ear protectors. I began to wonder if he was a hyperchondriac. To add to his hyper-tension and hyper-acidity problems, he suffered from hyper-acuity too, a fact which delighted one of our parrots, who reciprocated his hatred. Each time he passed its cage, it let out a piercingly shrill cry, like sheet metal being cut, and then watched with its head cocked to one side as he cursed and stumbled around with his hands clapped to his ears. I took deep breaths and cooked.

The *baguettes* were full of chemicals and noxious substances, he said. I bought biological ones, which cost over twice as much as the poisonous variety. Milk contained pus, so we had soya milk instead.

Renovating a derelict house is a daunting task for one man, and our man was clearly overwhelmed. The mess at the end of each day seemed to me to be disproportionate to the meagre progress. There were piles of rubble, sawdust, dirt, broken tiles and broken tools (ours), but almost no visible improvement. All the rubble had to be cleared away before the following morning: he wasn't going to work in such a mess and risk injury. In the absence of anybody else, it fell to me to undertake this task, and I staggered around with wheelbarrows loaded to the gunnels trying to find somewhere to dispose of the stuff. This activity began to eat heavily into my planning/shopping/cooking/washing-up time, and was something I hadn't bargained for and didn't particularly want to do, so I started hunting out another pair of hands. The first came in the form of a nice English lady whose much older husband was in poor health, and whose financial straits were dire indeed. She was a no-nonsense cheerful soul glad to do anything to help plump up her coffers, and set to with great energy as a builder's labourer, while I cringed at the sight of her manhandling piles of rocks and climbing ladders with buckets full of mortar. Sometimes it seemed to me she achieved more than our builder friend, and she certainly worked with a lot more enthusiasm.

'I can't say I fancy her,' he remarked one evening after she'd left. 'But if her old man pops off, I wouldn't mind marrying her. She's a damned good worker.'

I couldn't find a response, apart from a strained smile. After a week, she didn't come back, and I couldn't say I blamed her.

Our daily battles grew. While he had underlined at the start of the project that he wasn't a qualified builder, it seemed that in the interim he had become one, because for just about anything I asked him to do, he could come up with two technical reasons why it wasn't possible. He sent me to buy some hinges for the windows. Looking at my purchase, he shook his head with delighted disappointment.

'Wrong ones!' He waggled his finger merrily at me. 'Look – they don't work!'

'But they would if you put them the other way up,' I pointed out.

'Of course they won't. Honestly, you women.' He smirked with his most condescending smile.

'Well, just to humour me, could you please give it a try?'

That evening the hinges were correctly fitted, and the windows were in place. Sort of.

We seemed to be achieving little other than a hefty increment in our weekly shopping bill. Each evening I wandered round the site, trying to see what progress had been made, apart from more piles of debris. We'd started receiving enquiries for the renting of the cottages that summer, and time was moving too quickly; it was easily outstripping our builder who was already months behind the schedule he'd first drawn up. His updated timetable indicated that it would be at least another year before even one place was finished. Somehow we had to get more help. Fast. And our budget was already fully committed.

Terry put up a card in a supermarket in England, and a couple of young men contacted him who would be delighted to come out to France for the summer and work a few hours each day in return for board and lodging and as much as they could drink.

A few days later they arrived on our doorstep. One was thin and tanned with matted dreadlocks and a guitar; the other was plump and smiley with a small bundle of plumbing tools. Once they had showered and installed themselves in the empty loft space that we grandly called the spare bedroom, we sat down to a meal of salad, heaps of pasta, cheese and a couple of bottles of wine. They ate and drank heartily, and asked if there was anything more to drink, so I dug out another bottle of wine, and, at their request, a further one.

'You'll have to tell me what you like to eat,' I said.

'Not pasta,' said Dreadlocks. 'We can't stand pasta. We only like roasts, lots of roasts. Can we have something to drink, please?'

I opened the fifth bottle of wine.

'Don't you have any beers?' asked Dreadlocks. 'We're not really wine drinkers.'

The next day I'd go on a shopping expedition to stock up on joints of meat and beers, I promised, and after downing the sixth and final bottle of château-bottled wine they went out into the garden where Dreadlocks twanged his guitar and the Plump One gazed at the stars. I left them to it and went to bed, wondering how much the weekly food bill was going to be now that it was to incorporate daily roasts and beer on top of the increasing list of biological products. Still, it was cheap labour whichever way we looked at it.

When I left to go shopping the following morning, Dreadlocks was up and about and taking instructions from our builder, who didn't look very happy with his new workforce.

'I'm not at all sure about these two. I think you've got a problem there,' he forecast with manifest satisfaction.

I had problems in several areas; one more couldn't make that much difference.

The two chickens and leg of lamb with which I returned from the shopping expedition did not elicit the most meagre interest from Dreadlocks, who clamped his tanned fist over the two six-packs of beer in the boot of the car and disappeared with them. There wasn't any sign of the Plump One.

I roasted the chicken and some potatoes, made a salad, laid out a cheese board, opened a bottle of wine (château-bottled), sliced the biological *baguette* and set the table, and went to summon the staff. The day's rubble pile was building nicely, and a window was

308

vaguely set in position, slightly off the perpendicular. A dozen empty beer bottles gleamed greenly in the sunlight and Dreadlocks had taken off his shirt.

The builder despatched most of the chicken, and Dreadlocks slaked his thirst with a few more beers. He didn't seem to be hungry. There was no sign of the Plump One.

Mid-afternoon Dreadlocks came to announce that we were out of beer for that evening, so off I set and bought another two dozen bottles.

The Plump One materialized rather blearily later in the day, after the builder had left, and downed a dozen or so bottles of beer, apologizing for his non-showing but assuring me he would be up ahead of the larks the following morning and champing at the bit in his eagerness to work.

Between the two of them they polished off the remains of the cold chicken and the rest of the beers, and opened a couple of bottles of wine which they took into the garden where they strummed and star-gazed contentedly, while I lay awake mentally counting how many bottles they had consumed in the twenty-four hours since their arrival.

Dreadlocks surfaced for breakfast the next day, and took a shower.

'How do you wash your dreadlocks?' I asked. 'How do you get them clean when the hair is all matted like that?'

'Oh, I don't wash them. Just wet them. I haven't washed them since I grew them three years ago. And in any case, I never use any kind of soap on my body. It's bad for the skin.'

'How do you get clean, then?'

'I just use water. That's all you need.'

Actually, my olfactory sense had already indicated that there was something amiss in somebody's personal hygiene department. The builder didn't use deodorants,

309

and several visitors had remarked that they felt it would be a good idea if he did, especially during the very hot weather we were enjoying. But apparently all deodorants contain aluminium, which is very harmful to the body, which is after all our most valuable asset, as he pointed out regularly. So my waking hours were spiced with assorted hot male body odours that did nothing to enhance my pleasure in the day.

On the second morning of their stay, the Plump One did not appear again, and I asked Dreadlocks if he was unwell.

'Yeah. He's got a bit of a cold. But don't worry, he'll be OK soon.'

But he wasn't OK soon, and on the fourth day without any sign of life from him before 6.00 p.m., when he blundered from his sick-bed to drink lots of beer, I said that he'd have to see a doctor if he wasn't fit the following day.

The next morning he appeared at breakfast with a wan smile. He really didn't look frightfully well: his eyes were red-rimmed, his face was pale and shiny and he was a bit wobbly. However, he pronounced himself to be feeling much better and shortly afterwards was working in the garden sorting out plumbing fittings, and sipping from a bottle of beer.

'Kill the germs,' he explained rather sheepishly.

Dreadlocks joined him and after an hour we were once again out of beer.

'I'm off shopping. What would you gentlemen like for lunch?'

'I'll come with you,' said Dreadlocks. 'You don't seem to know much about beer. I'll show you what to buy.' He climbed into the car and off we went.

'What's the matter with the beer I've been buying?'

'Well, it's just not good beer. It's not strong enough, and it's not the beer we like drinking.'

I was a bit surprised, as in less than four days they'd drunk over a hundred bottles of the stuff, and quite a few bottles of wine they didn't like too, but if they wanted something different, that's what we'd get.

Dreadlocks collected a trolley and aimed it at the beer shelves. 'Ah! Great! This is the stuff.' He started scooping shiny golden tins into the trolley.

'See? Five point nine per cent. The best.'

As he filled the trolley to the brim and then started constructing a small pyramid of cans upon that solid base, so that he was pushing about one hundred tins of beer all told, I noticed the price. One tin cost almost as much as the six-packs I'd been buying – the ones they didn't like but drank anyway.

'Now hold on. Sorry, but this is far too expensive. If you're going to drink half a dozen cans a day, that's fine. But I'm afraid it's out of the question to buy all this lot. We just can't afford it.'

We negotiated for a few minutes and compromised on half a dozen of the shiny cans, and two dozen bottles of a less expensive brew that he thought might just be drinkable.

When we arrived home, the Plump One was nowhere to be seen, but happy little snoring sounds were coming from the spare bedroom and there was a pile of empty green bottles in the garden next to his abandoned plumbing tools. I felt slightly irritated.

'Doctor this afternoon.'

'No, don't do that!' Dreadlocks exclaimed. 'He'll be fine by tomorrow.'

'Sorry. Look, the agreement was as much as you could eat and drink in return for a few hours' work a day. We've stuck to our part of the bargain, but while we're keeping two of you, only one is doing any work. If he's ill, he needs treatment.'

311

'I'm doing the work for two. I'll keep on doing it, but don't call a doctor.'

'I think you'd better level with me,' I said. 'What exactly is his problem?'

'Heroin. He's an addict, and he's come here to go cold turkey. He's feeling really bad now, but if he sticks it out for another week or so he'll be OK. He really wants to come off the stuff.'

Wow! What was it about me? As if it wasn't sufficient to have had one drug addict on our doorstep in the shape of Elsa's brother during their visit to Gloria, now we had one actually staying under our roof.

'What about you? Are you on it?'

'No, of course not. I'm far too smart. Just stick to pot.'

'Have you brought any with you?'

'You bet! Half my backpack's stuffed with it!'

What fantastic news! Our neighbour had not long before been implicated in drug smuggling. I was under a certain amount of suspicion not only because I was English and his neighbour and had been frequently out and about with him and his wife, but also because my surname was identical to that of the man driving the second truck who'd been found in possession. Now our house was full of drug fiends. Could things possibly get any worse?

I'm soft in the head and a sucker for a sob story, and the Plump One, despite being a self-confessed feckless good-for-nothing who had never done an honest day's work in his life, had a certain charm. He had a gentle nature and was endearingly honest about his wicked ways. He recounted strings of offences from stealing cars to assaulting policemen; as a registered drug addict he was in the care of a social worker, and at every court appearance he was discharged as a hopeless case. From somewhere he had acquired a pharmaceutical encyclopedia, from which he was able to discover exactly what kind of effect each drug would induce. When he found one that sounded like fun, he looked up what ailment it was prescribed for, then researched the symptoms for that particular condition and trotted down to the doctor's surgery. There he reeled off a string of symptoms and told the doctor what the prescribed treatment was, and came away with the requisite prescription. His doctor, he said, was a very good sort. Generous state benefits ensured that the Plump One lived in comfort and enjoyed a self-indulgent lifestyle at the expense of the tax-payer. While I should have been shaking my head in dismay, there was a child-like naïveté about him, as if he really didn't believe he was doing anything wrong, and I couldn't dislike him.

'Where do you get the money to buy heroin?' I asked.

He smiled. 'Don't ask! There are ways and ways. My sister's a lesbian, and she and her partner want a baby. If I make her partner pregnant, so the baby is like their own real biological baby, they're going to pay me five hundred pounds. But my mum's not very happy about the idea.'

'Oh,' I said. 'But now you've decided to quit the heroin?'

'Yeah. I know it's crazy, I've seen the error of my ways and I really want to get myself together. But I'll leave if you want me to.'

Well, I admired his efforts and agreed he could stay for as long as it took him to sort himself out, as long as it didn't stretch into years.

For the next couple of days Dreadlocks worked, the Plump One went through the motions, and they drank beer, beer and more beer. We were going to need a skip to clear all the bottles.

Terry had arrived for a visit, and as it was the weekend we asked our helpers if they'd like to spend a day in town. Yes, they would very much, so we drove them to

313

Poitiers, gave them each 500 francs to enjoy themselves with, and arranged to collect them that evening from the *hôtel de ville* at 10.30 p.m.

It was a foregone conclusion that something would go wrong. At 10.30 p.m. Dreadlocks was waiting at the agreed meeting place, but predictably there was no sign of the Plump One.

'I've been looking for him for hours. Checked out every bar in town. Heaven knows where he's got to,' said Dreadlocks.

Well, what were we meant to do? How did we find one chubby person with a drugs problem on a Saturday evening in a town with a population of approximately ninety thousand? We drove around for an hour, peering into low dives and seamy bars, and returning periodically to the appointed spot, where the Plump One still was not.

'There's not much more we can do, except go home and wait for him to call. He's got our phone number and address, hasn't he?'

Of course he hadn't.

Dreadlocks wasn't concerned. 'He's always getting lost. He got robbed in Thailand and lost everything: passport, money, air ticket, all his clothes. But he sorted it out. He always does. Don't worry, he'll be back tomorrow.'

But he wasn't. While his friend spent the day happily sitting in the sunshine and working his way through the beer, we tried unsuccessfully to work out a way of being reunited with our troublesome guest. Each time the phone rang we pounced upon it, but the news we were hoping for didn't arrive.

We followed Dreadlocks's lead that evening and drowned our worries, and wobbled to bed hoping that the following day our lost soul would turn up.

The phone woke us from bleary and confused sleep at just after 2.00 in the morning.

'Madame Kelly?'

'*Oui*.'

'This is the *hôtel de police* in Poitiers. There is a young man here who is lost, and he thinks maybe he is staying with you. Will you speak to him, please.'

Having ascertained that it was indeed our missing young man, the nice policeman asked if we could come and collect him immediately. As the least inebriated driver I was elected to drive the 30 kilometres, and walk as steadily as possible into the police station and retrieve the prodigal, who was for the first time since he'd arrived sober, embarrassed and apologetic.

'I got lost,' he explained rather unnecessarily. 'Started going from bar to bar, and then found it was daylight and I didn't know where I was. I thought it was near Paris where your house was, so I followed the signs in that direction. Then I got lost in an industrial area, and I was really tired. So I managed to find my way to the police station. I wanted to phone my mum, but I didn't have any money.' The 500 francs had all been drunk by that time. 'The police tried phoning her for me, but she'd gone out for the day and didn't get home until after midnight. So I sat around in the police station all day until they finally managed to speak to her. Luckily she had your phone number.'

Aren't mothers wonderful?

The following week unfolded much like the previous one; Dreadlocks dug trenches and drank quantities of beer; the Plump One did his best, which wasn't very much. On the Thursday evening, we took them out to a restaurant where they ate and drank to their absolute limit. We had also invited Ken, who took the two of them back to his house and plied them with further quantities of alcohol. We heard them staggering back in the very early hours, and weren't surprised when there was no sign of them the next morning, apart from loud snoring interrupted by guttural belches and spluttery farts.

We left them to sleep it off until after lunch, when I shouted up that perhaps they could think about getting up.

'Fuck off, stupid, it's Christmas,' was the cheery response from Dreadlocks.

An hour later I tried again. Same response, but now they were playing a noise on the cassette machine, at full volume. I pulled the plug and asked them politely to come down, have something to eat and give us a hand. Nothing happened, so I went off shopping. When I came back our builder, who was looking pale and shaky, way-laid me.

'Look, I wouldn't go into your house,' he said. 'There's a lot of shouting going on. I'm staying out of it until it's all over.'

Well, I didn't want to have to stay out of my own house, and anyway, if there was shouting going on, I wanted to be part of it.

Terry and Dreadlocks were sitting glaring at each other. I asked exactly what the problem was.

Up until then Dreadlocks had been a pleasant, well-spoken and apparently reasonable young man, who spent several months of the year, he said, making jewellery in Thailand, and the summer season on a Greek island selling his wares and running a bar. Now, oozing alcohol from every pore and leaking at the seams, he had worked himself into a frenzy of resentment. Did we think they were slaves? How dare we buy them cheap beer, and take them to cheap restaurants! How dare we tell them when to get up! If we thought we were going to tell them what to do, we were very much mistaken. He plugged the tape player back in, deafening us with some kind of noise that sounded like a battlefield. I pulled the plug out again.

He turned to where the beer was kept, but we'd moved it out of sight. He stamped to the wine rack and took a couple of bottles.

'You're not having anything more to drink until you've sobered up.'

We took the bottles from him with some difficulty, while he stood glaring and shouting and trying to get round me to plug the noise in again.

The Plump One appeared and tried to help himself to the wine.

'Sorry, not now. Once you've sobered up, but you've really had enough for the moment.'

He fell into some sort of fit; yelping, shaking, waving his hands in the air, gasping.

'Gotta have something to drink. Gotta have something to drink.'

He really was in a dreadful state, so we gave him a bottle and he clambered back to the bedroom.

Dreadlocks had totally lost it. He ranted and raved and threatened and the pleasant face he had worn for the previous ten days fell off. He shouted and yelled and whirled around in circles until I said, 'You're leaving. Get your things together. We'll take you to the station.'

Still cursing he started packing his bag. The Plump One appeared. 'Shut up,' he said to his friend. 'These people have treated us very well, and we've been pigs. They don't deserve this. I really am sorry. We'll go now. Thanks for putting up with us.'

'If you want to stay until you've got over your problem, that's OK.'

'No, thanks all the same. Better go.'

And so they left, the Plump One full of apologies and promises to keep in touch, Dreadlocks muttering about exploitation and slavery.

'You people think I'm nothing. You think I'm just a

beach bum. Well, you're wrong. Let me tell you, on the island' – he named a Greek one – 'I'm a big, big man. I'm the cannabis king. Everybody knows me. I make a fortune. I could buy this place ten times over if I wanted to.'

OK, your majesty, farewell. Go and buy yourself some decent beer. And some soap. Terry drove them to the station.

Our builder couldn't hide his delight at this turn of events, but at the same time he wanted to know how he was expected to continue working without helpers. It was downhill at full speed from then on. His hyperacidity and hypertension became contagious, and I hated the sight of his car, arriving later and later each morning, and leaving earlier and earlier each evening. He'd been with us for almost a year; all the money we'd inherited had been spent, and we'd had to borrow more to complete the project. The work simply wasn't getting done. A window he had put in fell out; he drove huge nails through the new floorboards, leaving the heads sticking up like small metallic mushrooms. He couldn't drink coffee because of hyper-something, so I bought chicory substitute, which was quite expensive. With a month to go before our first guests were due to arrive, the cottage was still no more than a shell full of rubble. One day I went out for several hours, and came back to find a deckchair set up in the back garden, surrounded by half a dozen coffee cups. We'd have got better value from our money if we'd burned it as fuel.

I could see the pressure building up in him, ready to explode, and wished it would. I felt close to exploding myself and longed to be rid of him. However, knowing his financial situation and how much he needed the money we were paying him, I dared not add to his stress by dispensing with his services, such as they were, in case he keeled over with a heart attack. We continued our daily ordeal, becoming increasingly frosty with each other.

It was the pizza that was the final straw. Despite our strained relationship, I was still feeding him and he was still eating and drinking with gusto. On the fateful day of the pizza, I had an appointment which would keep me away from home until a little after lunch, so I'd prepared some salads and a cheese board, and bought the biological *baguette* and a giant, luxury eight-person pizza (non-biological).

'If you want to eat before I get back, it's all in the fridge, so help yourself. The pizza just needs fifteen minutes in the oven.'

Throughout the morning I looked forward to that pizza and the potato salad I'd made. I mentally tasted the bubbling cheese, the olives, anchovies, capers, garlic and tomatoes, and the mayonnaise-smothered potatoes.

When I got home, he was sitting in the garden in a deckchair.

'Was lunch OK?'

'Yes.'

I found only a stack of empty plates and dishes sitting in the sink waiting to be washed.

There was no pizza in the oven, no potato salad in the cupboards or the fridge. I wondered where on earth he had put them, so I asked him.

'There wasn't anything left over.'

He'd eaten all the pizza, and all the potato salad. And most of the cheese, and every crumb of the biological *baguette*.

'You didn't leave any for me, then?'

'No. I didn't think you'd want any.'

I added greediness to the hyper-list.

Enough was enough. He'd got to go. He was going to have to find another source of income and meals.

Swallowing my temper because I didn't want to frighten

him into cardiac arrest, I said: 'I think we've got a bit of a problem here. I know you're not happy, and, to be honest, neither am I. What are we going to do about it?'

'I don't want to be involved in this project any more.'

My heart grew wings.

'You're a complete laughing stock. You're wasting your money on this dump. Nobody's ever going to want to come here on holiday. You're living in a dream world. Everybody's talking about you and your crazy ideas. How could you think people on holiday would want to come to a place like this?'

I felt better now. 'OK. I understand, and I accept your resignation. I'll pay you up till today.'

'Hang on a minute! I can't leave just like that. What am I going to do for money?'

I had no idea. I paid him off, and he marched to his car red-faced, shouting over his shoulder: 'You didn't expect me to work here, with all your fucking animals around me, did you?'

And that was the end of the whole episode.

The next day a new builder started. Because of the way things had been going, and because the cottages absolutely had to be ready in time, as our future guests had already paid for their holiday,s and we'd already spent the money, I'd discussed the possibility of taking over the project with another builder about a month before things had finally come to a head.

The two cottages were both finished just in time for the holiday season – well, almost. When the first guests arrived the varnish on their staircase was still sticky, and three hours before the arrival of our second guests the 8 tons of crushed limestone we'd ordered for the courtyard was delivered in a great heap, and took three of us several fevered hours of raking and tramping to flatten. In the meantime Ken had started clearing up the exterior of his house, so our guests weren't faced with the eyesore that Bill had created.

Wandering round looking at the neat tiled floors, the plastered walls, the double-glazed windows and the fitted kitchens, I was quite envious. We still had a very long way to go before our house reached that standard.

Despite the doubts expressed by our erstwhile builder, our guests fell under the charm of our little hamlet; unlike him, they enjoyed the company of our dogs and cats, and feeding the horses. They loved the peace and quiet, sipping wine in the sunshine, helping themselves to raspberries and herbs, watching the birds, and the fact that within a short distance they could reach several large towns for shopping, or the Atlantic port of la Rochelle. Cognac was an hour's drive away, and Limoges just a little further. Children and adults alike were enthralled by their visits to Monkey Valley, and to Futuroscope. There was a wealth of nearby lakes and rivers for swimming and water sports, and restaurants in abundance. Seeing their pleasure I soon forgot the anguish and aggravation of the building project: it had all been worthwhile. And several of them were soon hunting for their own property in the area.

Chapter Nineteen

Another Christmas was on the horizon, and in the middle of December my old *bête noire*, Michelle, launched a new campaign to drive me mad. Since the shopping episode I hadn't heard from her, but she phoned very late one night, as if nothing had passed betweeen us, and asked in her bleating voice if I would make a Christmas pudding for the children she taught. Instead of taking the sensible route and just saying no, I explained that even if I was so inclined, which I was not, the pudding needed to have been made very much earlier in the year and left for at least a few weeks to mature. However, I did happen to have one left from last Christmas, which she could have.

She berated me for several minutes: what kind of person was I that I should suggest she give seven-year-olds something to eat that was a year old? When the verbal flow had trickled to a halt, I further dug myself in by pointing out that the alcohol content of the pudding gave it a very extended lifespan, during which it continuously improved. This information she relayed to her mother who was in the background, and it evoked an even wilder diatribe based on the fact that now I was trying to corrupt young children with alcohol. Here I withdrew my offer of the redundant pudding, hoping to bring the mad conversation to a close. But this woman was famous for not only her irrationality, but also her fearsome tenacity. If she did agree to risk the health of the little children by feeding them this thing, how should it be cooked? Reheated by steaming for three hours is the traditional way, I explained. Steamed for three hours, she shrieked. How did I think she could steam it for three hours in a classroom? I'd no idea, but blundered on to suggest a microwave oven, which would reheat the thing in seven minutes. Where did I think she was going to get a microwave oven? What did I care, I asked myself. Perhaps she could borrow one just for the morning? And who did I think would lend her a microwave oven? How would she get it to the school?

The remaining method would be to reheat it in a pressure cooker. This idea she favoured, as it would 'kill all the bacteria and destroy the alcohol', and she did actually own a pressure cooker. What a relief. Would she have to pay for the pudding, she wanted to know, or could she have it for nothing? To anybody else I'd happily have given it, but I was smarting from her rudeness and said that she'd have to pay what the pudding had cost us, which was 40 francs. She exploded. I obviously didn't want it myself or I would have eaten it a year ago, so why was I exploiting her? Calmly and very tiredly, I said if she wanted the pudding it was 40 francs, and if she didn't that was fine.

So she said she would go to the shop that sold English products, some distance away, and try to find a fresher, less alcoholic and far less extortionate pudding.

The following evening she called again to say that the shop was very expensive and the people had been rude to her, so she would after all take my pudding. But she couldn't come and collect it; I'd have to deliver it. We reached an impasse, and after long and difficult negotiations it was agreed that I would leave the pudding in our letter box. She would collect it some time later the next day, at a time that she was unable to specify in advance, and would reluctantly leave 40 francs in the box.

I dutifully left the pudding in the box, where it sat uncollected, until Christmas had long passed. When I retrieved it, it looked so inviting that I cooked it (pressure cooker method), and ate nearly half of it at one sitting. Gave me frightful indigestion.

The scenery changed dramatically with the seasons. Hectares were ploughed in winter, the steel ploughshares mixing the jagged stubble into the upturned clods of glistening crimson mud; then the tractors harrowed those same clods into neat narrow ridges of a fine crumbly tilth that bleached to a soft beige after a few hours of wind or sun. Shortly afterwards there was a just-discernible flush of green as the first tips of the new crop pushed their way upwards. The tips fast turned into shoots that raced each other skywards. In the winter months the crops were wheat, oilseed rape and cabbages. The wheat turned from green to fawn, and then darkened to golden brown and rustled crisply in the spring breeze, and in the summer there was hay, sunflowers blazed briefly in their yellow glory, and maize covered the land in rows of rustling green spears like Roman legions on the march. During late autumn the withered sunflowers and the maize were harvested, the machinery working round the clock, leaving the fields stark and empty, ready for the return of the plough and another cycle. It was then that you could see the quantity of rocks and flints that carpeted the earth, and you had to marvel at how things as fragile and vulnerable as new shoots could possibly force themselves up through the ground past these shoulder-to-shoulder chunks. Nature is extraordinary.

There seemed to be no pattern to the weather. We'd

worn T-shirts and eaten in the garden in December, sunbathed during January and February and had to light the fire in August. We'd seen severe drought, and endured torrential rain for days on end. Despite the fact that it didn't get cold here (remember the estate agent's assurance), we had recorded minus 18°C, and on summer afternoons the thermometer more than once registered 50°C. There were days when violent winds rattled the shutters and window panes, the roof visibly moved, the trees were bowed almost double and the chickens were lifted off their feet and blown around like paper bags. The weather forecasters used terms like '*détestable*' and '*catastrophique*'. But none of it could have prepared us for the weather that swept away the last few days of the twentieth century.

On 26 December 1999, parts of France, including Paris, were attacked by a fierce storm that seemingly caught the weather forecasters unawares. It lifted bus shelters from their moorings, tossed park benches around like kites, and toppled construction cranes. On the coast boats were lifted from the sea and dropped into the fields. That night the forecasters advised people not to travel the following day, as more high winds were likely.

On the 27th, just as night was falling, the second storm approached, sweeping its way from the Atlantic across Europe. It came gently at first, a soft hissing, caressing almost, and the trees danced to its rhythm. The hissing turned to a howl, tearing across the landscape, bending the trees; exhilarating to listen to, even inviting to venture out into. There was a darker than usual quality to the night sky. The dogs and cats crouched unhappily in corners, whimpering. We could comfort them, but we were anxious about Leila alone out in the field. Cindy had been put to sleep at a great old age the previous summer. We dared not shut Leila in the barn, in case it collapsed, but she sheltered each night beside a tall

325

concrete post, and we were worried that this, or the oak or the linden trees, might fall on her. But we could do nothing except pray and rely on her to keep herself safe until the storm blew itself out.

As the violence of the storm increased, the whole house shook, the windows rattled, the tiles shifted on the roof, and outside we could hear constant crashing. The wind's howl had turned to a furious shriek, an ear-splitting banshee screech as it reached speeds of up to two hundred kilometres an hour. The electricity died. The telephone lines went down. Crazy thoughts went through my mind: we were witnessing the end of the world. It was almost the last day of the twentieth century, and this was it, the end of everything. And despite the fear, it was exciting. Terry and I had to fight an impulse to stand outside and feel the unleashed power hurtling past us. It was just as well we did, because four large sheets of corrugated iron which formed part of what had been Bill's roof were lifted in their entirety, together with the huge oak beam which supported them, and carried 70 metres through the air and down to the bottom of the garden. Tiles billowed around like leaves. And utterly helpless, powerless to do anything, we climbed into bed and lay through the night with the animals all around us, listening for the storm to exhaust itself, which it did towards morning, crooning as it died, leaving behind it a calm just like any other early morning.

I was afraid to look outside when daylight came. 'Will you look?' I asked Terry.

'Leila's fine. She's standing patiently by the fence with her ears pricked towards the house waiting for her breakfast. But the walnut tree's down.'

We walked round the hamlet to see the damage. Astonishingly our ancient buildings were unscathed; so were the huge oak and the tall lindens. The only casualty was the walnut tree which had been tipped over on its side, but saved from being completely uprooted by one of its branches which kept it propped at an angle of about twenty-five degrees. We filled all around its exposed roots and it survived, putting out new growth which reached upwards, and giving us a good crop of fruit, too. Our whole little hamlet had withstood the terrible force of the storm with, apart from the corrugated iron sheets, no visible damage except a few dozen broken roof tiles.

But the landscape was devastated. There was not a single road not blocked by fallen trees. It was a sight to make you weep, poor, lovely trees lying dead, their roots poking up at the sky in pathetic defiance. In a copse of poplars just down the road every one had been snapped in half like a toothpick.

At a nearby cemetery three great pines had collapsed onto the wall and several of the gravestones, smashing them into fragments. Ninety-two people in France were killed and an estimated three hundred and sixty million trees destroyed. In some historic forests not a single tree was left standing – the landscape was likened to the aftermath of a tank battle. It was estimated that it would take a hundred and fifty years for the countryside to recover. The electricity supply was out of action in some areas for several months before normal supplies were resumed. Hundreds of the giant pylons that carried the power across the country were crumpled like paperclips. France had to import engineers from all over the European Community to help with the repairs. I sometimes wondered if a hurricane of such violence could possibly have approached without the weather forecasters noticing it, or whether they knew it was coming but didn't want to cause panic by announcing it.

Although our region took a terrible battering from the storm, we and our fragile property had survived unscathed. We were absolutely astonished when we spoke to friends and family in England, because they had heard nothing about this shattering event.

Four days after the hurricane, just before midnight, Terry and I stood in the Place du Maréchal Leclerc, in Poitiers, the beautiful city where Eleanor of Aquitaine and Joan of Arc had once walked, that had once, for a few brief years, been the capital of France. There were tens of thousands of French people here, some in fancy dress, some singing, some drunk, but all peaceful, happy, and friendly. A semi-toothless vagrant came up and serenaded me with a catchy and lovely song, '*Jolie Môme*', in a fine voice that did not match his tattered clothing. Lasers projected messages of world peace onto the front of the marvellous *hôtel de ville*, and recorded voices read the messages aloud.

As the midnight hour struck, the sky blazed with fireworks and the champagne corks flew into the twenty-first century. It was a supremely throat-lumpy moment.

Postscript

We arrived in France in 1995 to start our new life in the little hamlet, in the old farmhouse that needed so much work. It still does, although it has come a very long way since then. There were times, as I looked round, when I felt that the house would never be finished. There was always something else that needed doing: another roof to mend, another floor to lay, another window to install, the chimney to repair, the damp wall to deal with. But then, when I thought back to our arrival, and remembered the task that faced us, I saw that Terry's hard work, his unflagging optimism and his tremendous energy had achieved miracles. Not once, in all the years, had he shown any sign of wanting to give up. Every improvement was due to him. And with blocked pipes, leaks, collapsed fences, broken-down cars, and who knows what else, there was *always* something that needed doing over and above the building work. I'd made the garden and looked after the animals, and painted a few walls here and there, but it was a minuscule contribution to the overall project. Terry's was a breathtaking achievement for one man.

We'd both been put to the test of coping with the unexpected, surviving crises and dealing with tragedies. In the garden were many little islands, each island marking the resting place for one of our pets: Natalia and Hecate, Wizzy and Vulcan, Max, Amy, Virgil and Beau all had their own little plots, planted with roses and lavender, lady's mantle, aubrietia, lilies and nandinas. They had shared our lives, and had been our reason for moving to France, and our home was where they belonged.

Fred and his wife sold their house and disappeared from our lives.

Michelle stopped phoning.

Red and Paul, Christopher and Joseph, moved back to England.

Nothing more was heard from Mrs Malucha.

Carole and Norrie remained our friends.

Ken worked hard and tidied up and developed Bill's house. The sacks of cement and bundles of wire were replaced by fruit trees, a lawn, and rose bushes.

The small house that was snatched from under Bill's nose was partly renovated, and then abandoned.

Our *gîtes* were successful; many of our guests became friends and returned to stay again.

I missed Gloria's bright blonde hair, her chirpy voice, and our mad escapades. She phoned from time to time. She was happy living in England, near her children, still working as a companion to the elderly, and promised to visit us one day.

Bill rebuilt his life and his removals business and became a successful businessman; in the summer of 2001 he bought the only remaining vacant property in the hamlet, a large ruined house and barn that he plans to renovate for his retirement.

A close friend bought the cottage that stood between Ken's house and ours, and it was completely renovated.

Our granddaughter Catherine spent an entire summer with us; she was delightful company, and loved the animals, and playing cards by candlelight. She could often be seen wandering around with what she called a 'chicking' tucked under her arm, or spraying unsuspecting people with the hosepipe.

To keep our old horse Leila company, we bought two baby goats, Tuppence and Thruppence. The three of them became inseparable.

We are still here, and still enchanted with our home. This year, we are looking forward to seeing all our grand-children here together in the summer.

Leila and the goats are grazing in the meadow. Louis and Tigger, our remaining cats, are curled asleep in the new kitchen. In the living room our puppy, Talisman, a Hungarian Vizsla, is stretched out on a settee, next to the two parrots. We have four new chickings who provide excellent free range eggs.

All our French neighbours are still here; they haven't changed. There's a crisp, perfect lettuce on the table, freshly picked for me this evening by Mme Meneteau from their garden. Because this has been a rather wet and cold month, their strawberries haven't ripened, and the asparagus hasn't come up yet. She told me that M. Meneteau doesn't have much luck with radishes – they only grow leaves, nothing else. But their potatoes are doing particularly well.

Terry is still commuting, and comes here every fort-night to continue to work on our house.

Susie Kelly
Poitou-Charentes, 2004

BEST FOOT FORWARD
From La Rochelle to Lake Geneva – the Misadventures of a Walking Woman
by Susie Kelly

Why would an unfit, fifty-something Englishwoman embark on a solo walk across France from La Rochelle on the west coast to Lake Geneva over the Swiss border?

And why would a total stranger from San Antonio, Texas come to live in her crumbling French farmhouse to house-sit for a multitude of boisterous and unpredictable animals?

With no experience of hiking or camping, not to mention using a compass, Susie Kelly found out the hard way that it is possible to be overloaded and ill-prepared at the same time. Scorching days, glacial nights, perpetual blisters, inaccurate maps, a leaking tent and an inappropriate sleeping bag were daily vexations, but as she hobbled eastwards, the glory of the French landscape revealed its magic and the kindness of strangers repaid her discomfort in spades.

Best Foot Forward is an hilarious and heart-warming tale of English eccentricity, the American pioneering spirit, and two women old enough to know better.

'An inspired and heart-warming account'
The Express

A Bantam Paperback

0 553 81490 7

FROM HERE, YOU CAN'T SEE PARIS
by Michael Sanders

A fascinating memoir about life in Les Arques (population 159), a hilltop village in a remote corner of France untouched by the modern era. It is the story of a dying community's struggle to survive, of an artist whose legacy begins its rebirth, and of chef Jacques Ratier and his wife, Noelle, whose magical restaurant – the village's sole business – has helped ensure its future.

The author set out to explore the inner workings of a French restaurant kitchen but ended up stumbling into a wider, much richer world. Whether uncovering the darker secrets of *foie gras* or absorbing the lore of the land around a farmhouse kitchen table after a boar hunt, Michael Sanders learned that life in Les Arques was anything but sleepy. You will discover its vibrant history and traditions of food, cooking and rural living, sharing a family's adventures as they find their way in a place that is sometimes lonely, often wondrous, and always fascinating.

'A rich textural tapestry of everyday life in the Lot . . . Honest, funny and endearing'
Ken Hom

A Bantam Paperback

0 553 81566 0

FRENCH SPIRITS
A House, a Village, and a Love Affair in Burgundy
by Jeffrey Greene

When Jeffrey Greene, a prizewinning American poet, and Mary, his wife-to-be, discover a moss-covered stone presbytery in a lovely village in the Puisaye region of Burgundy, they know they have to live there. With an unabashed *joie de vivre*, they begin the arduous process of procuring their slice of paradise amid the wild beauty of the French countryside.

French Spirits is the magical tale of their odyssey to become not just homeowners but Burgundians. In lyrical prose, Greene recalls their experiences in turning the 300-year-old stone building – which the locals believe houses numerous spirits – into a habitable refuge. He brings to life their adventures in finding wonderful bargains with which to furnish their new space, including a firm mattress and some rather suspicious 'antiques' bought from the back of a van.

Greene offers the unexpected joys and surprises of village life, from celebrating his and Mary's simple backyard wedding to toiling in a verdant garden. He shares the experience of surviving his mother's decision to move in and humorously introduces the locals – both human and non-human – who define his and Mary's new world. Woven throughout this luscious tale are the pleasures of rural France: wondrous food and wine, long-held rituals and feasts, dark superstitions and deeply rooted history. A memorable feast for the senses, *French Spirits* will entertain and enlighten all who succumb to its charms.

'Charming and hilarious'
Michael Korda

A Bantam Paperback

0 553 81479 6

LIFE IN A POSTCARD:
Escape to the French Pyrenees
by Rosemary Bailey

I wake to the sun striking gold on a stone wall. If I lean out of the window I can see Mount Canigou newly iced with snow. It is wonderful to live in a building with windows all around, to see both sunrise and sunset, to be constantly aware of the passage of the sun and moon.

In 1988, Rosemary Bailey and her husband were travelling in the French Pyrenees when they fell in love with, and subsequently bought, a ruined medieval monastery, surrounded by peach orchards and snow-capped peaks. Traces of the monks were everywhere, in the frescoed 13th century chapel, the buried crypt and the stone arches of the cloister. Gradually these fragments revealed the spirit of the place.

For the next few years the couple visited Corbiac whenever they could, until, in 1997, they took the plunge and moved from central London to rural France with their six-year-old son. Entirely reliant on their earnings as freelance writers, they put their Apple Macs in the room with the fewest leaks and sent Theo to the village school. With vision and determination they restored the monastery to its former glory, testing their relationship and resolve to the limit, and finding inspiration in a small mountain community that welcomed them.

Life in a Postcard is not just Rosemary Bailey's enthralling account of the challenges of a new life. It is also an exploration of the rugged beauty of French Catalonia, the southernmost corner of France, the pleasures of Catalan cooking, and a celebration of an alternative, often magical, world.

'An inspiration for anyone thinking of moving abroad . . . a fascinating account'
Choice

A Bantam Paperback

0 553 81341 2

A SELECTION OF RELATED TITLES
AVAILABLE FROM BANTAM BOOKS

THE PRICES SHOWN BELOW WERE CORRECT AT THE TIME OF GOING TO PRESS. HOWEVER TRANSWORLD PUBLISHERS RESERVE THE RIGHT TO SHOW NEW RETAIL PRICES ON COVERS WHICH MAY DIFFER FROM THOSE PREVIOUSLY ADVERTISED IN THE TEXT OR ELSEWHERE.

All Transworld titles are available by post from:
Bookpost, PO Box 29, Douglas, Isle of Man IM99 1BQ
Credit cards accepted. Please telephone +44(0)1624 836000, fax +44(0)1624 837033,
Internet http://www.bookpost.co.uk or
e-mail: bookshop@enterprise.net for details.
Free postage and packing in the UK.
Overseas customers allow £2 per book (paperbacks) and £3 per book (hardback).